Privilege

PRINCETON STUDIES IN CULTURAL SOCIOLOGY

Paul J. DiMaggio, Michèle Lamont,
Robert J. Wuthnow, and Viviana A. Zelizer, *Series Editors*

A list of titles in this series appears at the back of the book

Privilege

THE MAKING OF AN ADOLESCENT ELITE AT ST. PAUL'S SCHOOL

Shamus Rahman Khan

Princeton University Press
Princeton & Oxford

Requests for permission to reproduce material from this work should be
sent to Permissions, Princeton University Press

Published by Princeton University Press, 41 William Street,
Princeton, New Jersey 08540

In the United Kingdom: Princeton University Press, 6 Oxford Street,
Woodstock, Oxfordshire OX20 1TW

press.princeton.edu

Fourth printing, and first paperback printing, 2013
Paperback ISBN 978-0-691-15623-1

THE LIBRARY OF CONGRESS HAS CATALOGED THE CLOTH EDITION OF THIS BOOK
AS FOLLOWS

Khan, Shamus Rahman.
Privilege : the making of an adolescent elite at St. Paul's School / Shamus Rahman Khan.
p. cm. — (Princeton studies in cultural sociology)
Includes bibliographical references and index.
ISBN 978-0-691-14528-0 (hardback : alk. paper)
1. St. Paul's School (Concord, N.H.)—History. 2. Boarding schools—
New Hampshire—Concord—History. 3. Boarding schools—Social
aspects—New Hampshire—Concord. I. Title.
LD7501.C822K53 2011
373.742′72—dc22   2010021520

British Library Cataloging-in-Publication Data is available

This book has been composed in Adobe Garamond

Printed on acid-free paper. ∞

Printed in the United States of America

9   10

For my parents, whose enduring love and support I have had the privilege of enjoying all of my life

The barrier has changed shape rather than place

—ALEXIS DE TOCQUEVILLE

Contents

Privilege

Introduction: Democratic Inequality

> The direction in which education starts a man will determine
> his future in life.
> —PLATO

> My story is part of the larger American story.
> —BARACK OBAMA

I am surrounded by black and Latino boys.

As I looked around the common room of my new dorm this was all I could think about. It was September 1993, and I was a rather young fourteen-year-old leaving home for the first time. My parents, who had helped me unpack my room and were about to say good-bye, noticed as well. We didn't say anything to one another. But the surprise on their faces was mirrored on my own. This was not what I expected, enrolling at a place like St. Paul's School. I thought I would be unlike everyone else. I thought my name and just-darker-than-olive skin would make me the most extreme outlier among the students. But though my parents grew up in small rural villages in Pakistan and Ireland and my father was not white, they had become wealthy. My father was a successful surgeon; my mother was a nurse. I had been at private school since seventh grade, and being partly from the Indian subcontinent hardly afforded one oppressed minority status. For the other boys around me, those from poor neighborhoods in America's urban centers, St. Paul's was a much more jarring experience.

I quickly realized that St. Paul's was far from racially diverse. That sea of dark skin only existed because we all lived in the same place: the minority student dorm. There was one for girls and one for boys. The other eighteen houses on campus were overwhelmingly filled with those whom you would expect to be at a school that educates families like the Rockefellers and Vanderbilts. This sequestering was not an intentionally racist practice

of the school. In fact the school was very self-conscious about it and a few
years prior tried to distribute students of color across all houses on campus.
But the non-white students complained. Though their neighborhoods of
Harlem and the Upper East Side might border each other, a fairly large
chasm separated the non-elite and elite students. They had difficulty living with one another. Within a year the minority student dorm returned.
Non-white students were sequestered in their own space, just like most of
them were in their ethnic neighborhoods back home.

I grew up in a variety of neighborhoods, but like most Americans, none
of them was particularly diverse.[1] My parents' lives had not been much different until they met one another. In no small part this was because they
grew up in rural towns in poor nations. My father's village consisted of
subsistence farmers; things like electricity and plumbing arrived during my
own childhood visits. My mother grew up on a small farm on the weather-
beaten west coast of Ireland. At the time she was born, her family pumped
their own water, had no electricity, and cooked on an open hearth. Modern comforts arrived during her childhood.

My parents' story is a familiar one. Their ambitions drove them to
the promise of America. Early in life I lived in New York's rural Allegany
County. But seeking to make the most of American opportunities, my
parents moved to the suburbs of Boston where the schools were better
and the chances for me and my brother were greater. There was more to
this move than just new schools. The Pontiac that was standard in the
driveways of rural America was replaced by a European luxury car. The
trips to visit family in Ireland and Pakistan were augmented by tours of
Europe, South America, and Asia. My parents did what many immigrants
do: they played cultural catch-up. I spent my Saturdays attending the New
England Conservatory of Music. Public school education was abandoned
for private academies. There was no more time for my religious education.
We became cosmopolitan.

For all these changes, my father never lost some of the cultural marks
of a rural Pakistani villager, and many in Boston did not let him forget his
roots. He was happiest working with his hands, whether doing surgery
or toiling in the earth. As he spent his free time sculpting the garden of
our home into a place that would soon be put on garden tours, he was
mistaken for a hired hand by visitors. During a visit to our home, one
of my father's colleagues exclaimed, "Where are your books!?" Never in

my life have I seen my father read a novel; his favorite music is still from the Indian movies of his childhood or the songs that greeted him when he arrived in Detroit in the early 1970s. He would not know Bach from Schoenberg. My father's reply to this cultural scolding by a New England blue blood was prescient: "Someday, my kids can have all the books they want." My parents were justifiably proud of what they had achieved, and the cultural tastes they would never develop they would instill in their children. We ate at fine restaurants. At one of these restaurants I saw my father, raised a Muslim, take his first sip of wine. The snobbery that always stung me—waiters handing me or my brother a wine list instead of my parents, who were clearly paying for the meal—seemed not to bother them. Compared to their achievements, these slights were trivial.

Attending an elite high school was the ultimate mark of success in our bourgeois suburban world, and I was determined to do so. My parents were not enthusiastic about my leaving home, but they knew the advantages of boarding school. Perhaps thinking of their own lives, they respected my desire to head out on my own. St. Paul's was on my tour of New England boarding schools. I didn't know anything about the place, but during my visit I was seduced. The school is a truly stunning physical place—one of the most beautiful campuses in the world. Luckily, I was accepted.

I was unprepared for my new life. The shock of moving from poor rural New York to rich suburban Boston was repeated during my first days at St. Paul's. This school had long been home to the social elite of the nation. Here were members of a national upper class that went well beyond the professional circles of my suburban home. Children with multiple homes who chartered planes for weekend international trips, came from family dynasties, and inherited unimaginable advantages met me on the school's brick paths. My parents' newfound wealth was miniscule compared to many at the school. And in my first days, all the European tours, violin lessons, and private schooling could not buy me a place among many of my classmates. I was not comfortable around this new group of people. I instead found a home by recessing into my dorm, away from the entitlements of most of my classmates.

For my entire time at St. Paul's I lived in the same minority student dorm. But as I became more at ease at the school, as I began to understand the place and my classmates, I also began to find ways to fit in. Upon graduating I was elected by my classmates to represent them on the board of managers of the alumni. While this respect of my peers made me proud, I was not sad to be moving on. I had purposefully not applied to the Ivy League schools that my classmates would be attending. St. Paul's was a world I had learned to fit into but one that I was not particularly happy in.

The source of my discontent was my increasing awareness of inequality. I kept returning to my first days: both my surprise at my minority student dorm and my discomfort among my elite classmates. The experience remained an aggravating curiosity. Why was elite schooling like a birthright for some Americans and a herculean achievement for others? Why did students from certain backgrounds seem to have such an easy time feeling comfortable and doing well at the school while others seemed to relentlessly struggle? And, most important, while students were repeatedly told that we were among the best of the best,[2] why was it that so many of the best came from among the rich? These were all questions about inequality, and they drove me away from the world of St. Paul's. But learning more about inequality also brought me back.

Democratic Inequality, Elite Education, and the Rise of the Meritocracy

No society will ever be equal. Questions about inequality are not "Is there inequality?" but instead "How much inequality is there, and what is its character?" Inequality is more tolerable if its character is perceived as "fair." Systematic, durable inequalities[3]—those where advantages and disadvantages are transferred from generation to generation—are largely unacceptable to our contemporary sensibility. We are unhappy if our poor always remain poor or our rich seem to have a stranglehold on wealth. We are similarly uncomfortable with the notion that ascribed characteristics like race help determine our life chances. Levels of inequality are slightly more contentious. Some of us do not mind large gaps between rich and poor if the poor receive a livable income and the rich are given the capacity to innovate to create more wealth. Others feel that larger and larger gaps generate social problems. The evidence seems to show that inequality is bad for societies.[4] Following these data, I am among those who believe that too much inequality is both immoral and inefficient.

One of the curiosities in recent years is how our social institutions have opened to those they previously excluded, yet at the same time inequality has increased. We live in a world of democratic inequality, by which I mean that our nation embraces the democratic principle of openness and access, yet as that embrace has increased so too have our levels of inequality. We often think of openness and equality as going hand in hand. And yet if we look at our experiences over the last fifty years we can see that that is simply not the case. This is most notable in elite colleges, where student bodies are increasingly racially diverse but simultaneously richer.

In 1951 blacks made up approximately 0.8 percent of the students at elite colleges.[5] Today blacks make up about 8 percent of Ivy League students; the Columbia class of 2014 is 13 percent black—representative of the black population in our nation as a whole. A similar change could be shown for other races, and women today are outperforming men, creating a gender gap in college attendance in favor of women.[6] Without question our elite educational institutions have become far more open racially and to women. This is a tremendous transformation, nothing short of a revolution. And it has happened not only in our schools but also in our political and economic life.

Yet at the same time the overall level of inequality has increased dramatically. When we think of inequality we often think of poverty. And when social scientists study inequality they tend to focus on the conditions of disadvantage. There are good reasons for this—understanding the lives of the poor should help us alleviate some of the difficulties of poverty. But if we want to understand the recent increases in American inequality we must know more about the wealthy, as well as the institutions that are important for their production and maintenance. This becomes clear if we look at what has happened to the incomes of American households over the last forty years. From 1967 to 2008 average American households saw their earnings increase about 25 percent. This is respectable but hardly laudatory. But as we move up the income ladder, we see something quite dramatic. The incomes of the richest 5 percent of households increased 68 percent. And the higher we go, the greater the increase in income. The top 1 percent of American households saw their incomes increase by 323 percent, and the richest 0.1 percent of Americans received a staggering 492 percent increase in earnings.[7] Why has inequality increased over the past forty years? Mostly because of the exploding incomes of the rich.

se dual tranformations of increasing openness and inequality run
st many of our intuitions about how social processes work. How is it
tnat some of our most elite and august institutions—those that are central
pathways to reaching the highest levels of economic success—have transformed into being more open to those they previously excluded, yet the
overall levels of inequality in our nation have increased so dramatically?
How is it that our democratic ideal of greater openness has transferred
into a much better life for the privileged few but stagnation for most of
our nation?

Part of the explanation emerges once we look at class. The "openness" I
have highlighted is racial. But if we add class to the mix, we see something
quite different. While elite private colleges send out press release after press
release proclaiming how they are helping make college affordable to the
average American, the reality of college is that it is a place dominated by
the rich. As my colleague Andrew Delbanco has noted,

> Ninety percent of Harvard students come from families earning
> more than the median national income of $55,000, and Harvard's
> dean of admissions . . . defined "middle-income" Harvard families as
> those earning between $110,000 and $200,000. . . . Today's students
> are richer on average than their predecessors. Between the mid-
> 1970s and mid-1990s, in a sample of eleven prestigious colleges,
> the percentage of students from families in the bottom quartile of
> national family income remained roughly steady—around 10 per-
> cent. During the same period the percentage of students from the
> top quartile rose sharply, from a little more than one third to fully
> half. . . . And if the sample is broadened to include the top 150 col-
> leges, the percentage of students from the bottom quartile drops to
> 3 percent.[8]

Harvard's "middle income" is the richest 5 percent of our nation.[9] This
alone should tell us a lot about our elite educational institutions. While
they look more open to us, this is in no small part because to us openness
means diversity, and diversity means race. But class matters.

Though poor students experience a host of disadvantages—from lower-
quality schools to difficult access to out-of-school enrichment programs
to the absence of support when they struggle—colleges are largely blind

to such struggles, treating poorer students as if they were the same as rich ones. This is in stark contrast to students who are legacies (whose past family members attended the college), athletes, or members of a minority group. Though students from these three groups are provided special consideration by colleges, increasing their chances of admission, poorer students are afforded no such luxury.[10] They may claim otherwise, but colleges are truly "need blind" in the worst possible way. They are ambivalent to the disadvantages of poverty. The result is a clear class bias in college enrollments. College professors, looking at our classrooms, know this sad truth quite well. Put simply, lots of rich kids go to college. Few poor ones do.[11]

As I discuss inequality I keep returning to education, and elite education in particular. This is no accident. One of the best predictors of your earnings is your level of education; attending an elite educational institution increases your wages even further.[12] Schooling matters for wealth. If the competitive nature of the college application process is any indicator, it's clear that most Americans know this story quite well. Given that increases in inequality over the past fifty years are in no small part explained by the expansion of wealth, and elite schooling is central to becoming an elite, we need to know more about how elite schools are training those who are driving inequality.

Before casting elite schools as the villains of our story, we must pause. For all my criticism of elite schools as bastions of wealth, we must remember that these are not simply nefarious places, committed to producing the rich. And as far back as 1940, James Bryant Conant, the president of Harvard University, declared it our national duty "to afford all an unfettered start and a fair chance in the race of life." Conant imagined creating a Jeffersonian ideal of a "natural aristocracy" where the elite would be selected on the basis of talent. At his core Conant was a Tocquevillian, hoping to strike a blow at the heart of the undeserving elite and replace it with what he imagined made America great: equality of conditions.[13] Over the past sixty years elite schools have made attempts to shift away from being bastions of entitled rich boys toward being places for the talented members of all of society. Many accepted black students long before they were compelled to do so by the pressures of the civil rights movement. They similarly transformed into places that do not just "allow" women; they created the conditions in which they could thrive. These schools' religious foundations led them to imagine that they were not simply places for the education of the advantaged but places that lead to the betterment of society.

In no small part this leading has meant attempts to create a meritocracy of talent. Things like the SAT—a test seeking to evaluate the "natural aptitude" of students and move away from favoring their wealth and lineage—emerged out of the ideal.[14] The test was imagined and instituted by Henry Chauncey, a descendant of Puritan ministers who arrived in this country in the 1630s. His family were firmly part of the American WASP establishment; they were among the very first students at the Groton School, one of the nation's premier boarding schools, and Chauncey himself was a graduate of and later a dean at Harvard. Through the SAT Chauncey sought to level the playing field and in the process transform elite schools and thereby the elite. The paradox of open inequality shows how this project has been both a tremendous success and a tremendous failure. Who is at elite schools seems to have shifted. But the elite seem to have a firmer and firmer hold on our nation's wealth and power.

One reason is that there is nothing innate about "merit." Though we tend to think of merit as those qualities that are abstract and ahistorical, in fact what counts as meritorious is highly contextual. Many scholars have pointed to the ways in which our definitions of merit change over time, depending on cultural and institutional contexts.[15] The term "meritocracy" was coined by Michael Young. In the 1940s Young had been asked by England's Labour Party to help institute and evaluate a new educational system meant to allow all young Britons the opportunity acquire the best education, should they be able. Young soon became cynical of the kind of technocratic approach to human character that such an education seemed to promote. Struggling to think of a word to describe this new system, he played off "aristocracy" and "democracy." Rather than "rule by the best" (aristos) or "rule by the people" (demos), this system would establish "rule by the cleverest people."[16] Though we often think of the word as something admirable, Young invented it to damn what he saw as the cold scientization of ability and the bureaucratization of talent.

At its core, "meritocracy" is a form of social engineering, aimed at identifying the talents of members of society so that individuals can be selected for appropriate opportunities. In the case of the SAT this means evaluating particular mathematics, reading, writing, and vocabulary skills and using them as indicators of academic ability.[17] This move toward meritocracy has sought to decollectivize formerly valued attributes and instead individualize new ones that are "innate." Rather than accept students because they manifest a character that revealed good heritage, this new system would look beyond the trappings of society and reward people's inherent individual talents. When meritocracy began to make its way into college admissions, then dean of Harvard admissions, Wilbur Bender, worried, "Are there any good ways of identifying and measuring goodness, humanity, character, warmth, enthusiasm, responsibility, vitality, creativity, independence, heterosexuality, etc., etc., or should we care about these anyhow?"[18] As Jerome Karabel has shown, many of these traits were used as proxies for elite status.[19] Bender, the child of Mennonite parents from Goshen, Indiana, was no elite WASP. But he expressed concerns that echoed throughout the world of elite education in the 1950s and 1960s: what might happen to the elements of character that so marked the old American elite? Would the rise of the meritocracy mean the death of the old elite?

With "merit" we seem to have stripped individuals of the old baggage of social ties and status and replaced it with personal attributes—hard work, discipline, native intelligence, and other forms of human capital that can be evaluated separate from the conditions of social life. And the impact of the adoption of this approach has led to rather contradictory outcomes. It has undercut nepotism. It has been used to promote the opening of schools to talented members of society who previously were excluded. But it has also been used to question policies like affirmative action that take into account factors other than performance on select technocratic instruments. It has been used to justify the increased wages of the already wealthy (as their skills are so valuable and irreplaceable). And most important for me, it has obscured how outcomes are not simply a product of individual traits. As I shall argue, this meritocracy of hard work and achievement has naturalized socially constituted distinctions, making differences in outcomes appear a product of who people are rather than a product of the conditions of their making. It is through looking at the rise of the meritocracy that we can better understand the new elite and thereby some of the workings of our contemporary inequality.

In exploring St. Paul's I will show how the school produces "meritorious" traits of students. We will see how these attributes are developed within elite settings that few have access to. What seems natural is made, but access to that making is strictly limited. Returning to my first days at

St. Paul's, we can see some of these tensions. The school had worked hard to recruit the talented members of minority groups; more were on campus than ever before. And these students did not represent diversity as mere window dressing. Instead St. Paul's hoped to take seriously its elite role within the great American project of equality and liberty. But for all these ambitious ideals, such a project was not a simple one. Admission was incredibly competitive; a condition of being an elite school is exclusion (or at least exclusivity). The acceptance of talented minorities did not guarantee integration. And openness did not always mean equality. The rich students still seemed to dominate the school. Yet structured around the new meritocracy, it seemed these outcomes were a product of different aptitudes and not different conditions. The promise of America was not fulfilled in my days at St. Paul's School.

The question is why. It is not due to a lack of commitment on the part of elite institutions. Nor is it because of the failure of the disadvantaged to desire mobility. In order to make sense of what is going on, this book leaves social statistics behind and explores my return to high school as a teacher and researcher, chronicling a year in the life of St. Paul's School.[20] Upon first imagining this project I was pretty sure I knew what I would find. I would return to the world of my first day at the school. I would enter a campus populated by rich, entitled students and observe a few poor, black, and Latino kids sequestered in their own dorm. I would note the social and cultural advantages of the students who arrived at school already primed to be the next generation of elites. And I would see how advantages were protected and maintained. But the St. Paul's I returned to was a very different place than the one I had graduated from just ten years earlier. My ethnographic examination of St. Paul's School surprised me. Instead of the arrogance of entitlements I discovered at St. Paul's an ease of privilege. This book is a story of a new elite—a group I had to rethink in light of my second time at St. Paul's—and how knowing about this elite reinforms our understanding of inequality within a meritocracy.

Returning to St. Paul's: Privilege and the New Elite

Before us stood two enormous closed doors. Heavily carved slabs of thick oak with large looping braided wrought-iron handles, it was clear that opening them would be no easy task. Standing in a hallway outside we could look out through the arched windows upon the immaculate lawns, ponds, buildings, and brick paths of the school that surrounded us. Behind those doors we could hear the muffled sounds of an organ and the murmurs of hundreds. I glanced around at the faces lined up behind me: excited, terrified, curious, tired. Some were nervously chattering, others frozen in place; surrounding me was a group of teenagers in their Sunday best, unsure what lay beyond. Behind those doors was our future. We waited.

As the doors opened a quiet overcame everyone. A deep, steady voice began announcing names. With each name another one of us stepped into a dark silence beyond those doors. Our line shortened; our time grew nearer. Soon I could peer into the building we were about to enter. Standing in the bright outside, I could just make out the contours of a cavernous space, softly lit with chandeliers that hung so far from the ceiling they seemed to float. I saw vague rows of people.

My name was called, and I stepped through the enormous doors. The Chapel was long and narrow. My eyes were slow to adjust. I told myself I shouldn't be nervous. After all, I had been through this before, years earlier. But it was hard to suppress my nerves. Dressed in a black gown with a blue and red hood and newly purchased shoes, my soles clicked too loudly against the cold stones. Some of the new faculty members walking in front of me looked around frantically, like rural tourists walking among skyscrapers for the first time. Others kept their eyes fixed on the distant altar, as though it were a beacon guiding them to the safety of their seat. As I casually and slowly walked between the pews, I spotted faces I recognized and places I had occupied years ago as a student. I was the last new faculty member to enter; after me came a stream of incoming freshmen, sophomores, and juniors. They swarmed in quickly behind me, unable to hide their anxiety, stepping on my heels until I took my seat.

This was our first ceremony at the school, "taking one's place." Through this ritual new members were formally introduced to the school and shown where we belonged among the community. Each new member had a designated seat—one we would occupy almost every morning for the next year. The seating is arranged like bleachers in a football stadium—four rows of wood-carved seats face one another, with the aisle we had just paraded down separating them. I belonged in the highest, back row, where all faculty members sat. To my right sat returning faculty, arranged in order of seniority; to my left were the new hires. In front of and below me were row after row of our students. As the new students took their place they filled out the very front row, closest to the aisle. Like the faculty, their place was arranged by seniority, with the seniors sitting in the row just below the faculty, and the new freshman in the lowest front row.

Stretched before me were girls and boys who had fought to gain entry to St. Paul's School. The pews were bursting with the weight and the promise of monumental success. The seniors closest to me knew that next year the college they were most likely to attend was Harvard—almost a third of them would be at the Ivy League, and nearly all of them at one of the top colleges in the nation. And college placement was merely the next step in their carefully cultivated lives. Just as this seating ceremony endowed them with a specific place at St. Paul's, so too would graduation from St. Paul's endow them with a place in an even more bountiful world. As they all had doubtlessly been reminded by eager parents, they would be part of an even broader community—a member of a group of graduates who occupied powerful positions throughout the world. The students around me, though fighting sleep and the hormonal haze of adolescence, knew that they were sitting in seats once occupied by the men and women who had led American commerce, government, and culture for the last century and a half. For the boys and girls around me, their own challenge was no less daunting; they were the new elite.

Since 1855 St. Paul's has been one of the primary homes for the adolescent elite of our nation. It is a strange feeling to know that you are partly responsible for shaping the minds and hearts of children who are expected to one day lead the world. Doubly strange because I had once been one of those students, watched over by many of the same faculty members with whom I now shared the back row. Here I was again. Only now my motives were far more complicated. I was here to mold these young men and women, but I was also here to study them.

How is it that a boarding school endows the future success of its members? What do these students have, develop, or learn that advantages them in the years to come? Just a few decades ago these questions might have been easy to answer. Students came from families that already had astounding advantages. For more than a hundred years, America's aristocracy used institutions like St. Paul's to solidify their position as masters of our economy and government, to pass that power on to the next generation. St. Paul's helped transfer the birthright of each new group of students into credentials, relationships, and culture, all of which ensured their future success.

Today, the dominant role of the elite has become less straightforward. Looking at the faces before me I saw boys and girls from every part of the world. St. Paul's could never be mistaken for a public high school. It has an intentional diversity that few communities share or can afford. Sitting next to a poor Hispanic boy from the Bronx—who forty years ago would never have been admitted—is a frighteningly self-possessed girl from one of the richest WASP families in the world. St. Paul's is still a place for the already elite. Parents who visit often do so in a sea of Mercedes and BMWs, with the occasional chauffeured Rolls Royce; on sunny days, the campus seems to shimmer from the well-appointed jewelry that hangs carelessly from necks and wrists and fingers. But it is more. Today the school seeks to be a microcosm of our world. Rich and poor, black and white, boys and girls live in a community together. As they share their adolescent lives in classrooms, on sports fields, at dances, in dorms, and even in bed, they make up a diverse and idealized community. Sitting there in my Chapel seat, I saw before me a showcase of the promise of the diverse twenty-first-century world. And I began to understand the new ways that St. Paul's instills in its members the privileges of belonging to an elite.

In the pages that follow I present a portrait of what I call the "new elite"—a group of advantaged youths who don't quite reflect what we typically imagine when we conjure up a vision of the well-off. They are not all born into rich families. They are not all white. Their families did not arrive on these shores four centuries ago. They are not all from the Northeast. They do not share a preppy culture; they don't avoid rap music and instead educate themselves in the "finer" cultural things.

We also don't know much about our elites. Though we eagerly read profiles in *Vanity Fair*, watch the latest exposé on the evening news, or smugly smile through television programs that show the grotesque underbelly of wealth, we lack a clear sense of how they acquire, maintain, and protect their positions. Who are the contemporary American elite? How are they educated? What do they learn about the world, the place of others, and how to interact with them? And how have they adapted to the changing social environment of the past fifty years? How have they dealt with the demands for openness by those who for much of modern history have been excluded from their rolls?

I will argue that the new elite are not an entitled group of boys who rely on family wealth and slide through trust-funded lives. The new elite feel their heritage is not sufficient to guarantee a seat at the top of the social hierarchy, nor should their lives require the exclusion of others. Instead, in certain fundamental ways they are like the rest of twenty-first-century America: they firmly believe in the importance of the hard work required to achieve their position at a place like St. Paul's and the continued hard work it will take to maintain their advantaged position. Like new immigrants and middle-class Americans, they believe that anyone can achieve what they have, that upward mobility is a perpetual American possibility. And looking around at their many-hued peers, they are provided with experiential, though anecdotal, evidence that they are correct.

Instead of *entitlement*, I have found that St. Paul's increasingly cultivates *privilege*. Whereas elites of the past were entitled—building their worlds around the "right" breeding, connections, and culture—new elites develop privilege: a sense of self and a mode of interaction that advantage them. The old entitled elites constituted a class that worked to construct moats and walls around the resources that advantaged them. The new elite think of themselves as far more individualized, supposing that their position is a product of what they have done. They deemphasize refined tastes and "who you know" and instead highlight how you act in and approach the world. This is a very particular approach to being an elite, a fascinating combination of contemporary cultural mores and classic American values. The story that the new elite tell is built on America's deeply held belief that merit and hard work will pay off. And it also harnesses a twenty-first-century global outlook, absorbing and extracting value from anything and everything, always savvy to what's happening at the present moment. Part of the way in which institutions like St. Paul's and the Ivy League tell their story is to look less and less like an exclusive yacht club and more and more like a microcosm of our diverse social world—albeit a microcosm with very particular social rules. This book will take us into the world of St. Paul's School to draw out three lessons of privilege that students learn.

Lesson 1: Hierarchies Are Natural and They Can Be Treated Like Ladders, Not Ceilings

Students learn to emphasize hard work and talent when explaining their good fortune. This framing is reinforced by a commitment to an open society—for only in such a society can these qualities explain one's success. However, students also learn that the open society does not mean equality—far from it. A persistent lesson is the enduring, natural presence of hierarchy. Within the open society there are winners and losers. But unlike the past where these positions were ascribed through inheritance, today they are achieved. Hierarchies are not barriers that limit but ladders that allow for advancement. Learning to climb requires interacting with those above (and below) you in a very particular way: by creating intimacy without acting like you are an equal. This is a tricky interactive skill, pretending the hierarchy isn't there but all the while respecting it. Hierarchies are dangerous and unjustifiable when too fixed or present—when society is closed and work and talent don't matter. And so students learn a kind of interaction and sensibility where hierarchies are enabling rather than constraining—in short, where they are fair.

Lesson 2: Experiences Matter

Students learn this through experience. Many St. Paul's students are from already privileged backgrounds, and it would not be unreasonable to think that they would have an easier time learning these lessons. Yet adjusting to life at the school is difficult for everyone. The students who act as if they already hold the keys to success are rejected as entitled. In learning their place at the school students rely not on their heritage but instead on *experiences*. There is a shift from the logic of the old elite—who you are—to that of the new elite—what you have done. Privilege is not something you are born with; it is something you learn to develop and cultivate.

Lesson 3: Privilege Means Being at Ease, No Matter What the Context

What students cultivate is a sense of how to carry themselves, and at its core this practice of privilege is ease: feeling comfortable in just about any social situation. In classrooms they are asked to think about both *Beowulf* and *Jaws*. Outside the classroom they listen to classical music and hip-hop. Rather than mobilizing what we might think of as "elite knowledge" to mark themselves as distinct—epic poetry, fine art and music, classical learning—the new elite learn these and everything else. Embracing the open society, they display a kind of radical egalitarianism in their tastes. Privilege is not an attempt to construct boundaries around knowledge and protect such knowledge as a resource. Instead, students display a kind of omnivorousness. Ironically, exclusivity marks the losers in the hierarchical, open society. From this perspective, inequality is explained not by the practices of the elite but instead by the character of the disadvantaged. Their limited (exclusive) knowledge, tastes, and dispositions mean they have not seized upon the fruits of our newly open world.

This elite ease is also an embodied interactional resource. In looking at seemingly mundane acts of everyday life—from eating meals to dancing and dating—we will see how privilege becomes inscribed upon the bodies of students and how students are able to display their privilege through their interactions. In being embodied, privilege is not seen as a product of differences in opportunities but instead as a skill, talent, capacity—"who you are." Students from St. Paul's appear to naturally have what it takes to be successful. This helps hide durable inequality by naturalizing socially produced distinctions.

This book is my attempt to understand the new elite and, through drawing out these lessons of privilege, to make sense of our new inequality. This work often emphasizes the way in which culture—students' dispositions, interactions, and ways of being in the world—defines elite belonging and thus helps drive inequality. Culture can be thought of as a kind of "capital"—like money it has value and can be put to work to acquire social advantages. In learning about the culture of the new elite I hope to elucidate some of the workings of inequality in a meritocracy.

My return to St. Paul's was inspiring. I saw how even our most august institutions could rewrite the assumptions of previous generations and attempt to create a more inclusive world. And yet like all good tales, this one has another side. Students from St. Paul's are undoubtedly privileged. They accrue extraordinary advantages, and the disjuncture between the lives of these students and the lives of other American teenagers—even those living a few miles down the road in Concord, New Hampshire—can be shocking. The elite adoption of the American Dream, however well-intentioned, happens against a backdrop of increasing social inequality. In embracing an open society and embodying privilege, elites have obscured the persistence of social closure in our world.

Throughout the twentieth century the battles against inequality were battles of access: could women, blacks, and other excluded groups be integrated into the highest institutions and positions in our society? These battles were largely won. Yet the results have not been what we imagined. The promise of the open society was not just more access but more equality. This promise has proven to be a fiction. Twenty-first-century America is increasingly open yet relentlessly unequal. Our next great American project is to find a way out of this paradox.

1

The New Elite

What is the future function of a predominantly Anglo-Saxon and Protestant
upper class in an ethnically and religiously heterogeneous democracy?
In many ways, this is the most important question of all.
—E. DIGBY BALTZELL

Some will always be above others. Destroy the inequality today, and
it will appear again tomorrow.
—RALPH WALDO EMERSON

I sat across from Chase Abbott. We were in my faculty office, a wood-
paneled room on the first floor of the Schoolhouse, one of the main academic buildings on campus. At times Chase seemed to claim my office, as
if it were his own. He stretched, sat back comfortably in his chair, almost
lounging. When he first entered he looked closely at the papers on my
desk, just barely resisting the urge to go through them. Before he sat down
he inspected the books on my shelf, even going so far as to take one down
and flip through it casually before putting it back in a different place. As we
talked his comfort and confidence were abundant; I thought at moments
that perhaps it was I who was visiting him. Yet despite his preternatural
self-assuredness, he was still a teenager. At other times he would avoid eye
contact, looking down at the floor or out the window to my right. He was
senior boy who felt both very at home and very lost at St. Paul's.

Chase had none of the angular, equine features of many of his classmates. His face was soft, his skin pale, with a ruddy hue on his cheeks and
nose. Late in the year I would see him in a seersucker suit with a pink tie,
boat shoes without socks, and straw hat; I never saw him so supremely
confident or comfortable than when in that outfit. In the Upper, where
many students live and all the school dines, the names of every graduate

are engraved upon the dark wooden hallways. As Chase ate his meals three times a day, he passed the names of several generations of Abbott men who had walked the same halls. Much of his life had been spent among graduates of St. Paul's and other elite boarding schools. Attending St. Paul's had been an expectation for as long as he could remember; to him, at least, it seemed his birthright. Yet his time at the school had not been triumphant. He was not a strong student. And he was not very popular. His enduring connections to the school had not translated into unbridled success. It surprised me to find that Chase—a boy who seemed to grow up in the very bowels of boarding school society—would struggle emotionally, academically, and socially at the school. If anyone was to be absolutely at home at St. Paul's, it should have been Chase Abbott.

After a particularly difficult first year, during which he didn't get along with his roommate and could not relate to his advisor or many of his teachers, Chase moved into Andrews House, where the other students were more "like him." They also tended to have long-term connections with the school. They were all fairly wealthy. They had summer homes on the same islands as various members of Chase's family. Many he had known before ever enrolling at St. Paul's. Most of the others he knew of through family and friends. And it was here where Chase began to find a home at the school.

When I asked Chase how he ended up at St. Paul's, he seemed to take offense at the question. He proceeded to tell me of the long series of family members who went to the school. He carefully mapped the history of the school onto the history of his family. He spoke of his father and grandfather, of uncles and great-uncles, all of whom were students under different administrations; he referred to former rectors of the school with a kind of intimacy that suggested that perhaps it was he who was at the school under the fabled reign of Samuel Drury in the 1930s. At the end of his story, and his history lesson about the school and his family, Chase turned the question around and asked, forcefully, "How did *you* end up here?" He betrayed just a hint of intentional surprise when I told him that I attended the same school his family had for generations, that my name was written among those of his family. That name and my appearance instantly revealed to Chase that I was not "like him"—that I could not construct the kind of narrative he had just provided me. As I explained my much briefer story—the child of immigrant parents who had become wealthy enough to send me to the school—Chase casually broke eye contact, looked indifferently out my window, and replied with a nonverbal grunt: "Hmmm."

Had this interaction happened fifteen years earlier, while I was still an anxious and awkward teenager, I suspect I would have felt a combination of shame and rage. But years later, as I was older and the school had changed, I could not help but chuckle. The interaction was reminiscent of a moment in Robert DeNiro's film *The Good Shepherd* when an Italian immigrant (and mobster), Joseph Palmi, asks an elite Skull and Bones member of the American government, Edward Wilson, what he and people like him "have" in life.

"Let me ask you something," Palmi says. "We Italians, we got our families, and we got the church; the Irish they have the homeland, Jews their tradition; even the niggers, they got their music. What about you people, Mr. Wilson, what do you have?"

"The United States of America. The rest of you are just visiting."[1]

Chase's "hmmm" was his try at a Wilsonesque reply. He "had" St. Paul's; people like me were merely visiting. In mapping his life and heritage onto the life of the school, in claiming its history as his own, and in romanticizing the school's past, he attempted to take ownership of the school. My chuckling was not just because I was older and more secure. There was something quaint and old-fashioned about his manner. What would have seemed a forceful utterance for much of the school's history now rang somewhat hollow. The power behind Chase's question and his response to my answer was empty. I knew that his attempts to claim the school were not successful. He sat before me in part because of his struggles. Though confidence and self-righteousness bubbled up periodically, much of the time he was not at home at the place that was practically his birthright.

Many members of the school were not as amused as I. After seeing me chatting with Chase, a boy I was close with, Peter, expressed what many others would time and again: "That guy would never be here if it weren't for his family. . . . I don't get why the school still does that. He doesn't bring anything to this place." Peter seemed annoyed with me for even talking with Chase. Knowing that I was at St. Paul's to make sense of the school, Peter made sure to point out to me that Chase didn't really belong there and that his presence and ideas would provide few insights for my project. Peter was from a wealthy town in Connecticut, from a family with ties to elite educational institutions. His parents had met at Harvard; they were not the first in their families to attend the school. Nevertheless, Peter and Chase understood their position at the school differently. For Chase it was a birthright. For Peter, it was his hard work.

When I returned to the school as a faculty member and researcher, one of my first realizations was that the sequestering of non-whites that so formed my own experience at the school was a relic of the past. Students of color lived all over campus. When I told my students that I had lived in a "minority student dorm" they didn't believe me. One went so far as to go to the library and look at old yearbooks to check my story. He returned, excited: "I can't believe it! You were right. They all *did* live together! I just saw your dorm picture!"

Just as I was shocked to discover that I had been sequestered in the "minority dorm" as a student, so too was I shocked to learn that there was a different kind of sequestering that was now occurring. Today it is the Chase Abbotts who live in an almost closed social group—a group of the most entitled students, some of whom come from the most established American families, families with long ties to St. Paul's and the Ivy League. Chase lived in a dorm with others "like him." Not all legacy students lived with Chase, but those who felt that such ties were important to belonging at the school—those who felt entitled—did. The school widely recognizes this. Though the school allows Chase's dorm to persist, it is in part because students can mostly choose where they live and mainly because few students want to live with others like Chase. Peter's complaints were not unique. Faculty, too, openly lamented the presence of students like Chase, who believe their family history matters enough that they need not work and can express disdain for those who explain their position at the school by such work. Most community members (faculty, staff, students, and alumni) point to students like Chase as examples of what is bad about St. Paul's. They question their admission and doubt that there will be a future for them at St. Paul's School—the dwindling number of students with Chase's attitude suggests that they are correct.

What happened to the American elite? How is it that the old, socially dominant elite who believe in the importance of their family breeding have lost their hold on an institution like St. Paul's? How have the entitled elite become more like the black students from just fifteen years ago—increasingly alone and isolated? Have they lost their power, or are they simply highly concentrated in one area but with power still firmly in their grasp?

And how have schools like St. Paul's continued to produce privileges for their students while rejecting the entitlements that for so long were tightly coupled with such privileges? What do the huge cultural shifts at a place like St. Paul's mean for the future of the elite and for the rest of us? In order to answer these questions, let's step away from St. Paul's for a moment and take a look at the slow transformation of the elite: from the ancien régime to the old elite to the new one.

The Fall and Rise of Elites

To understand our present elites, we must first place them in the recent context of rapid social transformations. The reader may be surprised to hear me refer to 250 years of history as "rapid," but given the comparative stagnation of elites for much of human history, our elites seem to be transforming at an exponential pace. The moment we must look most carefully at is "the long nineteenth century": from the French Revolution to World War I. Between 1789 and 1914 we experienced three revolutions: a political one in France, an industrial one in England, and, most important, the global rise of America. The effects of all three spread rapidly across the globe and changed our world. The balance of social power seemed to move from political to economic, and from the old world to the new. Monarchies fell, democracies emerged, and capitalists triumphed. During this time we saw an enormous extension of political rights and economic possibility, coupled with a massive increase in inequality. The ancien régime—the seemingly timeless aristocrats of Europe—lost their control of the world, and a different elite, what I am calling the "old" elite, emerged as the carriers of social power and influence.

Though less recognized, this period also gave us the ideological foundation of the "new" elite—the group I identify as emerging around us today. Transformations in our elite can be directly tied to the collapse of the ancien régime. Aristocracy as we knew it is dead. Symbolically we need only conjure up the image of a king and queen decapitated by their subjects (and in that instant, citizens) to understand the process. The triumph of bourgeois society was, in part, the emergence of our own individual rights and sense of possibility: inherited distinctions were, like monarchs' heads, severed. Change came shockingly fast. For much of recorded culture, human societies were ruled by kings or emperors or warlords and their descendants. The primary shift from the ancien régime to the old elite was from the inheritance of titles to that of wealth, and from the importance of ascriptive groupings[2] to that of individuals. And the shift from the old to the new elite is one that expands the potential participants in this process to include all members of society (namely, women and non-whites).

My focus is on the American case. And this too is no accident. America provided a new model for a nation. The long nineteenth century marked the demise of the old European way and the rise of a more American model. The liberties extolled by political thinkers in eighteenth-century Europe were made more real in America (at least to some). And Europe would soon look less and less like its past and more and more like an adaptation of the liberties made fresh in America. This nation has quite a different set of elites than those in Europe; this is part of why our nation is so unique: it is our "American exceptionalism."[3] Aristocratic influence endured in Europe long past the bourgeois revolutions like the one in Paris in 1789. In 1815 Napoleon reinstated a formal nobility, and France had far more kings and emperors throughout the nineteenth century than one would expect following a democratic revolution.[4] One of the central explanations for this is culture. Though monarchs varied enormously in the extent of their political power, throughout Europe the rising classes deployed aristocratic cultural marks as symbols of their wealth and position.[5] Americans, who lacked such an aristocratic culture, were more apt to deploy wealth as a symbol of itself.

The shift from an inheritance of honor, status, and title to an inheritance of wealth may seem trivial, especially if one considers that titles could be purchased. But it points to a vital rethinking of social life. Money can be earned; titles are granted. Central to the difference is the promise of mobility on the strict basis of what an individual does (and not, say, the generosity of the king). Under the ancien régime, there is a near fixed quality to social life wherein both privilege and poverty are granted at birth. The peasant knows he will remain a peasant all his life. But under the old elite there is the chance of potential advancement. The chance itself, no matter how slim, changed how people began to understand themselves and their relationships with others. Advancement was available; so too was the risk of ruin. For elites, these twin threats of the advancement of the poor and middle classes and the potential of ruin changed the fabric of social life.

The move away from a status-based aristocracy is often read as a quick embrace of liberal equality. And while a nice story, it is demonstrably untrue. For overwhelming periods of our nation's history, American laws have declared the majority of the world's population ineligible for citizenship, and for most of our history the majority of the domestic adult population has been ineligible for citizenship and full political participation.[6] While the capitalist process of industrialization is often tied to the emergence of democracy, the growth of capitalism has not been without its aristocratic worries. Upon his travels through America in 1831, Alexis de Tocqueville envisioned a relationship between democracy and aristocracy that was by no means exclusive.

> As conditions become more and more equal in the body of the nation, the need for manufactured products is universal and even greater; the cheap prices which bring goods within the reach of modest fortunes become a greater ingredient of success. Richer and better educated men emerge daily to devote their wealth and knowledge to industry; by opening great workshops with a strict division of labor they seek to satisfy the new demands which are evident on all sides. Thus, as the mass of the nation turns to democracy the particular class which runs industry becomes more aristocratic. Men resemble each other more in one context and appear increasingly different in another; inequality grows in the smaller social group as it reduces in society at large. Thus it is that, when we trace things back to their source, a natural impulse appears to be prompting the emergence of an aristocracy from the very heart of democracy.[7]

What Tocqueville imagined—this industrial aristocracy—many felt became a reality during the Gilded Age, a period between the end of the Civil War and the beginning of World War I. Though Americans were often less seduced by aristocracy than their European peers, an aristocracy of wealth has often been seen as looming just around the corner. And until very recently, certain birthrights remained immutable; it took centuries for the citizenry to abandon their deeply held racism and belief that men should, by natural right, rule over women.[8]

The transformations of wealth and elite culture during the Gilded Age offer some strikingly clear parallels to our own recent social transformations. The economy and social life were both reconceptualized. A second major industrial revolution began in the Northeast, creating the first real modern industrial economy. Soon American manufacturing production surpassed that of England, France, and Germany combined. A massive accumulation of wealth was concentrated in the cities of the Northeast and used to found or fund most of the nation's premier cultural and educational institutions that still survive today. Simultaneously, this process withered the civic ideal of white, landowning, public citizens constituting the backbone of American society as millions of migrant laborers poured onto the shores and were put to work building infrastructure and goods in factories. Many of these laborers were made citizens, participants in a great national project. Capitalists used them to amass staggering fortunes. Robber barons, men who dominated industries through anti-competitive and often unfair business practices, often directly exploited these diverse workers, taking advantage of their insecure position and the tensions between different racial and ethnic groups to pay wages that were barely livable. The Gilded Age was somewhat like our own: relatively open to made wealth, compared to the social strictures of previous centuries, yet this openness was coupled with massive increases in inequality, much of it along racial and ethnic dimensions. Just as wealth seemed to pile up in the banks of New York and Philadelphia, American cities seemed to increasingly teem with poverty and destitution.

The paradox of possibility and limitation was palpable. Ascriptive characteristics like race and ethnicity as well as gender and religious belief either prohibited or hindered advancement. And yet, the chance to "strike it rich" seemed ever-present. The era was particularly open to the possibility of self-made wealth or Horatio Alger–like stories; indeed, two of the greatest fortunes were made by men who began with nothing: John D. Rockefeller and Andrew Carnegie. On the backs of cheap immigrant labor (who often came to America with their own dreams), a different kind of elite emerged, replacing an older, more landed aristocracy.[9] You no longer had to own an enormous estate to be part of the American aristocracy. But you still had to be white (or white enough not to upset social mores) and a man. And now, you had to make or buy or sell a product, or develop new tools of finance to participate in the fabulous and complex capitalist marketplace that was coming to define our country.

As these Gilded Age elites became a distinct class, they removed themselves socially, culturally, and even spatially from their workers. Thus, at the same time as the world became economically more open, other forms of social closure emerged. A distinction between "us" and "them" was deployed by elites both to protect them from the unbridled advancement of others (sometimes the same ranks of striving men that they had belonged to just a few years prior) and to generate a sense of who they were. Wealth mattered enormously, and it was something that Americans actively displayed: think only of the country estates built up and down the Hudson, the emergence of planners like Frederick Law Olmstead, who, though famous for his public spaces, spent much of his time designing the grounds of the rich, and the success of firms like Tiffany's, which decorated the homes and bodies of the elite with the marks of distinction and difference. Mobility made elites insecure about themselves and their positions, and so just as elites opened economically an elite culture and a tightly regulated network of social connections gained strength, this culture and these social ties to one another made elites a more cohesive and closed social group. The inequality of the day can be understood in large part by this closure, by the ways that these elites put up fences and dug moats—both real and metaphorical—to separate themselves from the masses.

Perhaps the clearest way to see this fence building is in how New York's elite moved their homes away from the factories, mobs, workers, and migrants of lower Manhattan to the security of what is now the Upper East Side. Centered on the east side of Central Park, they sought to construct a space of their own—within the city but a world away from the Babel that was Five Points, the Lower East Side, and Greenwich Village. Their new enclave was built to exclude the other classes who lived just a few miles south, in their former neighborhoods. We can't forget that between 1877 and 1881, these elites actually built an *armory* for New York's 7th Regiment on the Upper East Side. Whereas the former armory had been downtown, as the rich migrated north, so did their fortress. Taking up an entire city block, between 66th and 67th streets and Park and Lexington avenues, the armory was "so constructed as to be defensible from all points against mobs."[10] Their new armory, with space to train their regiment, was also large enough to house many of the neighborhood's families in the event of class warfare. And it was fitted for not just their protection but also their comfort and tastes; no less than Louis Comfort Tiffany and Stanford White designed and constructed the decorations of its interior game, board, and social rooms.[11]

Beyond protecting themselves through the removed location and literal fortification of their homes, the elite also used cultural institutions to construct distinctions. It is no mistake that the Metropolitan Museum of Art, founded during the Gilded Age, is housed among the mansions that line Fifth Avenue. In the early nineteenth century, "fine" art was widely consumed across classes. Printers made copies of paintings and sold them cheaply in lower Manhattan (albeit primarily as pornography). Yet as they worked to create distance between themselves and the rest, elites isolated "fine art" in the walls of museums and used the anti-pornography Comstock laws to ban its wider consumption.[12] Though presented as "public" institutions, early museums were anything but. They worked to exclude the lower classes from art. Theaters were revamped to make it increasingly difficult for the mob in the pits to watch plays. As Lawrence Levine points out, we can look to *Huckleberry Finn* to see how, through much of the nineteenth century, what we think of today as highbrow cultural traits were actually quite common. In Twain's novel, the duke and king are driven out of a town for their attempted scam of performing Shakespeare. Yet the townspeople recognize the incompetence of the performance only because they intimately and deeply *know* Shakespeare. What would become an ultimate mark of highbrow taste, Shakespeare, was everyday knowledge among the rural folk of Arkansas. Similarly, opera was enormously popular among the poorer classes, particularly recent migrants, and opera companies would travel throughout the nation to areas then considered "backwaters," performing for appreciative crowds. But as theaters began to isolate plays and concert halls began to isolate orchestras and operas (and New York began to pay artists enough to keep them from leaving the side of the wealthy), cultural differences began to emerge as more dominant marks of class distinction.[13]

It was amid these turbulent shifts of nineteenth-century America that St. Paul's School was born. As we'll see, the tension over who exactly constituted the elite and how their elite status would pass from one generation to the next became an issue of great concern for America's old money and new money alike. The boarding school would become the site where the elites were made. Such schools helped form networks of association and common experiences for elites. Like the cultural institutions that created distinctions and geographical isolation, they aided elites in placing their children in a world apart from those who were darker, poor, quite different, and quite dangerous.

Boarding Schools

The first members of St. Paul's School were merely five; in 1856, three pupils, one master, and his new wife of seven days all arrived by carriage to a single-family home in Concord, New Hampshire. George C. Shattuck Jr., a Boston Brahmin and well-known physician, founded the school by donating his country seat, Millville. The first and only master, Henry Coit, was but twenty-four years old. Upon acceptance of the position, St. Paul's nascent board of trustees told Coit, "You have possession of the land and the buildings, but we can not promise you a salary." The pupils and Coit were expected to be self-sufficient. Today the story is told that immediately upon arrival, two began their studies while the third was sent to fish; they needed dinner. Their lives were to be spent in a familial, rural setting away from the corrupting life of the city.

  Six days a week, the school's first members arose at sunrise, prayed together, did their required chores (cleaning, farming, maintenance), ate, studied, prayed, and retired. They spent their Sundays at the Chapel. From this simple origin emerged a school that would become one of the primary homes of the American elite; by the end of his tenure Coit would wield an immense influence upon the American educational system, comparable to Thomas Arnold's impact through his leading of Rugby School in England.[14] Coit died in 1895, firmly at the helm until his final days. By the end of his forty-year tenure, St. Paul's had a faculty of 35 and a student body of 345.

  Two other famous American boarding schools, the academies of Phillips Andover and Exeter, were founded nearly a century before St. Paul's. They were far more similar to the British boarding school, using the model of the academy that granted a great deal of independence and movement for its boys. At Andover and Exeter, as at the traditional British schools founded centuries earlier, students lived off campus with families who would house them for a fee. In the early nineteenth century English boarding schools were not the kind of place one would want to send loved children—and certainly not places where they might be educated. As James MacLachlan has argued in his account of the boarding school, "At the beginning of the nineteenth century English education was at one of its lowest states—the universities moribund, secondary education so diverse that no generalization about it is possible."[15] August Heckscher has noted that such schools were "in a deplorable condition, scholastically lax, with student bodies prone to licentiousness and rebellion."[16] Famed schools like Eton, Harrow, and Rugby had classroom sizes of one hundred to two hundred pupils. Students did not live on a school campus (only the few poor students did) but were often housed in lavish private accommodation where they lived completely independent of the school authorities, and typically quite wildly: "A boy might get a very good classical education at one of these schools, but it had to be acquired much on his own initiative."[17]

Soon after the founding of St. Paul's, the American academies would move closer to St. Paul's vision and transform themselves into schools that also limited the independence of their students and encouraged the growth of a community. Before the 1850s, schools allowed young boys the chance to develop on their own.[18] St. Paul's would not take such a chance. It exemplified the mores of a new era and was founded on Victorian ideals that the already well-established British schools and American academies had yet to realize. The purpose was not to churn out servants to country or to wealth but to produce a community of "gentlemen." The idea that St. Paul's was a preparatory school for something later in life—university life, economic activity, and so forth—is entirely misleading. Its motto, "Ea discamus in terris quorum scientia perseveret in coelis" (Let us learn those things on Earth, the knowledge of which continues in Heaven), suggests its otherworldly, nonpurposive orientation. Only five of the first seventy graduates ever attended college: "Its ideal of a liberal and human curriculum, combined with religious training, active sports, and a richly developed community life, led the school along a path of its own."[19] This was done through a "gentle familial Christian nurture" of innocence. Students were highly regulated, placed in isolated familial surroundings that were free of corrupting or devilish influences,[20] and taught Christian values in this intimate setting.

As the long nineteenth century progressed, the young were considered dependent on their families and the institutions that trained them for longer and longer periods of time. The Victorians similarly expanded the period of childhood where boys were seen as more innocent and pure. Dependency and innocence went hand in hand; left alone they would quickly be corrupted. By the 1860s, the students at St. Paul's were the same age as most of the students at Harvard had been in the 1820s; its curriculum was much the same as Harvard's had been.[21] This delayed adulthood provided advantaged children three periods of development: first in their homes with their families, second in a school like St. Paul's that protected their innocence through isolation, and finally in either a university or an apprenticeship where students were less isolated and left to care for themselves. The hope was that the first two stages of this development would protect young men as they entered the third. This structure also distinguished middle- and upper-class children from working and poor children, who typically went straight from the home into the workplace. The rich were provided with "greater" moral development in their extended childhoods; this development provided a mark of difference—the mark of a gentlemanly morality.

The paternalism of such development should not be underemphasized. Boys, if left to themselves in the world, could not be expected to grow into moral beings. Rather, they required removal from corruption and vigilant surveillance. In his epic study of the social history of the family, Philippe Aries noted the ways in which boys were seen as requiring heavy management of their morality. Parents often hired preceptors to watch over, protect, and help their boys avoid moral pitfalls in life.[22] Quoting the biography of H. de Mesmes, a French nobleman, "My father gave me as a preceptor J. Aludan, a disciple of Dorat's, a learned man chosen for the innocence of his life and of a suitable age to guide my youth until I was able to govern myself as he did."[23] This paternalist moral protection of boys, shown here in sixteenth-century France, became even more vigilant in the Victorian age. Upon the founding of St. Paul's, simple surveillance was not enough (as it was for M. Mesmes); removal was also required. By the late nineteenth century in the United States, the preceptor transformed into the boarding school.

In its curriculum St. Paul's did not vary much from schools that had preceded it by even 150 years. At the inception of the school there were three courses: Latin, Greek, and mathematics. Twenty years later English, French, and history were added. Religious observation marked daily activities. For nearly the first century of the school there was daily chapel, three services on Sunday, and a Thursday evening sermon given by the rector. None of this was particularly novel for schools at the time. What was important about St. Paul's, what was emulated by later boarding schools, and what remains central to this day was the nature of living at the place. The image of a small group of students arriving with Coit and moving into a home with him and his wife is illuminating. Unlike their British counterparts, or those of the earlier American academies, St. Paul's students lived with masters in an environment that could be called a family or community.

As students were added the school insisted that new masters live on the grounds (with their families if they had them) so as to retain the school's fundamental sense of community. Coit and future headmasters and trustees struggled to maintain this community from inside and out. Over time they purchased all the lands surrounding the school, turning the originally modest fifty acres into a modern estate of two thousand. All faculty and their families continue to be housed on campus—many in homes that are attached to dormitories. They function in loco parentis, often viewed as dedicating their lives to their students and the school. The image of a pelican picking the meat from its own breast to feed its young is on the crest of the school, and it represents what students can expect of their highly qualified teachers: the ultimate sacrifice. Today, as in the past, not only do students and faculty live together; they spend much of their day with one another. Since its inception the school has met as a group with amazing regularity. In the early years the entire school was collected together upward of thirty times a week: eating all their meals together at high table, in the Chapel every morning and multiple times on Sundays, and on the sports fields six days a week. Dorms were designed with minimal privacy. To this day there are no locks on the doors of students' rooms, and faculty are encouraged to walk in at all times of the day and night. Housing is not arranged by isolating similarly aged children with one another. In the school's imagination, students live as siblings, the older living with and watching over the younger.

Still the school adapted some marks of the European system. For much of the school's history it was not a high school but a place for students from seventh to twelfth grade. Paralleling British schools, students entered in the first form and graduated as sixth formers. The "form" system is still in place. Students are not freshmen but third formers. The senior class is the sixth form, creating a symbolic distinction between St. Paul's students and their public school peers.

Suggesting that boarding schools protected the children of elites from "devilish" influences sanitizes an already familiar story of deep racism and class protectionism. In early America the model pioneered by Andover and Exeter served quite well—until a crisis confronted elites in the mid- to late nineteenth century. That crisis was the dual threat of urban poverty and immigration, combined with the increasing vulnerability of old elites to the wealth built by lucky migrants who defined the new economy of the Gilded Age. Elite children were no longer safe in the city, and families looked beyond economic dominance to social networks to solidify their status. They needed a protective refuge; the boarding school was just that.

Throughout the Northeast coast, as new European migrants flooded into cities like New York, Boston, and Philadelphia, as industrialization exploded and as class tensions rose, elites began to construct institutions that could protect their families from the threats of a modernizing nation. Just as cultural institutions—museums, orchestras, theaters—created symbolic boundaries between elites and others, and just as the Park Avenue Armory created a potential barricade against undesirables, other institutions, like the boarding school, physically removed children from the threats of the immigrant poor—protecting both their social position and their innocence.

Nicola Beisel has argued that family ties were essential to the elite. Indeed, at times maintaining quality familial relations superseded the interests of capital.

> The aim of the capitalist was not to accumulate as much capital as possible, but to establish a family embraced by the socially elect. To make it into high society one had to be rich, but being rich did not grant one's family admission; furthermore, a family maintained its position not by accumulating more wealth but by participating in social activities that further cemented ties within the social circle.[24]

Boarding schools helped families construct and solidify ties with one another and ensure that their children were well equipped to participate in activities with other elites. They were protectionist institutions aimed at providing not only the knowledge required to be successful but the culture, morality, and social ties that were essential to the American elite. The fact that the mere accumulation of capital was not the overwhelming interest of this old American elite is also a nod to an older, more aristocratic version of an elite who seeks to create barriers that prevent others from joining their rolls.

Boarding schools, then, might seem the least likely spaces to observe the emergence of a new elite and the opening up of our society. And yet we cannot forget the deeply valued sense of noblesse oblige—the belief held by our elite, today and a century ago, that with their advantaged position comes a responsibility or obligation to do some good for the less fortunate. Many truly believe that elite schools are the carriers of our nation's moral authority—particularly those from such schools. As the nation changes, the elites at places like St. Paul's do not imagine that they follow; instead they lead. Scholars have argued that the kind of isolationism and protectionism essential to the founding of such schools is still operative today.[25] A standard theory is that educational institutions function to prepare students for their future social and cultural positions. Thus, students are stripped of their individuality and built up to become "soldiers for their class." Boarding schools, in this formulation, are "total institutions,"[26] regulating their members' lives so as to generate a particular character.

> Since their inception the elite schools have had the responsibility of melting down the refractory material of individualism into the solid metal of elite collectivism. By isolating students from their home world and intervening in their development, it is hoped that they will become soldiers for their class. The total institution is a moral milieu where pressure is placed on individuals to give up significant parts of their selves to forward the interests of the group. . . . Thus the requirement that students eat, sleep, and study together creates and continuously reinforces a sense of collective identity.[27]

I believe that elements of this description were true a century and a half ago, in St. Paul's early years. But this standard view does not take into account the tremendous shifts and self-transformations that have occurred

within elite boarding schools and thus gives us a false impression of how
these places—and the elite itself—function today. Well over fifty years ago,
for example, St. Paul's presented itself as a model of the world, and one
that was representative of it. As the rector of the school, Matthew Warren,
wrote to the alumni in 1960, "We reach out to the world of which we are
a microcosm. Twenty countries are represented here in one way or another.
Every segment of American society is here. Nearly a fourth of the student
body is on formal scholarship."[28] This view of the school as a microcosm
runs against any argument of straight class reproduction and elite collectivism. It was in the 1950s, well before the watershed moments of social
protest during the civil rights movement, that St. Paul's hired its first black
teacher, John T. Walker. The school positioned itself not to reproduce the
world but often to transform it. This transformative process is a slow one
and not without its problems. But the ideal of the school as a microcosm of
the world—instead of a facilitator of class reproduction—marks an enormous shift from the class-based model of the old elite, where ascriptive
differences excluded much of the population and refined culture, morality, and social ties closed this social group from the vast majority of the
world. Further, the increasing emphasis on human capital that I witnessed
during my time at St. Paul's, as well as the value placed on the individual
distinction of the school's students and faculty, work against the standard
class-collectivist notion.

In no small part this increasing emphasis on one's own attributes and
abilities is due to a change in how the richest Americans who populate
elite schools acquire their money. In 1929 the vast majority of the incomes
of the richest 0.01 percent of Americans came from capital: 70 percent
of what they earned came from their ownership of things like factories,
while only 10 percent came from employment. By 1998 this had radically
shifted. Today, only 17 percent of the income of the richest Americans
comes from capital, and more than half their income, 52 percent, comes
from employment.[29] It is enormously important that today the rich explain their position by the work they do, not the capital they have or the
inheritance of their position. The difference between "us" and "them" is
not as it used to be—founded in the ownership of factories versus working
in those factories. Instead, the elite see themselves as just like everyone else:
getting up in the morning and going to work for their paychecks. The shift

in the structure of the economy and economic compensation has transformed the cultural understanding of the wealthy, where class collectivism
simply does not tell a compelling story of who the elite are or why they are
different from others.

To understand our new elite we require a new understanding, and
this will help us wrap our minds around the new forms of inequality that
strangle our nation. We need to make sense of the how the rise of the
meritocracy has created a new elite marked less by protectionism and more
by openness.

The New Elite, the Old Inequality, and the Rise of Meritocracy

As the Gilded Age came to a close the shine of possibility had faded for
many, the dream of America dimmed by the constant toil required in factories and shipyards. The immense engine of capitalism seemed to have
little room for individual betterment, requiring only an endless supply
of labor, of nameless and expendable cogs. Those who drove that engine,
the elites, had cemented their control and built a high fence around their
fortress. The first issue of *The Social Register*, a compilation of the lineages,
addresses, and marriages of the nation's two thousand elite families, appeared in 1887. That tiny number and the fact that they all were identified together testify to the exclusivity of the elites—their efforts both to
establish a network among only themselves and to solidify their positions.
Thirty years later Louis Brandeis documented the enormous concentration
of economic power in the nation. Through a study of the boards of direc-
tors of major corporations, Brandeis found that an inner circle of managers
was increasingly able "to control the business of the country and 'divide
the spoils.'"[30]

The image of a small interlocking group would dominate our understanding of the elite for the next hundred years. Elites were thought of
as a distinct class constituted by economic power, closed networks, and a
shared culture. While the early part of this story was one of conspiracy and
collusion of financiers, by the 1950s C. Wright Mills suggested we move
away from thinking about the ruling class as a ruling cabal and instead

realize that within capitalism there was a structural tendency toward the concentration of both social and economic power. Mills still thought of these men as having a kind of class coherence: "the leading men in each of the three domains of power—the warlords, the corporation chieftains, the political directorate—tend to *come together*, to form the power elite of America."[31] But rather than frame elites as a malicious villain, Mills suggested we look at how such a group might emerge within the economic arrangement of capitalism. As scholars looked more closely at the elites (often their own families), the cohesion of this group was seen to extend beyond boardrooms and into bedrooms. E. Digby Baltzell provided an account of the social-familial lives of what he thought of as "an American business aristocracy" who were "bound together by common interests."[32] Baltzell noted how the American upper class intermarried to preserve their culture and restricted membership.

The conclusion that scholars tended to draw from these myriad observations—from who was on what boards to what capitalism structurally looked like to who married whom—was that inequality is a product of closure and exclusion. The most recent and prominent of these voices is William Domhoff, who has argued that there is "persuasive evidence for the existence of a socially cohesive national upper class."[33] Our dominant way of thinking about elites and even inequality as a whole is now somewhat inaccurate—or at least not up to the challenges we face today. The new elite seem to exhibit an openness and generosity toward previously excluded members.

In order to make sense of this I chose to look at the culture of elites. The cultural restructuring of the American elite—from exclusion to omnivorousness—provides one of the clearest examples of how we might make sense of the puzzle I keep returning to. French sociologist Pierre Bourdieu employs the analogy of capital, suggesting that culture and social ties, like money in your wallet, aid in social advancement or limitation.[34] Bourdieu's insights can help elucidate the story of the old elite, where a particularly exclusive elite culture and social web helped create advantages that supplemented and even protected those garnered in the economy. But they can also be extended to help us see how, as the world has changed, culture continues to work for elites in creating distinctions. Today what is distinct among the elite is not their exclusivity but their ease within and broad acceptance of a more open world. *The Social Register* is dead. Chase

Abbott and his more aristocratic classmates are sequestered. Some of the most adamant defenders of the moral imperative of an open society that I have met are to be found among the faculty, admissions officers, and administrators of St. Paul's School. Schools work hard to frame themselves as intentional communities of racial, ethnic, and economic diversity. Rather than discriminatory fortresses, they purport to provide a model for what the rest of the world should aspire to be.

Such aspirations do not mean that these schools are *not* exclusive. A cursory look at St. Paul's leaves no doubt that the school is a place where already privileged youths spend their adolescent years; two-thirds come from families who can afford over $40,000 per year for high school. The college that students from St. Paul's are *most likely* to attend is Harvard, followed by Brown, the University of Pennsylvania, Dartmouth, Yale, Cornell, Princeton, and Stanford. The acceptance rates to these institutions are well above three times the national average. In recent years, 30 percent of graduating classes attended an Ivy League institution and around 80 percent attended one of the top thirty colleges and universities in the nation.[35] The school's annual per-pupil expenditure of over $80,000 for each student is approximately ten times what most high schools spend. St. Paul's also has one of the largest endowments of any educational institution in the country (nearly $1 million per pupil). For over a century the school has also been a place of national interest and intrigue. In recent years the inner workings of the school have featured prominently on the front pages of the *Wall Street Journal* and the *New York Times,* as well as national magazines like *Vogue.* Yet the exclusivity of these schools is now part of a new kind of belonging. The aristocratic belonging of Chase Abbott is on its last gasp. Elite schools exclude, but today they frame themselves as doing so on the basis of talent—accepting the best of the best. These best might be found anywhere in society, and so the elite work to find and include them.

This frame of a new inclusivity is not just some delusional fiction invented by the elite to justify their position. Instead, it has had support from some of the most powerful academic voices in the nation. Nobel Prize–winning economist Gary Becker has articulated what to many had become a popular and scholarly consensus: "low earnings as well as high earnings are not strongly transmitted from fathers to sons."[36] At the close of the twentieth century social commentators were widely heralding the promise of advancement that America held. While not denying elites, the view was that such positions were acquired "the right way." As David Brooks argues, "All societies have elites, and our educated elite is a lot more enlightened than some of the older elites, which were based on blood or wealth or military valor."[37] Ours may not be an equal nation, but it is a nation where you get a fair shake. Work hard, develop skills, and you'll get ahead. Our outcomes are not the product of your lineage but of what *you* do. This is a story of both potential and responsibility. It's a story of America, perhaps even the American Dream. You get what you earn. There may be people at the bottom, but if they have skills and they get to work, they could be at the top. Some even think of it as a story of basic fairness.

Most Americans want to believe in such an American story. We want to believe that our world is fundamentally fair, despite all of the injustices we see on the news and the awfulness we find in the paper. Such hope may actually be one of the things that the elite and the rest of us have in common. However, this common hope is quickly becoming a common delusion. One of the ways in which we can see this delusion is by looking at our evaporating middle class. After World War II elites were no longer on many of our minds. Instead, we were interested in the poor and rising classes. Openness was creating a more equal world, the world of the average Joe, who had political power and moral authority, and whose family and work were the heart of society. Elites were claiming smaller and smaller pieces of our collective pie. And after the civil rights movement many agreed that all Americans should have an equal chance at success, be they black or white, Asian or Latino. How would the civil rights movements play out economically? What would happen to our families if the feminist revolution succeeded? What were the long-term consequences of our middle class? As society opened up, what kind of new world could we expect? These were the hopeful questions on our minds—not those of a seemingly quaint aristocratic elite who were soon to be extinct.

However, it seems now that Becker's hopeful vision of a world where anyone can make it is increasingly wrong—that "the apple does not fall far from the tree," and perhaps it even falls closer than we imagined.[38] I chose to think of this as a "class" effect—that the origins of parents are good indicators of the destinations of children.[39] There is a good deal of evidence demonstrating that your life chances are highly determined by the wealth of your parents—that children more often than not seem to inherit advantages or poverty and, importantly, that the postwar period of optimism was not the culmination of a long and hard road of American progress where the middle classes were claiming the nation. As wealth begins to pile higher and higher in the accounts of the rich, perhaps it was really just a curious and unlikely moment in an America marked by relentless inequality.

The world is more open but still unequal. Class has a strong impact on future earnings, but elite institutions are aggressively claiming to be more welcoming than ever to the disadvantaged. We don't have good answers to why these seemingly incongruent observations go together. The new elite are acting differently than most of the elite before them. Robber barons earned their name by monopolistic practices and direct exploitation (and division) of ethnically diverse recent migrants. They did so not simply through economic practices within industry but also through social practices that explicitly denied most of the population access to elite positions. Today we have many examples of the reverse, of the comparative social openness of historically closed positions—for example, women CEOs and a black president. The minority rights revolution that began in the 1950s and continues today sought to eliminate discriminatory practices on the basis of group belonging.[40] Public and private institutions could make distinctions between qualified and unqualified membership, but they could not systematically exclude on the basis of membership in one social group. This has meant a radical opening up of institutions to those who, just a generation ago, might never have had access. Nearly every elite institution in our world looks different, and these differences matter enormously for understanding our new elite.

So let us now leave this history behind and enter one of these elite institutions. I will take you inside the doors of St. Paul's School, telling of the lives of students, faculty, and staff. Through this portrait I hope to provide a preliminary answer to how the elite have moved from an ethic of exclusion to one of inclusion. Again and again we will see the importance of meritocracy, where students explain their successes as the result of hard work and talents and reject the trappings of entitlement. But by looking at a year in the life of St. Paul's we will begin to see how, without exclusion or protectionism and within a context that emphasizes individual talents and work, elites are still able to reproduce their position for their children. I will show how heavily patterned inequalities can be maintained and obscured within a meritocracy. This great trick of privilege helps us see how the world can be more open and yet more unequal.

2

Finding One's Place

No member of the commonwealth can have a hereditary privilege
as against his fellow subjects; and no one can hand down to his
descendants the privileges attached to the rank he occupies in the
commonwealth, nor act as if he were qualified as a ruler by birth and
forcibly prevent others from reaching the higher levels of the
hierarchy . . . through their own merit. He may hand down everything else,
so long as it is material and not pertaining to his person, for it may be
acquired and disposed of as property and may over a series of generations create
considerable inequalities in wealth among the members of the
commonwealth. . . . But he may not prevent his subordinates from
raising themselves to his own level if they are able and entitled to do
so by their talent, industry and good fortune.
—IMMANUEL KANT

It is not a sign of arrogance for the king to rule.
That is what he is there for.
—WILLIAM F. BUCKLEY JR.

Twice a week, St. Paul's students dress in formal attire and eat dinner with
a faculty member. I found the meals fascinating, painfully awkward, and
occasionally even terribly boring. But since these teenagers were objects of
my curiosity, I always looked forward to my Tuesday and Thursday evenings. What the students seemed to look forward to, however, was the end
of the meal. The heavy wooden chairs would scrape in ugly unison against
the floor, and the hive of students would rush from the dining hall into the
Upper Common Room for coffee.

For faculty, the student bodies crammed into a small space presents a
challenge of escape, as to leave the dining hall they must squeeze through
the Common Room that the students have just overtaken. For students,
this moment is a social high point of the day. Pressed together in an almost

indiscernable mass, students wiggle through to find boyfriends, girlfriends, classmates, roommates, and friends. Standing on the outside it appears that there is nothing but chaos and sound. But there is a strange kind of order here.

Looking at the boys in blazers and ties and the girls in evening dress is almost to look into the future cocktail parties of the American elite. In these moments, the students are learning a vital piece of upper-class culture: how to act casually while dressed formally. As they move ably between groups as if the room were not impossibly packed, or as new students stand uncomfortably in the corner, it becomes clear that students all know their place in this room; they know where they do and do not belong.

Hidden behind the students in the far corner of the room is a comparative refuge: a maroon leather couch that envelopes you as you sit down. It looks out upon the crowd. But to sit there is not to observe others; instead, it is to be seen. This place is strictly reserved for seniors. To suggest a sacredness to this object might be to go too far. But the ritualized respect granted to this couch makes clear its importance in the psyche of the student body. While the rest of the Upper Common Room is crowded during after-dinner coffee, this couch, tucked away in the corner, provides space for those who occupy it. A line of students flanking the couch, like two sides of a rectangle, serve as a protective barrier for this sanctuary. This barrier is maintained by non-seniors who are talking to their senior friends. And it is so organized because no non-senior is allowed to stand on the rug upon which the couch is placed. With their toes resting just on the edge of the "senior rug," non-seniors afford respect and protection to the graduating class.

Midway through the year, I had Sunday brunch with Inger Hansen, another young faculty member, fellow graduate, and sister of one of my classmates. Inger and I discussed some of the challenges the school had experienced, particularly a rather dramatic hazing incident in a girls' dorm that I'll say more about in chapter 4. Both of us felt the consecrated hierarchies of the student body were part of the problem, and as we left the dining hall we decided to do something capricious: sit on the senior couch. It was the first time either of us had done so since our own senior years. The mere act of us sitting would serve as an intentional breaching transgression—a small challenge to the order of things.

It felt strange. As students walked by the couch, they all noticed us; some looked surprised and others even a little uncomfortable. We began to invite students over to chat with us. None was a senior. Everyone came over politely but respected the barrier of the rug. Then we invited one student, Ryan, to join us on the couch. As he stepped onto the senior rug for the first time, he did so with a great tenderness, as if not wanting to burden the rug with the weight of his body. Ryan attempted to sit gingerly next to us, but the couch was too soft; he could not help but be reclining within it. While Inger and I were delighting in the plush comfort, Ryan looked terrified in his sunken posture. As a senior joined us, and as talk moved to college, Ryan grabbed the opportunity to quietly leave. In his mumbled good-bye and his eager footsteps out of the room, I realized that what we had asked him to do was unfair.

The senior never said a word about Ryan's transgression, nor did he seem at all bothered by the underclassman's presence. More disturbing, it seemed, was ours. He made a point of asking us what we were doing there. There was no real hint of accusation, but it was clear that we all knew something about our sitting on the couch was not right. This couch was not a place for us. We may have been both alumni and faculty, but this was not where we belonged.

As we begin to get to know life at St. Paul's—a place where most of our nation doesn't belong—we must start with the importance of finding one's place. Many of the students at St. Paul's already know their importance long before they arrive as freshmen. Their entitlement—through their family's wealth, prestige, or connections, or all three—has been a fact of life for as long as they can remember. But the school introduces a tension—perhaps for the first time in these students' lives—between "knowing one's place" of entitlement and "finding one's place" of privilege.

Finding one's place at St. Paul's means learning the relentlessness of hierarchical relations (from whom to talk with at a cocktail party to which couches are yours to sit on), the endless and often obscure rules that have forever been a part of elite institutions. But here, among the new elite, there is a twist: the hierarchies can be used like ladders. You must acknowledge the order of things, just like your fathers and grandfathers did, but you can also work your way up this order and advance yourself one rung at a time. Hierarchies are not limiting or oppressive, as they have been for much of America's history, but instead the key to enabling advancement and success. Crucial to the perpetuation of the elite, then, is that each new generation learn to negotiate these hierarchies. This negotiation is an interactive and corporeal skill—what Pierre Bourdieu calls habitus. As we shall see, the development of these negotiating skills is one of St. Paul's most important—although not often acknowledged—responsibilities.

Taking One's Seat

St. Paul's is an Episcopalian school. Much of the daily life of the school revolves around the Chapel: four days a week the school day begins in the Chapel and many of the official rituals of the school—from announcement of alumni deaths (and the ringing of the bells) to the pageants that commemorate the religious seasons to the evensongs that take place every term—take place there.

The Chapel resembles a cathedral more than a church, and its tower can be seen from just about any point on campus. The building is also situated firmly—and intentionally—in the center of campus; even on days when the community is not inside it, they must walk past its imposing façade. Inside, the pews are all formed of beautifully carved wood and the sides of the building are lined with wood paneling. Hanging from the immense ceiling are wrought-iron light fixtures that look as if they hold candles rather than lightbulbs. The space is softly lit, creating an otherworldly beauty. The innumerable hours that students spend here make it less imposing as the days pass. By the end of their years at the school, many students will arrive at morning chapel in pajamas. Through one's time at the school the Chapel is transformed from an intimidating space to a kind of living room: an everyday place that can be inhabited with ease. It is also within this space that students literally learn "their place" in the school, as well as the organizing principles of the school.

As I described earlier, all faculty and students have assigned seats in the Chapel. Having a seat is itself an important symbolic marker: not all people in the community are afforded this right. Staff members, for example, from the school's many cooks to the cleaning crew to administrative members, are not granted seats. Students, on the other hand, are instilled from their first days with the idea that there is a place for them at the school, reserved for them alone to occupy. From the earliest incarnations of Christianity, having a seat has marked the importance of a community member; such sitting was an expression of power and the position from which teaching was done. When Jesus gave the sermon on the mount, he did so sitting down.[1]

In their seats in the Chapel, students and faculty face one another. As students move from year to year in the school, they find that their seat "ascends" nearer to those of the faculty. As they move up, they get closer and closer to adulthood, looking down at the younger children beneath and the places they once sat. It is no coincidence that the space where the school community meets most regularly as a group, the space most central to campus, and the space on campus imbued with the greatest symbolic importance is explicitly arranged as a hierarchy.

The faculty themselves do not exist on an equal plane; they are similarly arranged in order of seniority with the most senior faculty seated toward the front of the Chapel, next to the rector and the deans. On an orientation tour for new faculty, Bill Faulkner spent much of the time in the Chapel. The most senior faculty member on campus, Bill pointed to the end of the faculty Chapel seats. He told us, rather affectionately, that that is where he sits. "And that is the place that we call 'Coffin Corner,' as it is we senior masters who are closest to our graves who sit here."

The school year is inaugurated by the portentous ceremony I described in the introduction, what the school calls "the taking of one's place." Once seated, students and faculty occupy their positions for the entire school year. The ritual of taking one's seat and occupying it for a year underscores the importance of constructing, respecting, and maintaining a specific set of social relations—exactly those relations that provide St. Paul's students with their extraordinary advantages. Through their daily sitting in the Chapel and countless other formal and informal experiences at the school, students are taught that the world is a hierarchical place and that different people are placed in different spaces within this hierarchy. As students move up, it is not the hierarchy itself that changes; the seats in the Chapel are fixed. The order of things is literally carved into what seems a timeless building; an almost ancient interior of the space gives the appearance of permanence. The students move within this order, adapting themselves to its dictates and procedures.

The Chapel is not the sole space where we observe the consecration of hierarchy—students and faculty and staff alike experience innumerable examples of formal and informal hierarchical arrangements. Though there is no ceremony for the after-dinner socializing over coffee, year after year students nonetheless participate in symbolic acts that reaffirm their positions. Each June, seniors graduate and leave campus before all the other students (who must remain to take finals). On the evening that seniors leave, and on several days and evenings that follow, the incoming senior class relentlessly occupies the senior couch and the senior rug. Though on most days during the school year the couches are vacant, for these first days after the outgoing senior class departs, the members of the junior class seem to have a rotation so that at least one student is always sitting on the social spaces reserved for seniors. These acts seek to remind the community that they are the new senior class on campus and as such are afforded rights and spaces reserved for them alone.

At first glance, the process of "taking one's place" may not seem especially remarkable. Indeed, it seems like an aristocratic ceremony, the likes of which have been replayed in various guises in churches and estates and government offices for millennia. The arrangement of the Chapel, or the agreed-upon social arrangement of the students' after-dinner "cocktail hour," could be read as an inculcation of fixed hierarchical relations, not very different from the kinds of relations we have come to expect from elites in the past or from those across the Atlantic. As juniors occupy the senior couches, they could simply be inheriting their rightful position. "Taking one's place" could be read as conferring the mark of nobility.

Yet it is not. As students ascend the hierarchy, they do something that would be nearly impossible within an aristocracy. In an aristocracy, members do not "climb"—indeed the very point of this organization is that relationships are fixed. In the example of the Chapel, students would never "move up." Instead, they, and the generations after them, would keep their seat. In an aristocracy, the seats are fixed, as are particular people to them. For the new elite, the seats of hierarchy are fixed and there is an order of things, but students learn how to work within these positions to ascend. St. Paul's does not so radically rethink the world; the hierarchy remains, but the possibilities within them are new. The students know that everywhere there are hierarchies. The key is to understand the principles of their organization, be they birth, wealth, race, talents, or something else. So what are these principles? How do they allow students to drop the entitlements of an aristocracy and embrace the privilege of being part of the new elite?

Stan was a senior who had not been enormously successful at St. Paul's. He had been admitted to a top liberal arts college, one that students at most high schools would have been proud to attend. But for students at St. Paul's, it was seen as a second-best option. Stan was from a wealthy family, but not a particularly established one. Other students and faculty seemed to like Stan. "He'd be the last guy to kill himself working," his advisor told me, "but he's a good kid." But when I asked Stan about his work, and about the seating in the Chapel, Stan presented a quite different view.

"I worked hard to get here," Stan told me as we looked at his seat in the top row of the Chapel. "I learned in class, I worked to make the varsity team. And it was hard. But I earned it. We all earned it. And I feel good when I get to chapel in the morning and I see how far I've come." As we walked into sleepy hollow, the very back of the Chapel far from the peering eyes of the school administrators, Stan smiled at me. "I think back to that kid who sat in the front row back in sleepy hollow and I almost have to laugh. I've come a long way. It wasn't easy ... I mean ... it's still not easy. It might even be harder ... but I did it. ... Not everyone does this, gets this far. It takes a lot. I know I'm not done," he told me cheerfully, "I've sorta just begun. But now I know that I can do it. I've got what it takes."

Stan explains his ascension in the Chapel through his own hard work and claims that such movement was the product of this work. He learns about himself in the process, his own capacities and abilities, and can now declare, "I've got what it takes." He freely admits that "it wasn't easy," but these difficult experiences are essential to his sense of self. And these difficulties are what prove his hard work and merit. Stan's natural movement up across his four years at St. Paul's does not feel inevitable. It does not come out of entitlement—an ideal that would directly clash with American mores—but is reinterpreted through the classic American codes of merit and work.

When Stan tells me, "Not everyone does this, gets this far," he is entirely inaccurate. In fact, *everyone* at St. Paul's "does it." There are very few students who do not complete their schooling.[2] And those who do not are never seen as failures. When a student left the school at the end of my year there, the rector explained that she "would get the experience she needs at home." The student did not fail; she simply did not fit. But Stan, like other students, willfully ignores the inevitability of his advancement. Instead he thinks of his own actions as the engine of his achievements. The distinction here is a subtle but important one. Students work to frame their success not as deserved but earned. It is a product of what they have done and not where they are from. This framing—whether conscious or not—works against our very common, age-old suspicion of entitlement and the nagging feeling that the rich succeed just because of who they are. St. Paul's students seek to replace that frame with one that is based on achievement.[3]

This frame of achievement is found not just in the official spaces. As juniors began aggressively taking over the senior couches after graduation, I asked them why it was so important for them to actively occupy this space.

"Well, it's kinda like the forbidden fruit," James, a handsome, enormously self-assured young man, said to me. He was clearly looking forward to becoming a "big man on campus." "You know, we've never been allowed here before, and we really want to see what it's like."

"Yeah," his girlfriend, Emily, chimed in. "Plus, the couches are comfortable."

I was unable to control my exasperation at the suggestion that the comfort of the couch was why this pair had taken their turn at sitting on these couches, "Come on! Comfortable? You're sitting here because it's comfortable?"

James retorted, "Well, they are comfortable. You just said you might fall asleep."

But Emily understood what I meant. "This is going to sound ridiculous. But life here is tough. And this place, this was a goal for me. I mean, I would walk by every day and see seniors sitting here. And at first I thought, 'I'll never get there … I don't think I can do it.' But that motivated me. It's not just some 'forbidden fruit' for me. It was a goal. Something I could work toward. I'd see it every day and think to myself, 'I *am* going to get there … I *can* do it.' And guess what? Here I am. I've done it. I honestly don't care about the *couch*. But this is important for me. It proves that I did it. That all that work got me somewhere. That it was worth it."

Emily deploys the same frame for the couches as Stan did for the Chapel. Her ascension was a goal that came through work, not a deserved acquisition that came from time logged or inheritance. And in achieving their newfound status, Emily and Stan both appeal to their own capacity: Emily finds that she "can do it"; Stan, despite the lack of evidence, notes that he can achieve tasks he sets himself to in a way that not everyone can.

This capacity to achieve is not something that students simply mobilize to explain their advancement; students also place enormous importance on their own experiences at the school. Both faculty and students disciplined one another into drawing on their own experiences rather than simply displaying knowledge they had acquired from an advantaged position. Most commonly this happened with "work talk"; almost every conversation I had at the school returned to a discussion of how much work was to be done. Those who did not engage in such work talk were reminded that they should be working. Students often watched movies and television on their computers in their rooms instead of in common spaces. This was in part for privacy, but more often it was to avoid being seen not working by faculty and their peers. Students and faculty did not work all the time, but they engaged in practical and discursive practices to make it seem as if they did. Students like Chase Abbott who rejected the importance of such work were scorned, rejected, and even punished for doing so.

Evan Williams was a new ninth-grade student. He looked young, having barely begun to enter puberty. His face was not yet marked by acne, as was the case for many of his peers. He was slightly round—not fat, but still carrying a softness of childhood that would be lost in the years to come. His bowl haircut made him look even younger than he was. Even his speech betrayed his youth; his voice was still that of a boy, and occasionally it awkwardly squeaked as it began to drop. Yet on his first days Evan was confident, even arrogant. His sister had graduated from St. Paul's a couple of years earlier, and Evan arrived at the school knowing everything. He was from a "classic" St. Paul's background—an elite private middle school in an exceptionally wealthy community, with parents who both had deep and long connections to the world of boarding schools. Upon meeting them I immediately knew that this was not the first time they had stepped on St. Paul's campus. After unloading his suitcases and personal items into his dorm room, Evan quickly tried to assume a leadership role among the new third formers.

To Josh, a new student from the Midwest, he announced, "Well, I'm moved in. I'm going to go to Tuck! Anyone want to go?"

"What's 'Tuck'?" Josh wondered.

Evan snorted at Josh's ignorance. He resisted the urge to roll his eyes but took the opportunity to braggingly reveal that he knew everything about Tuck without ever having been there. "It's where people hang out. They have food that's way better than the Upper. And pool tables and things. But mostly people hang out downstairs. It's where sixth formers go after we have to check in and they still have time."

Josh looked at Evan with surprise and a hint of worry that he was going to be more over his head than he ever imagined.

"The Tuck Shop isn't open yet," said a stern female voice, as if emerging from nowhere. "It'll be a while before it is."

"Oh yeah. I forgot."

Mrs. Brown, an advisor in the dorm, took the opportunity to continue schooling Evan. She would not allow him make Josh feel even more inse-cure on his first day than he already did. "Are you sure everything is ready, Evan? You should use this time to make sure you know where everything is. You never know where your mom may have put things. And the school year really picks up soon. Now is the time to get organized."

His eyes welling, Evan fled to his room. Events like this were not in-frequent—those in which Evan attempted to display his "knowledge" of the place, only to find out he was wrong. He would become very upset, either lashing out at other students or quickly going to his room so others would not see him cry. Mrs. Brown's correction of Evan, her observation that he was moved in because his mom had put everything away, and her statement that he might soon be overwhelmed revealed that behind his bravado, Evan knew little of what was to come. She sought to remind Evan that his inheritance did not afford him all he expected it to.

New students like Evan, those who attempt to display knowledge of the place that they could not possibly have, are treated severely by older students (and even faculty). Students actively police the knowledge of St. Paul's. While Evan was initially respected by new students for his "insider knowledge," he soon learned that his displays of such knowledge were met harshly by returning students. In fact, returning students were meaner to him than to his fellow incoming students. They reminded him again and again that such knowing was not something you carried in your head or inherited from others. Evan could know everything about St. Paul's—from the Tuck Shop to secret tunnels, from what dorms were "cool" and what dorms weren't—but these details were mere bits of trivia in the minds of the older students. Real knowledge came only through *experiencing* the place. These students insisted that the only valuable knowledge was corporeal—inscribed on oneself by the experience of living at St. Paul's.

Evan once talked about a play performed two years earlier, when his sister was a student. A junior, Jonny, who had been in the play, overheard the conversation and quickly swore at Evan. The phrase "Shut the fuck up, Williams" was uttered in front of me and other faculty members on numerous occasions. On every occasion, it was said after Evan flaunted some piece of knowledge that he could not have experienced himself. Jonny knew that I would hear him and that I would punish him rather severely; I had done so to another boy a month before for swearing at a new student. Yet he still chose to reprimand Evan. Students would continue to police Evan in this way, even though they knew they would be punished by faculty. When I asked Jonny about this, about why he would swear at Evan when he knew I was there and would do something about it, he said to me, "I'm sorry, Mr. Khan. But Williams is so full of shit sometimes. It drives me crazy. And he's got it easy here in Ruggles. If he were in Barclay [another dorm, where Jonny had been a new student] he would get it a lot worse. He needs to know that. He keeps pretending like he's something he's not. I mean, don't tell me about a play *I was in*. He's been here like half a year. And he acts like he's a senior. He has no clue about this place ... about how it really works."

Jonny's objection to Evan is twofold: first, he doesn't know his place, "he acts like he's a senior"; second, he makes claims about St. Paul's without actually having experienced it, "he has no clue about this place ... about how it really works." Evan actually knew a lot about St. Paul's; though I had lived at the school for three years, and Evan only three months, I learned things I'd never known from him. But that knowledge has been gained in the wrong way and thus went against what the school valued as important.

When I began researching St. Paul's, I suspected that students like Evan Williams—those with insider or family knowledge of the place and previous experience at elite institutions like St. Paul's—would be the most successful. They would already know what to expect from St. Paul's and, more important, would have developed some of the embodied aspects of privilege. He would have the kind of skills and dispositions essential to belonging. But this was not always the case—in fact, it was more often the opposite. Instead, as students attempted to claim about things that they could not possibly have experienced, they were chastised for being "full of shit."

Evan quickly learned that to embody the school took experiences of his own. New students like him were broken down harshly by their older peers: a quick punch in the arm when no one was looking; flushing the toilets while they were in the shower, resulting in extremely hot water; the disappearance of your keyboard and mouse; or being ignored for a day—as if you weren't there—only to be spoken to the next day without comment. As these events piled up, and they did so quickly when students acted entitled, new students learned that their ability to claim St. Paul's would only come with time. These encounters challenged attitudes of entitlement. It did not matter to students what you knew because of who your family was. Instead, it mattered what you had lived through, what you had seen with your own eyes. Just as Chase Abbott and his friends were sequestered into the entitled students' house and treated as if they "didn't get" St. Paul's, so too were entitled displays like Evan Williams's met with contempt because really, he had "no clue." In order to be comfortable at St. Paul's and in order to advance within the school, students do not rely on entitlements based on who they are but proclaim the experiences that they have had.

Invisible Individuals

At St. Paul's there are many people who work very hard and experience none of the promise of the students. Indeed, there are many people who stay at the school for far longer than four years. These people are the staff, the men and women who make the school function day in and day out.[4] They are some of the most intriguing and most overlooked people on campus, and they offer a radically different vision of what entitlement, privilege, and experience mean in our country.

Though these individuals are often invisible, the school runs on the work performed by those behind the Gothic doorways and the immaculate campus grounds. So we must ask: How does the St. Paul's community bridge the interactions of people who seem to come from two different worlds—on the one hand, the American elite, and on the other, those who feed and pick up after them? While living at St. Paul's one is disciplined into recognizing the hard work of the staff. Staff members are celebrated in the Chapel after every five years of service to the school, and students in dorms are regularly reminded of the hard work that staff members do to keep their spaces clean. Each year the seniors coordinate the purchase of a Christmas gift for the custodial staff in their dorm. And these seniors typically demand payments from every student in accordance with their ability to pay.

Many of us probably assume that these students, like most impudent teenagers, would be utterly oblivious of the staff. However, the reality is far more nuanced. With some surprise, I found what Alexis de Tocqueville had seen a century and half ago as he traveled across our then new nation. Rather than act like European aristocrats, who maintained what seemed to be immutable distinctions between classes, Americans seemed to be striving for the removal of such distinctions: "In the United States the more opulent citizens take great care not to stand aloof from the people; on the contrary they constantly keep on easy terms with the lower classes: they listen to them, and speak to them every day."[5] Yet these observations were in part due to the shock Tocqueville, himself an aristocrat, experienced and in part a kind of wishful thinking. As I asked students and staff alike about the gap between elites and the workers around them, I identified some of the crucial distinctions that mark elites and that differentiate them from all others. We commonly assume that the gap between the wealthy and the rest of us is due to differences in cultural knowledge, or perhaps we simply cannot get over the differences in wealth. Or maybe interactions between these groups are doomed to fail—people are unable to cross that enormous chasm and interact with one another in meaningful ways. But after my time at St. Paul's, I believe that it is none of these things.

Joyce is getting close to retirement. She is no longer middle-aged but an older woman, with rough hands from cleaning with chemicals day after day. She must still have the considerable physical stamina required to clean day in and day out. But to look at her is to look at someone who seems tired from a lifetime of work. She had cleaned the Schoolhouse during all my years as a student, and I was saddened to see that she was still at work when I returned. I was embarrassed that I did not remember her. This isn't unique. While some of the people students are fondest of are staff members who clean their houses, serve them food, or deliver their mail, the majority of the staff recess to the background of students' awareness. In fact, many students interact with most staff by ignoring them.

Yet members of the staff know things about the school that few others do. They find condom wrappers and alert faculty to where students are having sex; they clean up vomit from bathrooms after students are sick (or, more likely, have been drinking too much); they notice what students eat or, more important, who is not eating. Sometimes they protect students' secrets, sometimes they reveal them, and most of the time they just do their jobs and go home at the end of the day. Home is in the surrounding towns; as they get into their cars to leave at the end of the day, their departure and separate lives from the school help construct a symbolic boundary between students and faculty who live on campus and staff who have lives somewhere else.[6]

Joyce was rather happy to talk to me (and proved to be so throughout the year). She arrives every morning at 4:30 A.M.; she works until 12:30. She has to do most of her cleaning before the students arrive in the building at 8:30. The job is clearly a difficult one and harder, she tells me, as she gets older. The Schoolhouse is the largest building on campus, housing dozens of offices, classrooms, bathrooms, and hallways. During class times about a third of the school, or some two hundred people, are in the building. Joyce is close to her seventies. I cannot imagine doing her job. Yet for all its difficulties, Joyce expresses pride in her work and none of the sadness (and perhaps bourgeois guilt) that I felt.

"I've been working at St. Paul's for twenty-three years," she tells me. "My old boss was having trouble with this person before me. She took a lot of time off. With a building like this you can't be like that. So he asked me if I'd do the job. And I've been doing it for fifteen years." She is clearly proud of her continued capacity for one of the most difficult custodial jobs on campus. "I don't know what they're going to do when I retire. When I take off people all tell me and my boss, 'I wouldn't want to do that building.'" Joyce smiles at me. She could do a job others couldn't imagine. "But it's getting harder." Six days a week classes are held in this building; she arrives hours before any of the rest of us just to deal with the aftermath of five hundred students, one hundred faculty members, and many staff.

Like Stan, she talks about just how hard she's worked at the school. Like Stan, she expresses pride in the work she has done. Yet unlike Stan, she has not advanced. She never had the same opportunities. After finishing public high school she soon married and began a life of work and family. The job she had at St. Paul's was a good, steady one. They pay was not high, but it was reliable. Jobs that might pay more were largely unavailable to Joyce. She had not attended college, and the manufacturing jobs that had once paid higher wages had long ago left the Northeast.

I thought of her as stuck. But Joyce thought differently. She is proud of her work, her family (whom I never met but heard much about), and herself. And she is proud that she works at a school around students who are being given chances she never had. Her pride in this work is not connected to advancement, as Stan's is. While students consistently employ the language of hard work, so do staff. The difference is that for students, this work got them somewhere; for the staff, like Joyce, the hard work gave them something: a sense of pride. Though both employ the codes of hard work, the meanings of those codes are quite different. For one, it is work hard, get ahead. For the other it is pride in a job well done and being part of a school that is one of the best in the world.

Yet it would be foolish of me to suggest that the staff were blissfully happy, duped into thinking their lives were like the elite around them. They saw the inequalities walking by on campus and knew what their life chances were. Most staff rarely chose to interact with me (or with any other faculty or students). I continually and clumsily asked about this; in one of my less admirable moments I inquired, "Why is it that we don't know your name? That we don't ever interact?" These questions were avoided, except on one occasion, late in the year, when a cleaning woman said to me, coldly, "Because you don't have to, *Shamus*; and we know not to." As she said my name, she pointed forcefully to the upper left-hand area of her shirt. Suzanne wears a nametag. The message was clear: she knows and is expected to know my name; no such expectation exists for me. I am provided a tag to look at when needed. Suzanne's terse statement seemed a painfully accurate summary of relations between staff and the "real" people at the school. Students learn from the distance created around the staff; they realize whom they need to know and interact with and those who can be invisible to them.

During my years as a student, if one of us broke a major school rule—if we were caught using alcohol or drugs or out of the dorm after check-in, or if we engaged in academic dishonesty—we were assigned "work duty." This meant that the student had to perform manual labor with the staff.

Yet the school recently eliminated work duty because it was perceived as demeaning to the staff—when students acted poorly they were punished by doing the work that staff did every day as a job. The change struck me simultaneously as an intriguing instance of enlightened thinking and as yet another means for the students to avoid interacting with those who serve them. When I asked staff, they understood the school's decision but didn't think the issue was particularly important. As one janitor, James, said to me, "When my kid gets in trouble I make him work around the house. That work is good for him. He learns a lesson. Same with these kids. But the thing is, my wife and me do that work every day. It's not demeaning to us to make him do the work that we would otherwise do. It teaches him a lesson he needs. I mean, when those kids worked with us, I didn't care. This is just my job." James looked me up and down quickly, eyeing me. I suspect he was trying to assess whether I could be trusted. "Want to show me you respect my work?" he asked. "Give me a raise."

The faculty and students' disregard of the staff and the administration's willingness to cut staff positions to save money often made the staff feel underappreciated. In the years before I arrived, the new rector, Craig Anderson, had worried that the school was relying too heavily on its endowment. And so he proposed that the school begin tightening its belt. Among other things, this meant cutting staff positions. As custodial and service staff members were fired, those who remained picked up the slack. This is an old and common story in organizations, where the worst paid are often asked to bear the brunt of sacrifices. What made it particularly hurtful to the staff—and what helped accelerate the eventual departure of Anderson—was that as staff positions were cut to save money, Anderson enriched himself, raising his salary from around $180,000 to $530,000. In addition to these riches, he had a mansion, a custodial staff, and a personal chef, none of whom was sacrificed to help save money.

Yet even amid this relative lack of appreciation or recognition, staff often found meaning in their jobs, and this meaning was similar to that of teachers; many staff expressed to me the importance of the fact that they worked at a school. "I used to work in this office," Cindy, a server in the cafeteria, told me, "and the work was fine. It actually wasn't that hard. And I even got paid more. But the job didn't do anything for me but pay the rent. I like the kids here. I like seeing them, being part of their day. I can tell when they're down and know how to make them smile. That makes it worth it."

Cindy was not alone in such sentiments. Tom, who maintained the Chapel, won a million-dollar lottery when I was a student. Yet he kept his job. As he explained it, "I like working here. I like the kids. And I know how to take care of this place. It's a big responsibility, but it's important. ... Sometimes it's really hard and I think about quitting. But then something happens and I realize I'm a part of something." I would regularly see Cindy do emotional work for students, lifting their spirits, listening to them complain about the latest adolescent debacle, counseling them about a breakup or an overeager parent.[7] She regularly did the same for me.

Though James points to a raise as the sign of an institution's "respect" for its workers, in one way or another almost all the staff did the unpaid—and often unacknowledged—work of helping care for and raise teenage boys and girls. And all of them placed value upon this experience. Many staff members are like Joyce: stuck in an area of the country where high-paying manufacturing jobs are long gone and a high school diploma provides little but low-wage employment. And so this care work also helps create meaning in a world where rewards are unlikely to come through wages. When telling me about her office job, Cindy remarked that it was much easier than her present job at St. Paul's. But for her the harder work is worth it. Students, faculty, and staff share not only a common belief in the value of hard work. They also share a commitment to the importance of the place where they work and the enterprise they are involved in. From this vantage point, staff and students would seem to have a lot in common. And yet for every moving interaction between student and staff member, there were a thousand moments where the two groups seemed to exist in parallel but utterly separate universes.

I have argued that part of the work done by American elites is to preserve hierarchies while making them invisible. If so, then how do young members of the elite deal with persistent, visible reminders of hierarchy around them and of the obvious inequality that emerges from such hierarchy? The most common way was to simply ignore the staff. When I asked students about the staff, few were able to actually name those who served them food on a daily basis or continually cleaned the buildings they inhabited, or any of those with whom they interacted on a regular basis.

And yet every student I spoke with objected to any suggestion of aloofness and mentioned a personal relationship with a staff member. These personal relationships were offered as examples of how staff were not simply ignored. Jessica, a junior from a wealthy New England family, argued that just because she did not know the names of cafeteria workers it did not mean that she did not know the staff. In fact, a few were a central part of her life. Speaking about one of the women who cleaned her dorm, she said, "I mean, actually, Gretchen is someone I really look forward to seeing every day. She's really sweet. Like an older aunt or something. And she'll remember something. If I tell her I'm stressed about a test on Thursday, she'll ask me about it on Friday. We talk. And I can talk to her in a way that I don't really talk to anyone else here. ... Part of it is that she's just not caught up in it all. Honestly, I don't know how I'd get through it all without Gretchen. She's really important to my time here." As she said this, she turned away from me, looking away into nothing, as if to have a personal moment of reflection.

Jessica was not unique. The stories I heard were often very touching; for one student it was clear that the small birthday present from a staff member meant an enormous amount to her—as much as her far more expensive present from her parents. And Cindy was not unique in arguing that the students similarly brought meaning to her work: unlike her office job, her work at St. Paul's was important—she helped educate students. This education was far more practical than what students learned in the classroom. But these everyday life lessons were seen as important by both the staff and the students. On an occasion where a new student sat down in the cafeteria and had a cafeteria worker come out from the kitchen to "serve" breakfast, an older student scolded her. When I asked the older student about this, she told me she had done the same thing when she was a new student, and the worker who brought her her plate had lightly joked that it wasn't his job to wait on her hand and foot. It was a valuable lesson she had been instilled with and one that we both revisited with students throughout the year.

Yet there are important differences between how students interact with staff and how they interact with faculty. Jessica referred to the woman who cleaned her dorm as "Gretchen." I never heard a student call a faculty member by his or her first name. I was always "Mr. Khan," even as students were sobbing in my office or telling me things that they would never tell their parents. Though there is enormous intimacy between students and faculty—they live together, after all—there are still symbolic boundaries of respect that are never breached. And as I pushed Jessica about Gretchen's life, it quickly became clear that she knew almost nothing about her life outside of the school.

When I asked Gretchen about why she knew about students' lives and why students didn't know about hers, she quickly argued that it was not because the students didn't care. "I don't want to bring my home to work. I like to keep that part of my life separate. These kids are ... well ... kids. It may seem like they're not. Because they're more independent than most kids. They live away from their parents. And they have a lot weighing on them. But it's part of being an adult. Kids don't know about your life. It isn't that they don't care. I don't talk about it. And how many sixteen-year-olds do you know who take an active interest in your life?"

I did not answer Gretchen's question. But during my year at St. Paul's, the answer was "a lot." Students often had a near pathological fascination with faculty lives. On countless occasions I heard students talking about faculty and their families, speculating about the ins and outs of their lives. Students were also eager to pump me for information about other teachers and were unafraid to ask me about my own life. For unmarried faculty, our romantic lives were the source of endless speculation. And for faculty alumni, of which there were many, students spent considerable time in the library, poring over yearbooks to find out details of their lives while they had been students at the school. Knowing about faculty was important to students; knowing about staff was not. In part this was because students did not "share" the relationships they had with staff; such relationships were far from the collective bonds that formed in a classroom. If students had any relationships at all with staff members, such bonds revolved around small intimacies, such as saying hi every morning in the hallway or chatting in the corner of the dining hall—moments that did not involve other students. But the lack of knowledge about staff was also simply because of the huge gulf that separated their lives. Staff and students were from different worlds, headed in radically different directions. The staff were likely to remain working at a school in Concord, or a place like it, for much of their lives. The students could reasonably expect the rewards of wealth and power in their future.

As I pushed students to think about the careers of the school's staff and why these men and women were in what many people (including the students' parents) would likely consider dead-end jobs, many initially expressed surprise at the idea. It seemed as though these students had never thought about the quality of the jobs performed all around them, their possibilities (or lack thereof) and their pitfalls. The obliviousness struck me as perfectly adolescent. And then, more often than not, the students began to relate stories about the staff that they had relationships with. These stories tended to emphasize the way in which staff were unlucky, had different values, or were from a past generation where opportunities weren't as available—or some combination of the three. Jessica suggested that Gretchen was clearly competent, as she "remembered things I never would," but that she was probably unlucky. "I mean, I've been really lucky to have so many opportunities. Some people don't get those. They've had really bad luck." Jason talked to me about Mike, a groundskeeper he had developed a relationship with, noting that Mike simply made different choices. "He really likes hunting. We talk about it. He's happy. Nearby he can hunt and fish. That's what Mike loves in life. And I totally get that. I mean, it actually makes sense. He's happier than a lot of people I know." And in thinking about Justine, an older cafeteria worker, another student argued that she probably wasn't afforded the same opportunities. "Forty years ago, women weren't allowed into places like this. We've come a long way. Things are different now." In each instance we see students constructing particular stories to explain a lack of mobility. The attendant difficulties in each staff member's life are unique. A result of this is that the students don't have to acknowledge how the staff as a whole is comparatively immobile. The durability of inequality is obscured, chalked up to individual difficulties rather than structural inequalities (or past inequalities that have been transcended).

As I asked students about the staff, I noticed that every student talked to me about two particular staff members: "Big Guy" and the "Milk Gnome." I was often asked if these two staff fixtures had been at the school when I was a student. Students seemed pleased when I told them yes, as if the longevity of these staff members proved a kind of universality and centrality of these two figures to the school. "Big Guy" is actually Bradley Mason; he has worked in the St. Paul's cafeteria for at least twenty-five years. All students know him because he makes an effort to know every student. He learns almost all the students' names each year and regularly talks to students. He also attends every student dance, and dances the entire night. He happily will tell you, "I'm the best dancer on campus!" Mason is called "Big Guy" because that's what he calls himself. He trains new students to interact with him in a very particular way. During the afternoon he will often walk through campus. As students approach, he will say, "Hey [student name], who's number one?" Students will almost always answer, "You are, Big Guy!" to which Mason will reply, "Woo!" and put his hand in the air, holding up his index finger. This makes most students smile. In talking to Mason about these interactions, he told me how he enjoys interacting with the kids on campus, having fun with them at dances, and making them happy. Mason is developmentally disabled; as a result, some students are uncomfortable around him and avoid interacting with him. Still others will interact with him in ways that are condescending, getting a laugh out of him.

By contrast, the "Milk Gnome" rarely interacts with students. Faculty are less tolerant of students referring to George Stevens as the "Milk Gnome" since, unlike Mason, it is not a self-given nickname. I am not even sure that Stevens knows of his given nickname. I was too embarrassed to ask him about it. Students have given Stevens this name because he is short and one of his many jobs in the cafeteria is to replace the milk as it runs out. The nickname has endured and has been passed down since at least my time as a student over a decade ago.

Unlike Mason's indulgent kindness, Stevens is far less gregarious and cheerful. He tends to interact in a much more gruff manner, demanding that students move immediately so that he can replace the milk or perform his other tasks at work. He is a hard and efficient worker, and seems to have no time to waste on the students. Like Mason, Stevens is also developmentally disabled. The students all know him, yet very few know his real name.

If Mason were the only staff member that most students knew, I would attribute his unique presence among the student body to his dynamic personality and continued interaction with and interest in students. But Stevens is the other staff member that all students know. Stevens shares none of Mason's personality and I never saw him interact with students other than to ask them to get out of his way. Their common features are two: they both work in the cafeteria, where every student goes two or three times a day, and they are both developmentally disabled. And as there are many other people who work in the cafeteria whom students do not all know or notice, the explanatory feature of both is their disability.

In the students' eyes, the staff members they individually know—and the fact that they may be "stuck" in their job at the school—are exceptions to the students' general faith in the American creed that anyone can make it. They are unlucky, have different values, or are unfortunate victims of past unfairness. The two members of the staff whom all students know, the two who do not recess into the background of students' daily lives and who are collectively acknowledged by the students, are the two who provide the least challenge to the way students frame their experiences. While staff could serve as a persistent reminder that there are other processes that might explain how some in society acquire privileges and others do not, the staff students notice do not. In short, students can comfortably notice Mason and Stevens and collectively share in their relationships with them because their disability offers an obvious explanation for why they don't advance.

The awkward position of staff members in the lives of St. Paul's students becomes even more interesting when you consider that a few of the students may actually have parents who are housecleaners, dishwashers, or office workers. About a third of St. Paul's students receive substantial scholarship, and the school makes a very conscious effort to recruit students from the lower rungs of the socioeconomic ladder. I assumed that these middle- and working-class students would have an easier time interacting with these overlooked members of the community, as their earlier lives would have been spent among the working and middle classes. I reasoned that wealthy students, by contrast, would be uncomfortable interacting with staff, as their privileged position would have prevented them from knowing what the lives of staff members were like. I was wrong.

It was actually the wealthy kids who "noticed" staff more frequently than did the middle-class kids; they were also more likely to build relationships with them. At first this observation struck me as improbable. I suspected that the students I spoke to were simply gregarious (perhaps because they were more comfortable at the school) and therefore more likely to strike up conversations with anyone. Yet as I pushed this idea I found that it was the wealthy students who worked much harder to argue with me about the importance of their relationships with staff members and the depth and shared quality of the connection. Wealthy students, it seemed, were intentionally developing the capacity to interact with those "below" them. This development is a useful and necessary tool within our democratized America; elite students will be required to interact with non-elites throughout their professional lives. And they will be held to account for these interactions. Learning to successfully negotiate them was an important skill to develop.

Non-wealthy students, by contrast, were much more concerned with developing a set of interactional tools that would aid them in navigating upward, through elite institutions and networks. Further, wealthy students could more comfortably recognize and interact with staff members, as their own status and position were clear. For the wealthy, already ensconced in their place, the staff's presence did not highlight the tensions inherent in the efforts to transition into the elite. For middle- and working-class students, the presence of the staff members brought into relief the distinction between their present lives at St. Paul's and their past lives at home. Non-wealthy students had to learn to manage the contradictions between their "exceptional" experience at the school and their former, "everyday" experience at a home that was very different from St. Paul's. For wealthy students, no such contradiction management was necessary. For middle-class kids, the staff were a daily reminder that the space at St. Paul's—with its opulent, wood-paneled rooms, its gorgeous buildings and sacred spaces, and its immaculately manicured grounds—was not where they came from or what they were used to. The staff were reminders of this contradiction, of the seeming foreignness of their presence; the staff made more difficult the essential task of displaying ease and knowledge of the place.

In learning to construct intimacy with staff members—those permanently below them—students developed the capacity to interact across the social boundaries of class. By learning these interactions, elites prepared for a future where dealing with the lower classes would be inevitable, and at the same time they made such boundaries seem artificial or unimportant. If you can chat with the cashier or trade jokes with the janitor, then you obscure the categorical distinctions essential for durable forms of inequality. There is no need to harp on class differences or the stark limits of the American Dream. Instead, students viewed the small slices of inequality, or the lack of social mobility, that they observed as "exceptional" cases— Mason and Stevens, as we saw, could not possibly advance—or through creating personal narratives, as with the other workers who were good people and were at the school as a result of bad luck, different choices, or past inequality. The lack of mobility, then, is not a systemic feature of social life; it is an exception, particularly among those who value the same kinds of things that students do: belonging to an educational institution and working hard.

Dense Intimacy and Distance

The relationships between students and staff could not be more different from the relationships between students and faculty. While the interactions with staff give the students unintended but vital practice at working within hierarchies, the faculty at St. Paul's occupy a radically different (though not uncomplicated) place on the school's hierarchy. I found that the faculty-student relationship can best be described as "dense," which means that the students and faculty interact with one another in myriad complex and at times contradictory ways. The density of the relationship with faculty allows for both intimacy and respectful distance. It is in learning to produce this relationship that students develop a particular interactional dynamic essential to privilege. Though the staff can at times serve to challenge some of the organizing principles, modes of interaction, and codes of the school, relationships with the faculty help reify modes of working within hierarchy.

Unlike in other spaces where children are raised, at St. Paul's adults are part of every aspect of students' lives. Most high school students live significant chunks of their lives outside the view of both their parents and their teachers. Yet the students don't leave St. Paul's to go home at the end of the day. And because of the community model of housing, every student dorm also houses at least two faculty members, so even at night students are no more than a few hundred feet away from a teacher. Faculty at St. Paul's are expected to teach, advise, parent, coach, discipline, watch, comfort, and console students—often exercising these multiple roles with the same student within one day. These multiple, often contradictory relations create an emotional density, which cultivates the conditions for both extraordinary growth and enormous difficulties. Learning to manage this complexity is key to a student's success at St. Paul's. These multiple dense relations teach students how to interact with those above them in a hierarchy in a way that is both familiar (even familial) but respectful.

But simultaneously, having faculty always present and available to students reinforces the sense of their own importance: the adults at St. Paul's have given their lives to them.

Students, as a whole, believe in St. Paul's. They look at the students around them and sense that they are surrounded by excellence. They look at their teachers and think that for the most part they are brilliant. And they look at past generations of students and see how their predecessors have entered elite colleges at astonishing rates. As alumni return they are introduced by way of their long lists of achievements; current students (and their check-book-wielding parents) are made well aware of what the alumni are doing with their lives and how St. Paul's helped nurture such invariably fantastic success. The school administration works hard to cultivate belief in the institution because, to be blunt, the school costs a lot of money. And for all that money it must do *something* for its members.

The history of the school is a "storied" one, and almost all the stories told about the school are good. Most students recognize that their classroom education is not the primary aim of their time in the school. Jennifer, a self-assured senior, told me, "I'm from Boston. There are lots of good day schools around my house. Actually I've heard that the test scores from my public high school are even better than the ones here. If I wanted some total academic powerhouse I didn't really need to come here. There were lots of other places I could have been."

Not all students thought of St. Paul's in such terms—many thought St. Paul's was one of the best educations you could have. But they emphasized that this was not the point of the place. Others, like Jennifer, pointed to schools near home they could have gone to that would have provided a very good education. What is it that leads students to believe in a place like St. Paul's?

Beneath the thrill of being at an elite institution, cloaked in all of its regalia, St. Paul's students consistently believe in a foundational ideal of the boarding school. Anyone can learn physics or calculus. You can take classes at any number of great institutions. You can study the classics in high schools across the nation and, if motivated—as these students all believe they are—on your own. Though there are curricular differences between elite schools like St. Paul's and other schools, it is not the content of what is learned in any one class that makes the St. Paul's difference. The true mark of the elite boarding school experience spills far beyond the classroom. In fact, in interviews with recent alumni many were startled by how little they had learned at St. Paul's. Yet in these same interviews they praised what they had learned at the school. The difference was not that they learned more but rather that they learned differently.

This was often tied to the excellence of teachers and the strength of their peers. Nelson Aldrich (a scion of the Rockefeller family) attended the school in the late 1950s. Over lunch he told me a story about going to see the film *Dead Poet's Society.*

"It really was quite a poor film," he commented. He then asked me if I'd seen it, and we both seemed to recall its absurd sentimentality. "There wasn't anything special about it. And yet as I walked out, tears started to pour down my face. There I was, a grown man, sobbing on the street corner of New York City after a fairly horrible film! And why? Because I remembered all those wonderful teachers who had given their lives to my education, to the education of us young boys. And I had never said, 'Thank you.'"[8]

Aldrich's sentimentality about his teachers is not unique. Among the faculty are some extraordinary teachers, and as Aldrich says, many give their lives to their students' education. This experience of teachers dedicating every aspect of their lives to students (living on campus, working with students from 7:30 A.M. to 11:00 P.M., always being "on call" should something happen) helps instill in elite students the importance of their lives and their worthiness. Counterbalancing the entitlement that might emerge through such an experience, students and teachers often develop what can only be called a loving, familial relationship. And so they learn to expect an enormous amount from the world around them; they learn to appreciate these things less as entitlements and more as gifts.

The image of self-sacrifice for children is not lost on the faculty; like most teachers, it serves as a dominant frame for what they do. Yet it was not uncommon for faculty to complain that we were always the ones doing the sacrificing. Late in the year, in an inebriated moment, a young faculty member, Peter, began to talk about the school crest, a pelican that rips the meat from its own breast in order to feed its young.

"You know what I've been thinking about? That pelican. That damn pelican. What do we teach them with that pelican?" He looked at me, drunk, tired, and searching. "I mean, it could be that they learn to sacrifice for others. That they're the pelican and the world is their children. But it's not. We never teach it to them that way. We're always the pelican. Sacrificing for them. But why should anyone sacrifice for them? ... I mean," he stumbled, hoping to find the right words, "don't get me wrong ... but sometimes I wonder why we teach them that. That there are those of us out there dying for them, that they deserve that ... I mean ... they're the last people ... I don't know."

The next day Peter was embarrassed about this conversation; his suggestion that students didn't deserve our sacrifice conflicted directly with our most basic role as teachers at St. Paul's: to be there for these young men and women. And yet his suggestion that rich students should not be the ones for whom we tear out our breasts but instead should be the ones sacrificing would resonate with many faculty. Peter's drunken musings point to a contradiction many teachers felt between what they were asked to do—sacrifice—and what we taught students—to think of the world as a space of possibility within which they could realize their interests. Yet for the most part faculty embraced their stalwart dedication to students; as Aldrich and the school crest suggest, we give our lives for the school and, like the staff, take pride in that decision. And the impact of that dedication was not lost on students.

"David Newman changed my life," a young alumnus told me. "There's no question about it. I sat in his Shakespeare class and my understanding was transformed. Then I started acting in plays. I had no interest in acting. I still don't. But I did it because of Mr. Newman. I just knew that I could grow with him in a way I couldn't anywhere else. And so, well, we never became friends, but well, my fondest memories of St. Paul's are sitting at his house with other students, just talking. That's what St. Paul's was about. I'll never forget him." As I talked with more and more current students and alumni about their relationships with their teachers at St. Paul's, I could not help but think of Freudian transference—about the ways in which students seemed to fall in love with their teachers, and how this deep sentiment made possible kinds of learning and development that would have been otherwise enormously unlikely.

"There's something they give you," Diane, a classmate of mine, recalled. "Something I can't explain. But it's special. Yeah, it's time. They give you more time than any other adult ever would when you're young. But it's more than that. It's almost like they give themselves to you completely in a way that no one ever does, or will again." Teachers, of course, do have their own lives away from students. Like Aldrich's story of sobbing in the streets of New York, Diane's recollection is more of a romantic memory than a reflection of what teachers really do. Regardless of its accuracy, however, the intensity of this intimate experience was shared by innumerable students. And it emerged from a set of dense, overlapping, and often contradictory relationships.

"God, I can't get away from you today," Adam Sise joked with George Billings as he walked into my apartment. George replied, "Yeah, I'm sick of you too!" He then turned to me and said, "Damn, this is a bachelor pad if I've ever seen one!" He didn't mean it as a compliment. I had moved to St. Paul's with only what would fit in my car. The apartment was sparse—decorated and furnished with a few of my books and whatever the school gave me. In many ways my apartment looked like no one lived there.

I replied, "Hey, at least it doesn't reek. Which reminds me. Keep your shoes on. I don't need that foot funk in my house. I get enough of it in your room."

We were in my apartment, cooking dinner. Adam and I were both advisors in the same house. George was a junior, one of the nine advisees we were cooking a meal for. Adam was in his early twenties, I was twenty-six; the boys were between fifteen and eighteen. Some of them lay sprawled on my couch, watching a movie. Others were clearly looking through my things, though they tried to appear not to be. As they realized that my own bathroom was upstairs, next to my bedroom, they all quickly took the opportunity to rush upstairs and see where I slept. Seeing that I had a case of beer in my fridge, one of the students jokingly called out to the others in the room, "Hey, anyone need a beer?" As Adam and I cooked with students, we chatted about heading into Boston that Saturday evening—something we never would have mentioned around students in their dorm. The setting was more fraternal than formal, and though it was an utterly ordinary moment for St. Paul's, I see now that from an outsider's perspective it was incredibly intimate.

Earlier that day I had observed Adam in the classroom. As George walked into the room, he said to me, "Oh! Hello, Mr. Khan. I guess you're observing Mr. Sise today. ... How are you?"

"Good, thanks. How are you?"

Correcting my English by example, George replied, "Well."

We shared a smile, recognizing what he had just done. "Good. I'll see you this evening?"

"Yeah. I'm really looking forward to it. I hear you can cook!"

"We'll see. It's a busy day," I said, betraying that the long school year was beginning to wear on me. "I'm not sure I'll have time to pull anything special together."

"Well, it will be nice to have something that isn't from the Upper."

In the classroom, neither George, Adam, nor I showed any of the intimacy that we would later display over dinner in my apartment. A few weeks later George would sit across from me at seated meal—a biweekly formal meal—and our interaction would again be far more formal, asking other students to "please pass the potatoes" and at the end of the meal asking me, "May I be excused from dinner?" After several years at the school, George had learned to make polite, casual conversation before class and respectful conversation over a formal meal, and yet still could joke with me about my bachelor pad and his smelly feet. He learned to traverse a range of relationships with me. Those that were more formal taught George how to "respectfully" interact with me. Those that were casual taught him how to interact with me more loosely, almost as if we were friends.

But the key word here is "almost." Had our discussion of smelly feet been between two students, rather than a faculty member and a student, we can all imagine the verbal sparring match that would have ensued. St. Paul's students, just like all other teenagers I know, love to talk trash. Yet when I jabbed back at George, he accepted my response and moved on. Though students work to construct levels of intimacy with some faculty members, they also learn to respect the authority of faculty. George knew he could not return the insult. Though he could playfully mock my apartment, he would not go much further; to do so would cross an unspoken but very clear boundary. My experiences with George are also true in the aggregate. Throughout the school, students learned to relate with the faculty as a whole in a range of ways. Some faculty were quite formal in their interactions, while others allowed for greater intimacy. Taken together, students learned multiple ways of interacting with those above them.

In other words, the teacher-student relationship at St. Paul's is not a relationship; it is a set of relationships. And as these multiple relationships pile on, so does the intensity of the connection. What do St. Paul's teachers do? It is not that they teach in a radically different way than public school teachers; it is that they relate to students differently than most adults relate to adolescents. And the educational ideal of the school is that these multiple relations are what make for a rich learning environment. As the school writes about the faculty, "Our faculty members live among the students in our fully residential community, making it easy for them to forge lifelong bonds with the students here. Teaching goes beyond the classroom, as faculty members serve as advisers, coaches, mentors, and friends."[9] It is not what you learn; it is how you learn it. The emphasis on process not only provides a learning environment laden with a wide range of emotional demands but also challenges students with multifaceted interactions. Students must learn to navigate the many different ways they can talk to their teachers—just as they have to learn how to experience St. Paul's in order to become knowledgeable about it. To be successful—both at St. Paul's and at whatever else life offers these elites—they must figure out how to embody these relationships.

They literally must know what the various postures feel like and internalize the many different poses necessary to succeed in the myriad dimensions of an elite existence. In learning to embody a variety of interactions—how to flop onto your teacher's couch and compose yourself at a formal dinner, each with equal ease—students learn to negotiate the dense, yet subtle content of hierarchical relations. By learning how to comfortably yet respectfully relate to those above them—teachers—students learn a crucial mode of elite interaction. This mode consecrates hierarchy by respecting it and by acknowledging the formality required in certain situations; at the same time, the ease with which the successful students navigate the density almost denies the existence of hierarchical relations. And there is a clear difference between this kind of interaction—respecting the hierarchy while making it disappear—to the one with staff—where it is the people themselves who disappear. The implications for the richly layered relationships between faculty and students are incredibly important for understanding privilege: they help students comfortably find a place they wish for in the world they return to after their time at St. Paul's.

It is with their teachers that students learn the dynamics of complex interactions. They learn to treat those with authority over them not simply as authority figures but also as confidants. Students learn not to impose upon the relationship—to act as if they actually *are* friends with faculty. But at the same time they learn to develop a closeness with those who hold authority over them, a bond unlikely between two people who only exist to each other as student and teacher. And so while students identify the "closeness" as what makes such elite schooling special, insofar as it allows for a different kind of learning, I find that even more essential is a dynamic where authority is respected but interacted with in such a way that it seems not to exist. Students learn to support and reify the hierarchy. Through such reification they voluntarily subjugate themselves to the many rules of the school—in sharp contrast to the staff, who have no choice but to submit to the hierarchy. Also in contrast to the staff, the students' relationships with faculty may be unequal, but they learn how to work within the density in a way that allows for advancement.

Thinking about this process, the "ideal" of St. Paul's is not a scholastic one; it is relational. The value of St. Paul's is in "being there"—the way students "find their place" is by experiencing the relationships that gird the school. As we shall see in later discussions, I found that this knowledge is not simply a set of things that students cognitively know; instead, how to negotiate relationships is an embodied interactional knowledge. The elites I have observed are not learning to construct, make, and embody distinctions. They are not moving to the Upper East Side and barricading themselves behind the armory. Instead, they are learning how to acknowledge these distinctions when necessary while also composing themselves as if such distinctions did not exist. The hierarchy is everywhere, on campus and off, but with the right skills the hierarchy seems to disappear. Students learn to comfortably interact with others above and below them, to produce meaning with staff and faculty alike.

It is important to note that when the hierarchies appear too strongly, or exist along what are unacceptable dimensions, they are made to disappear by the school. Two years after I left the school as a researcher, the school hired several non-white faculty. The school was enormously proud of this, as recruiting such faculty to Concord, New Hampshire, is no easy process. However, the school was immediately presented with a problem. In the Chapel, faculty are seated on the basis of seniority. The image of almost all of the non-white faculty sitting in the back was too reminiscent of pre–civil rights era blacks sitting in the back of the bus. And so the school decided to abandon its hierarchical seating arrangement for faculty and students. When the hierarchy highlighted categorical distinctions that showed some of the oppressive and exclusionary properties of hierarchies, the school was no longer comfortable with the arrangement. This is an important moment. And it would be particularly problematic for my argument if it continued. But after a couple of years—after these non-white faculty moved forward in their seats with seniority—the school again returned to its hierarchical arrangement. The hierarchy was reinstated once it no longer suggested that it was ascribed characteristics like race that mattered. As the non-white faculty moved up, the hierarchy could safely reappear, telling a story of progress and hard work (rather than reminding us of durable inequalities).

Here the new elite seem to think much like optimistic Americans of all classes: though hierarchy may be a structure that *marks* the world, it is not the one that *makes* it. Rather, inequality is a result of the characteristics of individuals—their hard work, their choices, and even their luck. But navigating these relationships, the students realize, is a delicate task. Though the ease of their interactions seeks to obscure hierarchy, St. Paul's students—unlike some of their more brash (read: poor) American brethren—are careful not to challenge it. As any of their parents will tell them, one must not forget that hierarchical structures are essential for any elite to be an elite.

Without a doubt these relationships are difficult to learn. Many students struggle with them. But for those who figure them out, the rewards are enormous. Aldrich praises the teachers who had "given their lives" to his education; in a similarly melodramatic moment, another young alumna commented about the ways in which teachers seemed to give themselves to her "completely." In the view of these and other elite students, the world is not simply a blank slate to be taken advantage of; the world actually gives itself to you. The sense of worth that underlies these statements—that "brilliant" teachers would dedicate their lives to you, even to their own detriment—shapes how students understand themselves. They believe that they are worthy of investment and the product of a community that deeply invests itself in them. The sense here is that St. Paul's students have the mark of the chosen.[10] Though such a mark is certainly a privilege, they take care to emphasize that their selection into the school and what they do there comes through their own work. In short, the mark is part of their own character. Though it seems appropriate that the world gives itself to them, they simultaneously believe that their place among the chosen few is something that has not been given to them but rather is something that they have earned.

Presumption and Reverence

As St. Paul's students navigate their way through the school, they gradually find their place. So what then does it look like when students have found their place? As they grew more comfortable at St. Paul's, students displayed a certain signature emotion, which typically existed somewhere on a continuum between presumption and reverence. As we'll see, both of these extremes are problematic for the students, and the most successful products of St. Paul's are probably somewhere in the middle of the continuum, betraying an emotion that I think of as ease.

The simplest example of presumption can be found in Chase Abbott—the entitled boy who walked into my office to chat, casually looked through my things, and acted aloof, suggesting that I was "just visiting" *his* school. In suggesting that his lineage is important and should be respected, Chase fails or refuses to acknowledge changes in the American elite. In interacting with faculty and other students the way he did with me—suggesting that he really belonged here and that perhaps I did not—Chase attempted to make the hierarchy visible, with him firmly perched at the top. Ironically, the student who complained about Chase was just as wealthy and from a traditionally elite family. But Peter had learned to interact in ways that suggested that it was *what he was doing* that explained his space at St. Paul's and not the fact that his family could buy him a place at any institution in the world.

On the other end of the spectrum are non-white and non-wealthy students who have a sense of reverence for the institution that affords them previously unimaginable opportunities. I met Matthew Courtney for the first time as he sat across me at our formal seated meal. I was completely taken by him. After two weeks of having him at my table I approached his advisor to tell him, "Matthew Courtney is the sweetest kid I've ever met."

"Tell me about it," Tony said to me, excitedly. "When I read his file I almost broke down. I gave it to Karen. We sat there like a couple of blubbering idiots. He wrote his essay about how he was homeless for a while, sleeping in a car with his mom."

Karen, Tony's wife and a math teacher at the school, shared in appreciation of Matthew and confirmed that Tony was not exaggerating about their tears: "It killed me."

"When we were putting kids in dorms I jumped all over him. I wanted him here with me. Kids like that are what St. Paul's is all about. He's unbelievable. He lives with this rich kid from California; they're great together."

At the end of each seated meal with me Matthew offered to do the least desirable task: removing the dishes. Soon I had to stop him, telling him that I would like another student to do it. Matthew replied, "I really don't mind." But I interrupted, "I do. It's time for someone else to pull their weight!" Matthew smiled and, regardless of my intervention, helped the student I had asked to do the task. Unlike Chase Abbott, who exuded entitlement within the institution and was generally disliked by those not like him, Matthew was well received by all students and faculty. I was not alone in being taken by his "sweetness." We all appreciated that rather than an expectation, St. Paul's was an opportunity for Matthew.

Matthew's appreciation for this opportunity bordered on reverence. In working on an academic audit of the school I noticed that black students took the most classes and received the worst grades. Some of this difference was due to the fact that black students were comparatively underprepared when they entered the school. Many had to start in lower-level math classes, for example, and often took more classes to "catch up." However, even if these catching-up classes were eliminated, black students still took more classes than other students. I asked an eleventh grader, Devin, about why he thought this happened.

"Mr. Khan, if you saw where I'm from, you'd know. You wouldn't have to ask. Look around here. How many places are there like this in the world? None! This is it. This place, is ... well ... it's something else. And I'm never going to be at a place like this again. Even if I go to Harvard, it won't be like this. This is my chance. And I'm making the most of it."

When I followed up by asking, "Even if it means you get worse grades than other kids?" Devin protested that he actually did pretty well. "You should know this by now. There's more to St. Paul's than grades." Devin wanted to get the most out of the institution that he could. And this was not the case only with black students. Non-wealthy white students employed a similar strategy. Susan, a girl from Idaho, argued to me that she didn't go into town on weekends because "I came to St. Paul's to be at St. Paul's. Concord isn't that different from the towns I left at home. There isn't much I can get out of there."

Coupled with "getting the most out of St. Paul's" is a high degree of respect for the institution and the people who work within it. Part of the reason teachers valued Matthew so much is that with him you could feel the appreciation. He took none of it for granted. We could contrast this to Jennifer, who told me that she could have gone to any number of schools around her home in Boston. Though she clearly appreciates the experience, she reminds me that she could have had an experience similar to this elsewhere. For students like Matthew and Devin, this was not the case. Staying home was not a comparable option. They had to leave to acquire the kinds of things that most students at St. Paul's take for granted. The resulting respectful reverence cuts against these students' capacity to interact with the institution in a way that makes the hierarchies appear to disappear. Whereas students like Chase were entitled and not respectful enough, students like Matthew and Devin were so respectful that they failed to create the intimacy and dense relationships with teachers so crucial to success at St. Paul's. Their abundance of respect is actually a problem, as it makes the distance between faculty and student feel greater and reinforces the hierarchical quality of their interactions. Their reverence hindered their ability to embody the experience of the school and its manifold relationships. And as we shall see in later chapters, reverence for the institution also hinders these students' capacity to negotiate the school—and the wider world of the elite—with ease.

Much of the day-to-day life of St. Paul's School highlights the persistence of hierarchical arrangements. Students learn that hierarchy defines the social relationships of the world—even in the most unlikely, "otherworldly" space of a chapel. But students also learn that they can work within these fixed hierarchies. The code that students employ to make sense of this work is the same one used by people across the country and across the socioeconomic spectrum: the American meritocratic code of "hard work." The faith that St. Paul's students evince in the value of hard work—and of the limitless possibilities that work creates—is astounding, incredibly sweet, and very naïve. And it is also very convenient because the flip side of this faith is a particularly malleable vision of hierarchies: though they certainly reflect natural inequality, they are not seen as systematic or producers of durable inequality. As these students find their place, they learn the value of "working within" such hierarchies and how such negotiations seek to preserve the relationship while obscuring it. Hierarchies thus become invisible in one's interactions—with people both lower and higher on the ladder—and instead what you accomplish on that ladder is the result solely of your own work.

Privilege, then, involves navigating through the Scylla and Charybdis of respect for hierarchy and intimacy within such relations that make them appear as if such a structural form did not exist. In learning to navigate these difficulties, students learn the importance of finding their place within the school and, as the years pass, advancing that place. Rather than think of the world as a space of equality, students learn to think of it as one of possibility; adopting the liberal frame, equality is not to be expected but a "fair shake" is. Where you end up is most often a product of *what you have done*—students feel they have "reached the higher levels of the hierarchy through their own merit."

3

The Ease of Privilege

The really efficient laborer will be found not to crowd
his day with work, but will saunter to his task surrounded
by a wide halo of ease and leisure.
—HENRY DAVID THOREAU

What we hope ever to do with ease, we must learn first
to do with diligence.
—SAMUEL JOHNSON

But I can't teach you my swag
You can pay for school but you can't buy class
—JAY Z, *SWAGGER LIKE US* (T.I.)

The girls scramble to get ready. They rummage through their closets. They anxiously wait for an open shower to wash off the grime of their afternoon sports practice. They rummage some more. For some, their clothes seem a tired reminder of previous dinners. They rush into each others' rooms, trading clothing, accessories, and advice. The girls look crisp. They want something sexy enough to catch the eye of their classmates, but nothing so bold as to raise an eyebrow and perhaps the ire of the faculty. Many settle on a little black dress, with a shawl to cover their shoulders. The excitement is palpable throughout the house. Somehow it is already time. All over campus, clusters of girls emerge from each house.

At the same time, the boys wait in lines to shower after sports practice. Some are amiable, joking in the long hallways outside the common bathroom; others are annoyed that they didn't just shower at the gym instead. Finished with a hasty shower and an even hastier shave, they puddle back to their rooms. The boys dress more casually—some wearing a vintage 1970s shirt beneath a jacket and tie, others sporting boat shoes and shorts. Casual, however, is far from careless. There is an intentionality to their preparation. Their excitement is quiet. Scraggly lines of boys quickly merge with the pockets of girls along the brick pathways that cut through campus. The teachers emerge from each house as well, some chatting with students, others happy to let the gaggles wander ahead, knowing their solitude will soon be over. It is 6:00 P.M. on Tuesday. The entire school is headed for dinner together.

Just before we enter the hallways of the Upper, we are greeted by blaring music. Each year one student undertakes the responsibility of providing a soundtrack to the school's biweekly seated meal arrivals. With speakers pointed out the dorm room windows and the stereo system cranked to its limits, hip-hop typically greets the formally dressed school as we hurriedly arrive to dinner. On the opening days of school the music seems a jarring contrast to the formal meal about to be undertaken. But as the days pass, it becomes less and less notable until finally, it's just another part of the ritual.

There are three dining halls at the school, and all three are used to seat the entire school at once. Two of them are open for every meal—one is a cavernous, utilitarian space that the school attempts to spruce up throughout the year with student artwork; this fails. The other is very similar in design but much smaller and more intimate. Both these rooms might be found in any high school across the country. The third would not. It has been newly minted "the Harry Potter room," as the dining hall in these novels and movies bears a striking, almost eerie resemblance to the upper dining room. New faculty with young children will often take them to this room on their first days at the school; this space, more than any other, instills in these young eyes the majesty and grandeur of the school. Like the Chapel, this room has impossibly high ceilings; mammoth chandeliers hover above heavy wooden tables and chairs; dark wood panels on which the names of the earliest alumni are engraved line the walls. Faded, almost ageless tapestries hang on the walls alongside pictures of once important men, long dead and forgotten.

As the school enters these rooms for dinner, no one sits. We remain standing behind our assigned seats, loudly chattering. One of the school's chaplains clears his throat and a hush overcomes the room. Sometimes our prayers are solemn: "Grant, oh Lord, that we never forget the fortune of your bounty. And as these thy gifts are enjoyed, let us remember those who might go hungry this night. Through your Grace, may such gifts soon be enjoyed by all." Yet at other times, the prayers are playful, even mischievous. Late in the winter, when the school is tired and the endless requirements of the day seem too much, the chaplain might simply say, "Rubba dub dub. Thanks for the grub. Goooo God!"

As the food arrives at the tables, carried by fourth formers, the excitement subsides. We are immediately reminded that the food at these formal meals is worse than that at any other meal. For the kitchen, preparing food for six hundred people who all must be served at the same moment is a nightmare. When I was a student, the standard Friday fare was steaks like hockey pucks. On the side were overcooked vegetables and a limp salad. But parents were pleased to hear about such lavish-sounding dinners. Knowing that their children were eating steak made parents feel their children were well fed and perhaps that their money really was being put to good use. But for those of us sitting through such seated meals, more food was pushed around plates than actually consumed.

Teenagers are hungry. They are growing, perpetually, it seems, and right before our eyes. As a keystone of St. Paul's traditional vision of a rounded education—and to keep the students out of trouble—they are kept busy and active. Except in their senior year, all students must participate in athletic activities each afternoon. This growth and their activity mean that students seize any opportunity for a meal. Even they have standards, however. The quality of food and the fact that they sit among people not of their own choosing limit what students eat. The quality of the food is often mirrored by the quality of the conversations at the table. Once at dinner the excitement of getting ready transforms into a listless twenty minutes. Throughout most of the year my tables could not wait to leave. At times my attempts to engage students seemed a kind of torture, and I was soon disciplined into eating a quiet, fast meal with them.

It is moments like these that make St. Paul's truly exceptional. Sitting in a stunningly beautiful dining hall and eating in formal attire twice weekly with other students and faculty is one of the unique experiences of St. Paul's. I had thought that meals like this would be central to what students learn at the school. The meals are obviously a training session: teaching students how to eat a "polite" meal, how to make table conversation with relative strangers, how to discern what is acceptable and unacceptable in formal interactions. But on most occasions students sat with downturned eyes, pushing their food around, thinking of little more than leaving the burdensome event. If St. Paul's was teaching the finer, more subtle points of table etiquette, I never saw it. What students seemed to learn was how to be ambivalent about a meal like this—ambivalent, and terribly bored. What happened at these tables was not something that I would want to subject anyone to.

Yet if the meal is so boring, why are the students excited to prepare for it? And if seated meal does not teach students the finer points of eating a meal—finer points that might help them later in getting a job—what does it do? Scholars of inequality often point to "the finer points" as some of the many things that produce inequality. The logic here is that people's position in the world is not just about the money in their pockets but their cultural aptitudes. Here, culture does not just reflect inequality (the notion that rich people like classical music, for example, or that poor people like heavy metal or hip-hop) but also works to produce it. From this view, St. Paul's advantages its students by giving them cultural resources that future institutions will then select upon and reward.

All of this is true: St. Paul's certainly does create such traits in students. However, these traits are not quite what we might imagine. Students do not memorize and practice the innumerable cultural codes of conduct that make up "elite tastes and sensibilities." When I was a student, as a hazing ritual older students in one house gave the new students the book *Tiffany's Table Manners for Teenagers*. The new students were forced to memorize this book and could be quizzed about it at any moment. Incorrect answers would be met with physical punishments, often resulting in a deep bruise on the arm. Upon my return, this was unimaginable. Rather than be forced to learn formal rules of etiquette, students learn to be comfortable around such elite tastes and sensibilities and, more often than not, even be indifferent to them. The students at seated meal are not uncomfortable in their formal attire, nor are they anxious about eating dinner with faculty members. In fact, the event is a non-event to them. They could care less. And this ease—which, it turns out, is far more valuable than merely revering and producing expertise—is what students at St. Paul's learn at seated meal and everywhere else.

The New Nobility

As we seek the historical roots of ease, we can do no better than consider the case of the French, who know elite culture better than anyone. It is particularly apt as we have begun with an enterprise the French basically invented and refined: eating a formal meal. And there is no better guide to the contemporary French elite than the social scientist Pierre Bourdieu. My own work and ideas are inspired by Bourdieu, who is similarly fascinated by the "Inheritors"—those at the top of the French educational system, the young men and women who are on a path to success in the French economy. Their success, it seems, is preordained, despite our rapidly changing world. "Many sociologists marvel at the ways in which the world changes," he has said. "I marvel at how it stays the same."

His questions are much the same as my own: what do schools do, how do they do it, and how do the advantaged fare within systems of schooling that are increasingly concerned with eliminating such advantages and being "fair"? How is it that elites manage to navigate a changing world economy? How is it, when there is no longer a nobility where status can be legitimately inherited, indeed, where such a notion is actively challenged, that elites still seem to be a kind of "nobility," transferring their position from one generation to the next? How is it, in short, that as the world around us seems to change, *who elites are* seems to stay the same?

As we all know, the world was irrevocably changed through the social unrest of the 1960s. The civil rights movement demanded nothing less than the restructuring of our entire society, from who could sit at a lunch counter to who could hold what jobs to what kind of rights and treatment we could expect from our government. The women's movement argued for much of the same thing: there should be no places reserved exclusively for men or limited to women. These changes were not just about economic and political rights—they forced us to radically rethink our families. At the core of these movements was a simple idea: the world should be an open one. Everyone should have an equal chance of achieving their goals, provided they had the talent required and worked hard. This essential argument was carried throughout America, across Europe, and into many other parts of the globe by innumerable other groups. There was a common thread across all these movements: we require a new world open to

all members of society, one where the voice of the diverse many—and
not the privileged few—would rule. Men and women, young and old,
called for a new elite based on merit; some even questioned the notion of
an elite itself.

Looking at the Grandes Ecoles—France's elite public schools—two decades after these protest movements, Bourdieu asked what, if anything,
had changed in these educational institutions. After the calls for revolution, how was the new world different from the old? In France, the famous student and worker protests in May 1968 had been aimed in part
at these elite schools. On the one hand they were seen as publicly funded
institutions for the elite. On the other, they were argued to be indifferent
to educating their students in anything other than a conservative morality. What Bourdieu found led him to marvel at how things seemed to be
the same. The elite still managed to get into these schools at astonishingly
high rates and outperform other students within them. And though the
Grandes Ecoles had adopted the language of 1968—merit, openness, rel-
evance—Bourdieu found that in fact they were still public institutions for
the "nobility." How could this be? In France, it is a truth widely recognized
that the nation was remade after 1968. But Bourdieu's findings suggested
that among the elite, this was a fiction. The nobility still had their systematic advantages.

Educational institutions have organizational logics that determine what
good work looks like, what kind of work is valued, and what kind of qualities students should have. After 1968, these standards were no longer supposed to favor the nobility. They were replaced by impersonal and objective standards, highlighting "what it takes" to be a good student, scholar,
and even public citizen. Yet Bourdieu found that the logic of this "new"
institutional organization still mirrored the dispositions of the nobility.
Put simply, the rules of the game still matched the ways in which elite
actors play the game. "Impersonal fairness" was a sham. The explanation
rests on the continued ease that the nobility feel within elite schools.

Thus, when, in the indefinable nuances that define "ease" or
"natural" talent, we think we recognize behavior or ways of speaking considered authentically "cultured" because they bear no mark
of the effort and no trace of the work that go into their acquisition,
we are really referring to a *particular mode of acquisition*: what we

call ease is the privilege of those who, having imperceptibly acquired their culture through a gradual familiarization in the bosom of the family, have academic culture as their native culture and can maintain a familiar rapport with it that implies the unconsciousness of its acquisition.[1]

Why, then, has the hierarchy stayed the same in the Grandes Ecoles and among French society more generally? Why are the elite still overrepresented within these institutions and more likely to be successful within them? Because throughout their lives before entering such institutions they have developed dispositions that will advantage them. They feel at home within the institutions that reward them for exactly the type of behavior that is already "native" to them. And the result is even more insidious than it had been in the past because today, unlike years ago, the standards are argued not to advantage anyone. The winners don't have the odds stacked in their favor. They simply have what it takes.

Does this explanation work for the United States? As we shall see, the idea of ease has a lot of explanatory power. But its combination with the frames of hard work and merit generates a uniquely American elite. At St. Paul's the students who enter the school with the presumption of ease are aggressively confronted and challenged, as we saw with Evan Williams. Ease is not simply inherited from experiences with families; it is made in interactions at the school. Daily life at St. Paul's is an education unto itself, and presumptuous displays without such experience are met harshly.

To return to the biweekly formal meals: instruction about the finer points of eating a formal meal is not what is important. Today's elite are no longer building moats around culture—preventing others from acquiring what they have. For the new elite, it is no longer about knowing particular things (like which is the salad fork). In today's age of free, accessible information, knowledge *about the world* is not a particularly easy resource to protect—nearly anyone can learn about Plato, or classical music, or what wine to order with dinner. And after the social movements of the last century, excluding people from such knowledge is no longer acceptable. However, knowledge of how to carry oneself *within the world* is a much more challenging resource to acquire. So eating that meal—ironically, the most common of things that we do everyday—is more challenging than knowing what to order. The latter requires cognitive knowledge that can be learned by anyone; the former requires corporeal knowledge that is developed through experiences within particular settings. The distinction is between learning rules, which are easy, and learning practices, which are far more challenging, as they require living the relations in question. The nearly ingenious trick—if I may call it so—is that the mark of privilege, corporeal ease, is anything but easy to produce. What appears a natural, simple quality is actually learned through repeated experiences in elite institutions. The result is a near invisible barrier. The apparent easiness of these characteristics implies that if someone doesn't know how to embody ease, it is somehow *their own fault*—they do not naturally have what it takes. This allows for inequitable outcomes to be understood not as the result of the odds being stacked in the favor of some but as something that simply "happens."

Rites of Initiation

There is a kind of arrogant stroll to the seniors as they return to campus their final year. I'm not alone in noticing. "There's such a difference when they arrive," the head faculty member in my house, Jane Clunie, happily comments. For her, it is like her children have returned; many of these boys she has had living with her for years. "God, you can really see a difference in them! It's not just that they look older—but Steve sure does—they walk and talk differently! Just look at Steve. He's got his arms back, his chest pushed out like a peacock!" Jane is soon overwhelmed by laughter, and I can't help joining in, even though this is the first time I've ever seen Steve. "He used to look down all the time when he was a third former. They act like they own the place now." Jane's laughter quickly turns to a solemn seriousness. Looking away from our seniors, directly into my eyes, she warns, "We're going to have to watch out for them."

This confidence has far humbler beginnings. During their first days of school, new students seem to walk as if carrying a great burden, with their shoulders curved forward and chins pressed low into their chests. These new students, who are thirteen to sixteen years old, almost always wander the campus in the safety of packs. They look less like they own the place and more like they want to leave it. Arriving at St. Paul's is a humbling and often difficult experience. Regardless of their wealth, most students are at least a little stunned by the school's two thousand carefully cultivated acres and its nearly one hundred Gothic brick buildings, all surrounded by carefully pruned trees and brick-laid paths that eventually meander to the school's several private lakes and streams. On the very day they arrive they must not only start their lives at the school, they must also leave what, for most of them, was the only life they knew. For ninth and tenth graders to pack up their rooms, put them into a car, and move into a completely unknown room they will most likely be sharing with a stranger[2] is incredibly daunting. They must also say good-bye to their parents—in many cases for several months. Though they have been emotionally preparing themselves for this new experience for months, almost no new students seem ready for what lies ahead of them.

Upon arriving at school new students go immediately to the Rectory to meet the head of the school. A mansion in the middle of campus and home to the rector and his family, the space is packed with new students and their families. There the students are asked to pick up a school pen and sign their name into the official rolls of the school—marking their entry into St. Paul's. Parents do not enroll their children; children enroll themselves. This offends some parents; I heard more than one father mutter, "Who do they think is paying for this?" Though no students are writing the check to the school, they are nonetheless instilled with a sense of self-management, responsibility, and authority in their first act at the school. They, not their fathers and mothers, sign on the dotted line. And this sense of independence will serve to transform the scared boys and girls who enter the school into the self-assured, often brash young men and women Jane Clunie and I couldn't help but laugh and worry about.

Immediately after signing their names into the school the "new boys" and "new girls"—affectionately, condescendingly, and persistently referred to as "newbs"—are met by their "old boy" or "old girl" (typically a senior) and shown the grounds and their room and are introduced to the school. While this introductory drama played out on my first day, I sat in the foyer of my house with the other advisors and the four sixth formers who lived there. It was 8:00 A.M.; the room was filled with the smell of donuts and wood cleaner. We were anxious, but quite soon bored as we waited for the new students and their old boys to arrive and set up their rooms. Sam, one of the four advisees I would inherit that year, was the first to arrive. A new fifth former, Sam was the son of another faculty member who was also an alumnae. As he began unpacking his things Sam was incredibly at ease in his new home. Unlike other students who had thought for months about what they would need for their new life and how it would fit into their room, Sam knew that if he forgot anything he could just walk to his mom's house across campus. He did not seem nervous at all to be joining the school. Even his clothing was indifferent. Whereas the other new students were wearingly newly purchased clothes for their first day—I observed the tell-tale fold marks of many recently unwrapped shirts—Sam showed up in an old pair of shorts and a T-shirt. With no one yet to compare him to, I thought at the time that his performance was completely normal. His confidence was exactly what I had expected from St. Paul's students. They would display the marks of comfort and ease produced from a life of privilege. However, I soon realized that Sam, having spent the last year on campus and being somewhat older, had a huge head start.

Some students were completely hyper, some refused to make eye contact, some seemed paralyzed, and some tried, incredibly unsuccessfully, to play it cool. What they all had in common was fear. I had suspected that students who acted as if they already belonged at St. Paul's—students who showed in the admissions process that St. Paul's fit them completely, that it was like their living room—would be the students who were accepted to the school.[3] I also expected that corporeal ease would vary among students, with those who came from "classic" St. Paul's pedigrees—those from established elite families—displaying the most comfort at the school. In short, I expected the corporeal inscription of ease that Bourdieu found in France.

On this first day, with the exception of Sam, the faculty child, I saw none of this ease. Most of what I saw was fear and attempts to overcome or hide it. William, an Asian American third former, barely shook my hand when I introduced myself before fleeing to his room; he never made eye contact. Josh, a third form faculty child, pretended to be too busy to interact (though his mother had already set up his room for him) and made himself as inconspicuous as possible. I saw him check to see who was in the house common area before entering; once he stalled for several minutes until a parent caught my attention so that he could walk through the common area without talking to me.

The parents were eager to keep busy. They worked frantically, trying to make things right, trying to ignore what they knew would come next. Several mothers insisted on setting up their child's room just like it was at home. Many of the fathers began tying all of their son's ties: "It's one less thing for you to think about." Two sons protested, saying they knew how to do it, but the fathers continued. "It will make your life easier. And your mother will feel better if she knows your ties are tied well. You know how she worries that you look good."

Soon after students unpack their rooms, and just hours after they have dropped off their children, parents are asked to leave. These are incredibly difficult times for new parents and students alike. Parents try to avoid getting their children too upset over the good-bye; students do not want to be seen crying on the first day. As they say their good-byes, many promise that they'll return for upcoming athletic games or for parents' weekend in mid-October. Other parents and children know—though it often goes unsaid—that they won't see each other until Thanksgiving break in November. This is a long two and a half months for most third and fourth formers and their parents. As they say good-bye, many of them know that they are saying good-bye for longer than they ever have before. Students respond to this specter quite differently than do their parents. Most of the teenagers standing on the steps of the house do not offer heartfelt good-byes. Most often students are indifferent. As parents hug their children, many students barely make the effort to place their own arms around their parents. Others are curt with their parents and act annoyed by their continued presence.

If we saw these good-byes on their own, we might think that boarding schools really do live up to their reputation: places where wealthy parents send unwanted or in-the-way children. Most parents try to seem happy to be leaving their children. Fathers tousle their sons' hair. A mother offers her daughter one last piece of advice with a wide smile, one even removing a long-cherished necklace and placing it around her daughter's neck. They wave while driving away; they honk their horns in a celebratory tune. Most students appear relieved once their parents actually leave. They hurry back into the house, eager for the next stimulus. Yet in the subsequent days, and for many, even the next hours, there will be real homesickness and real pain on the part of parents. I will receive multiple phone calls from crying parents, and though there will be fewer tears, students will suffer similarly in their rooms.

Parents leave by 5:30 P.M. At 5:45 the faculty and new students meet in the common room of their dorms. The students wander in. They look shocked. Many are wearing jackets that are slightly too big for them; parents know that they may not have an opportunity to buy new clothes for their pubescent children who seem to be growing overnight. The well-tailored clothes that I expected from the next generation of the elite are largely absent. Many boys look a little ashamed, as if they are wearing their father's suit. The protruding shoulder pads that extend well beyond their arms and the sleeves that cover much of their hands only serve to make the boys look even smaller than they are.[4]

Once the reluctant crowd is assembled, we head across campus to the first seated meal of the year. The new students know this evening is significant but don't quite grapple how. As we walk, we pass girls who have yet to figure out what to wear to these meals. Some look as if they might be going to prom or a formal black-tie event. Others wear girlish dresses, suggestive of the cute innocence of middle school. These girls do not know it yet, but soon all of these outfits will be shoved into the backs of their closets.

On our walk the boys from my house seem to recede farther and farther into their suits. We move as an almost silent pack. My attempts at talking to them mostly fail. The boys drag their feet and keep their eyes down, kicking pebbles across the path as we make our way to the dining hall. The purpose of this first gathering was to teach the new students the practicalities of seated meal. For this first meal the seating was easy. Unlike the constant shuffle of the coming years, tonight they would eat in the comfort of their house, with their head of house leading the table and their fellow new students around them. It seemed rather strange that I was about to teach thirteen-, fourteen-, and fifteen-year-olds how to eat. Yet that is exactly what we did. Jane Clunie, who had been at the school for decades and had shepherded countless students through the terrifying first hours, had no qualms about what needed to be said. Eight new students sat at the heavy rectangular table assigned to us; Jane and I sat as well along with another new faculty member, and the servers placed large platters of breaded chicken and overboiled vegetables in the center of the circle. Jane began the lesson almost immediately.

"Mr. Khan, would you be kind enough to serve us? Thank you. It is important to say please and thank you to the faculty member. Also, people are much too bashful about eating at seated meal. Do make sure that you actually eat. This is your only chance for dinner on Tuesdays and Thursdays." The students nodded agreeably. They seemed thrilled to have someone to pay attention to, something to follow to take their minds off what seemed to be an increasing terror. I began to disperse the plates, placing the chicken on each and trying, in vain, to arrange the food in a way that made it look more appetizing.

Responding almost immediately to our silence, Jane began, "There is nothing worse than sitting at a table where no one speaks. For much of the year you will be sitting with people at seated meal whom you do not know. You will sit with faculty whom you are unfamiliar with. But this is not a chore; it is an opportunity. Get to know people at your seated table. You never know the friendships that may emerge from these casual interactions. If you're very uncomfortable in this situation and feel awkward joining conversation on the spot, you might think of something to bring to the table before the meal."

George, a boy who grew up in the rural West, far away from anything like St. Paul's, wondered out loud, "What would I bring?"

Jane could not contain her laughter. Her fiery, amiable spirit erupted briefly, but almost immediately, knowing she might make George feel even more out of place than he probably already did, she turned to him, and shifting from laughter to tenderness, replied, "Oh no! George, I didn't mean an object—although that could be interesting—I mean a story, a bit of news, something interesting that happened to you that day, or something that's going on in the world. Okay? When you are done, place your fork and knife on your plate, facing you, like this." As Jane arranged her fork and knife on her plate, mostly cleaned of food, she looked around and saw that the boys had not shared in eating a meal. "Josh, you've hardly eaten a thing!"

"I had something with my mom this afternoon."

"Oh, okay." Jane decided not to push Josh any further. His barely audible reply revealed just how uncomfortable he was; she would not add to his torment. Deciding not to single out any more students, Jane continued her general instructions. "Now, many people rush to finish and leave. I hate when students do this. Please don't. Wait for everyone to finish eating. Be patient. After we are all done eating, someone at the table clears the serving dishes away. When you clear the serving dishes, you bring them into the kitchen. The kitchen staff will help you with them. Make sure to thank them. Then someone clears the plates away. Often no one wants to do this job. It's harder, the tray is heavier, and it takes longer. It is very nice if someone offers to clear the plates rather than making Mr. Khan ask."

Jane was silent, and picking up on her cue, I decided not to ask anyone to clear the plates. The silence was soon awkward, and the students looked up at one another, knowing they should do something but not quite sure what that was. Ben was the first to figure out what we were all waiting for. "May I clear the plates, Mr. Khan?"

"Thank you, Ben."

As he began to gather the plates in front on him and scrape the piles of uneaten food onto one plate while stacking the others, Jane became annoyed with this display of poor table manners. "Please, Ben, don't clean the plates at the table. Bring the plates to the serving table and clean them there." As Ben, embarrassed, clumsily lumbered to the serving table, trying to figure a way to bring the half-cleared plates with him, Jane's sympathy for this young boy led her to find a way to help him. "It is often nice if others help with clearing the plates."

As if on cue, the boys all quickly stood up and scrambled to bring their plates to the serving table next to our table. As she laughed, saying, "Thank you!" to the boys, I caught her eye, and Jane and I shared a smile. She had seen this many times before, and I knew that not so long ago I was one these same, lost boys.

Though it was a struggle—far more painful than any subsequent meal—we had made it through our first meal. The students looked largely unhappy. They had hardly eaten. The dining hall we sat in was "the Harry Potter room"; it has the effect of making one feel incredibly small. Its massive size, high ceilings, dark wood paneling, and pictures of dead men seem to emphasize the significance of the space and the insignificance of its occupants. Students were even smaller by the end of the meal, their shoulders rounded, their heads tucked like turtles into their shoulders, and their arms held close to their sides. As we ate, surrounded by the one hundred and twenty-five new and equally anxious students from other houses, the hall was eerily quiet. Beyond the instruction of faculty members, few people talked. We were continually reminded of our embarrassing silence as seniors walked by our hall, peering in and loudly laughing.

Even Evan, who had been trying to exude self-confidence since he arrived, was wildly uncomfortable. No students knew how to act in this new place. They had no real sense of the place, no sense of who they were within it, and no sense of how to carry themselves. Though many of these students had eaten formal meals with their parents before in restaurants, at country clubs, and at holiday gatherings, the skills seemed not to transfer. Perhaps it was the discomfort of being completely removed from the everyday comforts of one's life. But all students—rich and poor, black and white—seemed ill at ease in this, their first meal and first lesson.

Slowly, through eating meal after meal over the course of a year, these students would learn how to act during seated meal is if they were eating "normally"—as if they were not sitting with teachers, and students who were their senior, as if they were not in a jacket and tie or a dress. In short, they would learn to pull it off. In all my time at the school the seated meal would never become a triumph of easy conversation or a bastion of casual banter, with clever turns of phrase that showed these students to be masters of a formal dinner. But they would, eventually, turn into something comfortably mundane.

Yet at this early moment in the school year, none of the "newbs" knew how to pull it off. This first lesson was also a message: you do not yet know how to do the most basic of things, but we will teach you, from the ground up. This lesson and so many others like it were the seeds, the cultivation of a sense of self, that each student would likely rely on later. How to sit with someone who is senior to you, how to look comfortable in a suit or dress, as if it were an everyday piece of clothing, how to make casual conversation—all of these skills were yet to be developed but were in the process of being inscribed upon students. The school asserts itself at the top of the hierarchy so that the students learn how to interact with each part of the hierarchy, each rung on the ladder. It is through this relentless practice, in engaging the ladder, learning its rules, figuring out when to climb and when to stay put, that the students can eventually make the hierarchies not limit but enable their advancement—provided they learn the right way to climb.

After our meal, all new students and faculty head to the old chapel for the first night service—a tradition that dates back to the opening days of the school in 1856. The old chapel is one of the most beautiful spaces on campus: in the middle of the grounds, intimate, and too small to house the whole student body. Yet all new students spend their first night in this chapel before going to bed, and all graduating students spend their last night at a service here. These first and last night services are performed with enormous symbolic weight. Craig Anderson, the rector of the school and former bishop, was in command of the evening: "Now, let me *truly* welcome you to St. Paul's. Your time here begins now. And we shall start with a prayer. You will hear and learn many prayers during your time here, but this one is unique. It will become *your* prayer. It is our school prayer."

As he said these words, I wondered, "What is the school prayer?" It amazed me that after years at the school I could not know this one fundamental thing—the prayer that was supposedly *my* prayer. Before I became too anxious, thinking perhaps I did not know the school as well as I thought, Anderson began to pray, "Grant, oh Lord, that in all the joys of life, we may never forget to be kind. Help us to be unselfish in friendship, thoughtful of those less happy than ourselves, and eager to bear the burdens of others. Through Jesus Christ our Savior, Amen."

I was rather amazed. It had been nine years since I had uttered that prayer, or any other. Yet I did not need to read it—the words fell from my mouth as if by reflex. I remembered. And though not sentimental about my own time at the school, I still found it an emotionally stirring moment. It was my prayer, perhaps my only one. The new students, however, remained mostly lifeless. They did not say the prayer with any particular energy. The prayer itself did not yet hold the kind of symbolic weight that it did for me. The power of the lessons from a place like St. Paul's emerges from their accrual over time. How many polite conversations would these new students have with various faculty in the coming years? How many times would they recite the school prayer? And each time the lesson is laid down once again, the skills are embedded deeper and deeper into who they are. So deep that years later, they still know that prayer, and against their resistance, it still means something.

As students exit the first night service an enormous roar begins outside. Those still inside look startled. They shuffle down the aisle and slowly through the old wooden doors into the darkness. Surrounding the old chapel are all the seniors, prefects, and many faculty. They are cheering the new students. With this first night service, they have become a part of St. Paul's. This is the first real joyous moment of the day. The new students endured the tortures of setting up their room, parental good-byes, dressing up, learning how to eat a meal, and a rather sober religious service. But now their first day was brought to a dramatic climax. As tra-dition deems, they were cheered by those who in nine months will walk into the same chapel themselves and leave as alumni, to the cheers of the entire school.

The seniors in our house found our new students and hugged them, screamed around them, and clapped. Their shouts were incomprehensible. But the excitement and relief was palpable. School might just be a little fun and not all somber work. As we all walked back to the house together, the new students loosened their ties; some untucked their shirts. George looked at the other students, smiling, and said, "That was awesome!" They all smiled at him and nodded in agreement.

The weight of these events is not lost on the students. "Like, I thought I'd left the old me home," one new student, Jason, told me. "And then we did all these things and I realized that I was something new. I was a part of something new. I had to start over. And we did these things, like eating, that told me how to do it, and that I had to. . . . But it was good. I'm part of something now. I'm worried about it, but I know it will be really good. And these things made me feel like I was new, but part of something old. It's cool."

St. Paul's symbolic rites of initiation—from learning to eat to the first night service to the taking one's seat service a few days later—make "new" students. These lessons seek to radically transform each child from a frightened newb who is barely comfortable in his or her own clothes to something new, a "Paulie." Much of learning this new self is learning to embody a new set of relations and to gauge one's position within them. Certainly Jason, and all the others, knew how to eat: he had done so tens of thousands of times before; his parents had no doubt corrected him on the proper etiquette at the table. And yet still there was instruction. St. Paul's suggested that he needed to start over, from the very beginning. Past experiences of the entitled would not matter. Instead, the lesson seemed to be what mattered was what happened at the school—from this moment forward. It was in your hands.

What to Wear and How to Wear It

New students have all the wrong clothes. Boys bring turtlenecks, thinking that they will be much easier to wear to seated meals than a shirt and
tie. Parents supported this, thinking that they would be easier to keep
clean and wrinkle-free. These newly bought turtlenecks will make a single
appearance and never leave the closet again. Girls bring everyday clothing that is too feminine (a flower-print dress, for example) and formal
clothing that will quickly be deemed not sexy enough (austere, full-length
dresses). Much of their suitcases contain clothing for "girls"—they will
soon learn—for better and for worse—to dress like women. Almost all
new students, boys and girls alike, bring clothing that is too large. Though
practical for these growing children, the students themselves will soon re-
fuse to wear the oversized garments.

I first noted the shrinking of new students' wardrobes at the end of the
first month of school. My initial thought was that students were unable
or unwilling to do laundry and had simply run out of clean clothes. However, I noticed new students in my house fastidiously doing small batches
of laundry more than once a week, and I learned that many new students
subscribed to a private laundry service with a weekly pickup and drop off.
Students were not having laundry difficulties; they were choosing to wear
only a select few of their clothes.

The end of the fifth week of the fall term is parents' weekend,
during which many students go home for two days. Those who live
too far away often stay with their parents in local hotels (or travel to
Boston or New York and stay in hotels there). Most international students
"go home" with other new student friends who live in or around New
England.

Almost all students come back looking different. They have new hair,
new clothes, new shoes, new watches, new decorations for their rooms,
new music, new DVDs, and—sometimes it seems—new everything.
The transformation is often dramatic. When a student of mine, Michael,
returned from Connecticut, I barely recognized him. "Michael! You …
you've gotten a new haircut!"

"Yes, Mr. Khan." Michael's monotone response revealed his annoyance
at my noticing the change in his appearance.

"Michael really wanted a new haircut," his mom chimed in. "He's been going to Cindy for as long as I can remember, but this time he wanted something new."

"Mom!"

Michael had found out where a senior from his hometown got his hair cut and arranged with his mother, weeks earlier, to go to the same person. Michael had entered school with boyish hair—a kind of bowl cut that flopped up and down and swayed, emphasizing the still childlike curves of his face. When he returned in October his hair was closely cropped on the sides and spiky and angled on top. He was obviously spending a lot of time in the bathroom mirror, figuring out how to manipulate hair product. He was working to look more mannish.

Ken, a new student from New York City, returned to school with bags of new clothes. He had worn a Hawaiian shirt on the first three Saturday evenings of the term. He clearly liked the shirt and perhaps thought it festive for a weekend night around campus. But by the third weekend I overheard older students giving him a hard time about the shirt. I never saw him wear it again. His new clothes were exceptionally preppy. He brought back several brightly colored collared polo shirts and a pair of plaid pants flecked with bits of pink. On the first day after the holiday, he would wear two shirts, both collars popped, with these pants. He began wearing boat shoes without socks; these became such a persistent feature that late into the winter faculty began to tell him that he'd catch a cold—one even forced him to return home to put on socks.

After the break, I noticed new posters on walls and new music coming out of rooms. Grace, who used to drop by my office to talk about violin (she and I both played), stopped by to ask about something quite different. "Mr. Khan, um, have you ever heard of DMX?"

"You mean, 'It's dark and hell is hot' DMX?"

"Um ..." Grace had no idea what I was talking about, when referring to an old album.

"The rapper?"

"Yeah!"

"Sure. But not in a while. I don't really listen to rap." After I said this, Grace looked at me, slightly disappointed. Though I was a young faculty member, I felt, at that moment, old.

"I just got *Grand Champ!*"

"*Grand Champ?*" I wondered out loud.

"His new album!"

"I guess I'm out of it."

Taking a opportunity to bring me more up-to-date, Grace told me, "You should check it out." I was surprised by our conversation. For Grace, a girl from suburban Boston, this seemed an unlikely—and sudden—transformation.

It did not stick. Within a couple of months Grace and I were back to talking about violin repertoire and technique. Yet Grace had tried out hard-core rap, with great enthusiasm. Months later I asked her why she had bought that album.

"I don't know. I mean, I guess, you know, I went to the first dance here and I didn't really know any of the songs. In middle school I totally did. And it was fun. So I guess I felt left out. And Amber—in my dorm—she listened to DMX all the time. And so I guess I just wanted to learn it. I don't really listen to it that much anymore. It's weird. I mean, I still kinda like it. I don't know."

Months after this conversation I chaperoned a dance and there was Grace, singing along to DMX, jumping up and down, her hands bouncing from her shoulders to knees—mimicking the movements of the latest hip-hop video.

Michael, Ken, and Grace all returned to school looking and acting different. None of these differences was a onetime fix. They did not suddenly fit in, nor did they necessarily feel at home in their new hair, clothes, or music. Learning the difference between a salad and a dinner fork, knowing the difference between the classical and baroque period in music, or identifying modern versus postmodern art is not the most vital part of a St. Paul's education. Much to my dismay as a teacher, the essential learning has little to do with what might be happening in the classroom (though we'll see how this matters in chapter 5). Instead, these students are learning the seemingly mundane things that students learn at just about every high school: about clothing and hair, about how to move and respond to different kinds of music. In a million different ways, they're learning how to embody a new position.

With Michael, he becomes frustrated as his mother and I draw attention to his changed state—we highlight what he was hoping would be a natural transformation. Ken learned what he "should" be wearing as a preppy New Yorker. In Grace's case, this meant how to act as if she knows about and likes rap music. All three learned from older students how to transform themselves into a more appropriate "Paulie." Importantly, though these lessons are cognitive—the students recognize what was "appropriate"—they are at heart performative, corporeal transformations. What happens over that weekend in October is a flurry of changes inscribed on the body—a physical discipline in how to conform to the expectations of an elite.

These transformations have little to do with what we might consider classically elite practices. Indeed, they seemed to be the most mundane of high school makeovers. And yet, it is these seemingly superfluous details that are at the heart of daily life and are essential to positioning oneself effortlessly as a "Paulie." Though Michael, Ken, and Grace each were elites before they entered St. Paul's, they still had to learn from the ground up—their homegrown ease did not suffice.

Though their fathers may mutter about who is *actually* paying the bills as students are asked to sign their own name to the rolls of the school, such independence—however illusory—is key to St. Paul's. These experiences convey to the students a sense that it was not the work of their ancestors nor is it the inheritance of wealth—new or old—to which they owe their position. Instead, they are paying their own way at the school through hard work and the slow cultivation of necessary experiences. All students must learn anew: they remake themselves in the most basic and everyday of ways, from eating meals to getting dressed. As they take on their new bodies, these mundane social practices work to obscure just how different these students are from others. Much of what happens at St. Paul's looks like the same, hormone-filled displays that occur at any other high school. Yet this seeming similarity is key: the students learn to make distinctions disappear between themselves and other non-private school students, indeed, between them and the rest of the non-elite world. This helps construct a narrative that the difference between St. Paul's and other schools is not the obvious distinctions of privilege and wealth. They look just the same as the rest of us. It's not that they have access to privileged information that we are excluded from. It's not that they have bought their way into some exclusive club. Instead, when privilege is successfully embodied, the gap between them and us just seems natural, an almost inevitable result of "who they are."

Distinction

If students from privileged backgrounds do not capitalize on their preexisting privilege, perhaps they have other resources that nonetheless aid them in advancing through St. Paul's. One such resource could be the capacity to make fine distinctions. We might believe that what sets the elite apart is their capacity to recognize subtle differences that the rest of us might not be able to spot or embody subtle tastes that serve to advantage them. Did that suit you're wearing cost $1,000 or $10,000? You may know Bach's *Goldberg Variations*, but do you know the differences between its classic interpretation by Wanda Landowska, the idiosyncratic genius of Glenn Gould, and the daring modern synthesis of Murray Perahia? Could you spot the difference between a 1980 and a 1981 Bordeaux? Surely there is a whole world of such subtleties, a whole language that reveals your grasp of the finer things in life.

I assumed that being a Paulie meant fine distinctions. One evening, while sitting in the common area of my house, a new junior, Harrison, was talking to the freshmen about what to look for in dress shirts and where to buy them. They had all just come from formal meal. Harrison, well through puberty, towered over the younger boys. His voice was deep, and his accent had a strong current of a formal colonial British education. Harrison was well liked on campus and respected by younger students. It seemed to me that he reeked of authority. There was no conversation here; rather, Harrison was holding forth, demonstrating his knowledge and conveying to the others what they should know that he already did. I could not help but think that this scene was a perfect example of the transfer of the distinctions that mark elites from the rest of society.

"You need to pay attention to thread count. I mean, this Pink shirt is a 200—it's so much softer and lighter than my Polos." I was proud that I knew what Harrison was talking about. I had once thought of owning a Thomas Pink shirt—but my not-so-distant immigrant sensibility got the better of me; I could not justify the $150. Harrison continued, "But Pink shirts are still not really made for you. I mean, if you go to a place like Savile Row—it's just off Bond Street—you can get a *real* shirt. One made for you." Around the room I'm sure the other students wondered the same thing I did: "Where is Bond Street?" (perhaps it was in Concord or Boston, or more likely New York). But no one was willing to admit this. And so no one asked.

Harrison then moved to the care of such a tailored shirt. "The problem here is that there's no place to wash them. I mean, you can't put them in the laundry, and the dry cleaners ruin them. It's a real problem. I'm doing them in the sink now. I guess it works. Hand washing is the best. But it really is a problem here. Something I didn't think of."

I didn't know this. I had never thought of hand washing one of my own shirts. I didn't realize I was ruining them—but I soon remembered they weren't much to ruin. Though my brother had lived in London for the previous ten years, and I had visited him often, I still had no idea what Savile Row was or that the street was famous for quality tailors. It was clear that none of the other young students did either. As Harrison took his shirt off and let the other students touch it, I could not help but join in the ritual, appreciating the softness of the shirt. I was seduced by the moment. I was watching, so I thought, the training of the new elite.

The following Sunday, I drove the house seniors, James, Peter, and Ed, into Boston for dim sum. During the ride, they brought up the interaction that Harrison had had with the younger students.

"I heard you were on duty Tuesday when Harrison was talking to the newbs about clothes or something."

"Yes. It was interesting."

Almost before I could finish my sentence, Ed interrupted, "It was bullshit, is what it was."

I was honestly shocked.

"I mean, who owns shirts like that?" Peter asked, rhetorically.

"Not even my dad," James decided to answer. I knew James and Peter to be from fairly wealthy families. Paying what they did for St. Paul's, their parents could also have bought them shirts like the one Harrison was wearing.

"I know. I mean, maybe Larry."

Thinking perhaps my seniors were not like other seniors, I asked who Larry was.

Peter answered, "Oh, those guys from Hong Kong. They have crazy clothes."

But so as to emphasize that this was unique to Hong Kong, and not St. Paul's, James told me, "Yeah. But no one here does. Harrison doesn't know what he's talking about."

After Harrison's conversation with the new students, Ed had some of them come to his room and ask him about it. The new students were worried that even after their shopping sprees with their parents they still didn't have the right clothes. And so they went to Ed, a senior, for guidance. Ed proudly exclaimed, "My shirts are from the Salvation Army."

But his roommate, James, wouldn't put up with this kind of bullshit either. "No they're not."

"Okay, fine. But still, they're not some crazy $300 shirt. I mean, I buy them myself."

Peter was the most confused about what had happened. Though James and Ed seemed almost angry about it, Peter didn't get it. "I don't even know what Harrison was talking about."

As I explained about Savile Row—just off Bond Street—and that these London tailors were said to make some of the finest clothes, Peter's shock only intensified. "Where? Seriously?!? Do you have those shirts?"

"No," I said forcefully. "Never heard of the place. I had to Google it."

"But that's what I'm talking about," Peter said, calming down. "*You* don't know about them," suggesting that if I, an older Paulie, didn't know about them, then "no one does. And who would go to London to buy a shirt?"

James wondered even more broadly, "Who would have a shirt tailored?"

As the conversation continued, Ed told me that he and James had to spend a lot of time assuaging the new students' worries. "We had to take those guys aside and tell them that that was all bullshit. I even showed Smith my closet. No one cares about that kind of stuff here." It was only after the new students had seen the closets of the seniors and after they had touched these seniors' shirts and seen that they were just like the shirts they wore that the worries disappeared.

James ended the conversation by saying, "Harrison is weird like that." Ed and Peter concurred: "Yeah. He doesn't get it."

What I had witnessed in the common area was not an example of the importance of distinctions but an example of the differences between American and European elites. The performative display of fine distinction is read as "bullshit"—a form of trying too hard that does not display one's ease. Imposing these kinds of fine distinctions upon clothing was not an example of what elites need to learn but quite the opposite—an example of "not getting it." Harrison and the guys from Hong Kong might be forgiven for their tastes. But here in America things were different.

Ed's comment that his shirts are from the Salvation Army is telling. His friend James does not let him get away with his posturing; Ed's shirts

THE EASE OF PRIVILEGE 101

aren't *really* from the Salvation Army. Not any clothing will do. Students rarely tried to "slum it." Years ago as a student I had seen some students do this—holding together an old pair of shoes with duct tape when their trust funds could have allowed them to buy a shoe company. This was only done by extremely rich students as a sign to the rest of us that they had little or nothing in life to worry about. They could walk around as they wished, and still their wealth would protect them. But today clothes had become less about your social position—rich or poor, slumming or posturing—and more an expression of your individual character, something that students felt categories like class could not reveal. In doing his own shopping, Ed authenticates himself and emphasizes his own personal, physical experience.

As the school year progressed, I saw again and again how students rarely highlighted the distinctions between "them" and the rest of the world. Surely there were numerous ways that they were different from most American teenagers: from their homes to the place they would ski over winter break to the summer internships that might be waiting for them back at home. Yet none of these accoutrements of a wealthy life was bragged about. Harrison's discourse on shirts was not repeated, by him or anyone else, because as the weeks went by, the new students learned that simple truth again and again: it was not their shirts that made them different.

Students learned not to value elite knowledge or to savor (or hide behind) the things that distinguished them. Instead they learned to consume quite freely across cultural boundaries. They learned to absorb it all and to *want* to absorb it all. Grace learned to chat with me about both DMX and violin technique. Rather than construct boundaries using their wealth and particular knowledge, the students instead work in ways to suggest that the field is even. It's not the quality of the shirt on your back that matters; it's who is beneath that shirt.

Bullshit

The descriptions presented thus far in the chapter—the shared fun of dressing up for dinner, the across-the-board discomfort of opening day, and the rejection of elite clothing—seem to suggest that St. Paul's School is a world without class or social distinctions. That notion, as anyone who went to high school already knows, is both naïve and inaccurate. St. Paul's is in no way exempt from the endless hierarchies of the real world, nor does it make any effort to fashion itself into a cultural utopia. Just as students ignore the mantles of privilege and money and power that many will eventually inherit, so too do they devalue the fine distinctions of wealth that go hand in hand with the country club membership. The disappearance of these distinctions helps maintain the façade of an even playing field. Yet this story is far from complete. Along the quest for embodied ease, serious problems can arise.

Early in winter term as I was walking home from a rather long day, I heard two black girls, one senior and one freshman, talking about schoolwork. The senior, Carla, I knew casually. She was a strong student. The freshman, Lacy, was in the humanities class taught by a close friend. Recently, he had told me happily that she was starting to "get it." I eavesdropped unapologetically.

Carla, a role model, took her position seriously and kept tabs on how new students were adjusting. "How'd you do on that paper?" she asked Lacy.

"I don't know. I feel like I totally bullshitted it."

Carla, emphasizing that that was not the question, replied, "Well? How'd you do?"

"Fine, I guess," Lacy said uncomfortably. "But it was weird."

Reassuring Lacy, but in a way that seemed to directly confront the core principles of the school, Carla told her, "Well, that's what you learn to do here. Bullshit your way through."

The next day, when she walked by my office, I asked Carla about her exchange with Lacy. Carla did nothing but apologize. She was clearly worried that I was upset with how she was presenting the school to new students. And despite my assurances that I was just interested in what she meant, I was unable to get her to talk to me.

A couple of weeks later, Carla tapped on my office door. "I've been thinking about what you asked me a while ago," she said. I encouraged her to sit; she was now eager to talk. She was frustrated, but also eager to give voice to something she'd obviously been thinking about for a long while.

"I do really well here," she began, "but I didn't always. I did really badly at first. And I thought it was because I was stupid or something. Like I didn't get it. But that was the thing, I didn't get it. I wasn't dumb, I just didn't know how to talk like you want me to talk. I mean, I look back at my papers and I don't think they're worse. They're just different. And until I learned how to talk like you wanted me to talk, how to write how you wanted me to write, I was dumb."

Carla was lecturing me. I felt a finger of accusation. Her frustration was palpable. I had never taught Carla, but I knew what she meant. I was a representative of the expectations of an institution; I was part of the "you." And that "you" had a mode of operation, an organizational logic, that was not hers. Ten minutes later, Carla summed up her thoughts with stunning clarity: "I didn't get smarter. I learned how to say the same thing, only different. Not my way, yours."

This is what she meant when she told Lacy that students have to learn to "bullshit their way through" St. Paul's. It is the kind of accusation that runs directly against what schools like the Ivy League and elite boarding schools claim they do. Carla's recipe for success is simply one of translation. Her papers are not better, "they're just different." What made her smart was "learning how to talk like [teachers] wanted her to talk." Most important, at St. Paul's she had simply learned to say "the *same thing*" but in a language that was mine, not hers. Carla's description of learning at St. Paul's is startlingly different from what most students describe. But, of course, Carla herself is quite different from most of her classmates.

I began asking students to tell me about their own "St. Paul's moment"— a moment where they felt that they had suddenly "gotten it," where what had been eluding them became clear. Everyone seemed to know exactly what I was asking about, describing their transformations in ways that emphasized the enormous personal meaning to such events. Students talked about constantly working hard but eventually having an epiphany. The transition to "getting it" was not that the student decided to buckle down and start working but that they had *always* worked. One day, something just clicked. George, a white working-class boy whose family had been farmers, encapsulated the kind of narrative I heard again and again.

"I knew I was going to have to work hard here. My mom and dad told me about it. That all these kids would be really well prepared for school. I couldn't expect to be ready like they'd be ready. But they [his mom and dad] told me that I'd have something others wouldn't: I was used to working really hard for everything." George smiled at me. I thought he was proud of his work ethic. But instead he began to laugh at his naïveté. "Man, were they wrong! Everyone works hard. But one day I just got it. I was sitting there in Mr. Bellfour's class, and he was talking about our next paper. And I just *knew* what he wanted in the assignment. It was like I had been sitting in the dark before, and suddenly someone just turned on the light! I still work like hell. . . . But now I understand. I get it."

This kind of story could have been much like Carla's—only described in rosier terms. I asked George if he felt like he was "bullshitting" now—if his "getting it" was really just a way of translating his own experiences into a language of someone else's. It took George a while to answer. He didn't understand my question.

Eventually he told me, "Mr. Khan, you get it. But you're like older and smart and educated and stuff. I don't really know how this world works. But I'm beginning to. It's got nothing to do with 'bullshit.' It's learning how things work. That's what you're teaching us! Why else would people pay so much?!? I'm getting how the world works."

Carla agrees with George's sentiment. She is also getting how the world works. But George and Carla code this "getting it" differently. For Carla it's learning how to translate her own language into mine; Carla argues that both forms are equivalent—"the same thing, only different"—but that one way is privileged over the other in the elite world. For George it's learning how things (actually) work in the real world, as opposed to the world he came from. George's argument would be echoed by many other middle- and working-class kids at the school. With few exceptions they placed great value in this exposure to "how things work" in the real world of the successful. Though never made explicit, the implication was that this exposure was not something they could receive at home. In fact, I found that, in general, working- and middle-class students were some of the greatest believers in what St. Paul's does for its students.

As stories like George's piled up, I began to see the difference with Carla as a racial one. Carla questions the general legitimacy of a St. Paul's education. St. Paul's is a bullshit system you need to learn, not a legitimate understanding of how the world works. Or put less harshly, it's one among many legitimate ways of understanding things. What's "bullshit" about St. Paul's is not that the school's vision is invalid but that implicit to this vision is the belief that its particular way of understanding the world is *the* way. This is what frustrates Carla: that *her* way is not recognized.

Though Carla is recognized as an excellent student and is quite popular at the school, this approach to the school does make life difficult for her. Faculty feel something different in her work. They often told me they wished she were "warmer"; both her work and her personality were often "cold." She did good work, but it was "formal" and "distant." And students similarly told me that they felt a kind of "distance" from her. One of Carla's closest friends confided in me: "Sometimes I feel like we're just going through the motions here ... I don't know, with her it's sometimes different. Like we're not really connecting, almost like we are, but I remember it like something I saw in a movie, *not us*. Like it happened to someone else. Like our connection is someone else's, or something I saw. Not all the time. But it's weird. I don't get that from everyone. Or really anyone else."

Rather than learning to truly embody the school in a way that is natural, Carla learns, in her translation, to "act it." Her refusal to think of St. Paul's as *the* natural order and instead as one potential order among many results in a distance from the school and others within it. We might think of this distance in negative ways, or as a kind of oppositional consciousness, where Carla claims her "previously subordinate identity as a positive identification."[5]

Regardless, Carla is a clear example of a student who successfully learned the "hidden curriculum" at St. Paul's. Despite her difficulties early on, she did not struggle that much more than any other student. She worked hard. She excelled in her classes. She went on to an outstanding college. If anyone was able to discover something "hidden" within the curriculum at St. Paul's it was Carla; she was able to understand the unwritten rules of the school, translate her own understanding of things into these rules, and excel. Carla's experience at the school tells us that this is not enough. To her, the mere act of learning the hidden curriculum feels forced; her resistance to the school's lessons is apparent to the faculty and influences her interpersonal relationships. Because she did not believe the curriculum was legitimate—but just a different form of bullshit—she was unable to interact in ways that made the organization of the school, and her success within it, seem natural.

Carla's case forces us to acknowledge the assumptions of a St. Paul's education: ease only comes once you buy into the belief that the St. Paul's way of acting is really the right (natural) way to act. It's not some artificial form of bullshit; it's the way the world works. Carla was one of the few students who talked to me about all the students who *could* be at St. Paul's—who perhaps deserved to be—but were not. While the school and its students talk relentlessly of hard work, merit, and excellence, almost no one talked about what this emphasis meant for those who *weren't* at the school. In other words, if St. Paul's was a meritocratic place—if you got there because of your hard work and your own personal excellence—then why was the school made up of mostly very wealthy students? Why were there comparatively few black or Latino students? Why did blacks and Latinos not do as well as the white and Asian students? Why, though girls consistently did better than the boys, was the student body still half boys and half girls? Why did students tend to come from cities or areas just outside of cities? Why were they mostly from the East Coast? Why were many students the children of parents who went to boarding school, particularly St. Paul's? Most of these questions are rather easy to answer. In fact, the answers seem so obvious that we tend to dismiss questions like these. But if we *really* believe that the school is a place for those who are excellent, who work hard, and who deserve their place—and that nothing else should limit who applies, or gets in, or goes to the school—then these questions become very hard. Carla asked these questions. And her answer was that these privileged groups had a way of "knowing" the world that was their own. Not hers. As it turns out, her answer is quite a good one.

I have argued that students who presumptuously display their ease, comfort, and knowledge of St. Paul's are challenged to first experience the place—they are, as it were, "put in their place." The implication of this, I suggested, was that "elite" students did not necessarily have the mark of belonging before entering St. Paul's—or at least, that their lives before St. Paul's didn't matter in terms of their success at St. Paul's. However, in light of Carla's critique of the school, an adjustment is required.

Let us return to Bourdieu for a moment. Bourdieu argued that elite students were more likely to be found in elite schools because there was a correspondence between their dispositions and the logic of the institution. They shared the "correct" cultural tastes before setting foot in school. My experience at St. Paul's challenged this view; I found that students who came from "St. Paul's families," or who displayed a taste for the finer things, were met with a degree of contempt. All students, regardless of their background, initially felt uncomfortable at St. Paul's and had to learn their lives anew. Unlike the French case, there was a focus on experience within the institution. I believed that the emphasis on embodied knowledge ties directly to the exceptionalism of this American moment: the primary importance of experience suggests that it is *who you are* that matters, not *where you are from.* Yet Carla's interpretation of the school as a form of "bullshit"—a very particular social organization that pretends to be the way the whole world works—suggests that for some students, particularly non-white students, there are contradictions between their understanding of the world and the school's organizational logic. Carla was not the only black student to point this out to me. Her perspective is simply the most powerful one.

At the heart of this contradiction is the meritocratic frame itself. Carla saw the school's use of this meritocratic frame for what it was: a mechanism that obscured for most of us the enduring forms of inequality that for her were so visible throughout the school. Her observation allows us to read students like Chase Abbott in still a different way—that his entitled displays were not presumptuous but perhaps one of the most "honest" approaches to the school because the school is not, in reality, a meritocracy. That is, if you believe that the best students in the United States do not come overwhelmingly from the already extremely rich—from families able to pay $40,000 a year for high school—then it is not a meritocracy. And if you believe that the children of alumni should not have a far better chance of attending the school than children who are not "legacies," then the school is not a meritocracy. If you believe that boys should not win more academic awards than girls, even though girls outperform them, then the school is not a meritocracy. And if you believe that white Protestants should not be strongly overrepresented at the institution, then it is not a meritocracy.

Carla and other students like her sincerely express their appreciation for the opportunities that the school affords them. However, they also struggle to make sense of such a profound contradiction. They must confront the questions that inevitably arise as they walk the manicured grounds. *What about other kids from home who could be here but aren't? Why are so many of the students here so rich? Why do so few of the people here look like me?*

Students from advantaged backgrounds, by contrast, don't seem to be plagued by such questions—if they are even aware of them at all. After all, the only past experiences they have to draw on are likely far *more* homogeneous than St. Paul's. American schooling systems are strongly tied to neighborhoods, and these neighborhoods are very racially and economically homogenous.[6] It is very hard to get into a place like St. Paul's (the acceptance rate is well under 20 percent). Compared to their peers at home—peers who likely failed to get into St. Paul's—wealthy students have worked harder or proven more talented. So to these students the school really does look like a meritocracy. The relatively large numbers of "different" students at boarding schools—non-white, middle and working class—provide support for the view among the wealthy that the school is a meritocracy. Compared to past experiences, the school really does seem a melting pot.

But students who are comparatively disadvantaged navigate a much more bumpy terrain. Julie, a new African American girl, pointed out her excitement in the first few weeks of the school. "I sat there screaming in my head, 'This is real! It's really real!' I couldn't believe it. But I was really at St. Paul's now. And I thought of all these people who sat here before me. Even you! They went through the same thing. They sat in that same room and began what I'm about to begin. And they did it. They might not have had me fifty years ago. But there I was now, just like everyone else. Every right to be there." She knew that not that long ago students like her would not have been welcome. It is the American commitment to opportunity and the fights waged by her fellow citizens that have allowed students like Julie access to St. Paul's. But the insistence on using the American Dream to explain one's position at the school obscures just how durable some inequalities are. The opportunity of being at St. Paul's comes with a catch—the adoption of an orientation that sometimes runs firmly against one's own experiences and perhaps those of one's family, where perhaps hard work and merit were not so strongly rewarded. This is the kind of contradiction that wealthier students don't have to manage. And not having to manage these kinds of tensions makes ease at the school that much easier.

This leaves the difficult case of George, the white boy from the family who had been farmers. Though many non-white students would convey similar sentiments as Carla, by contrast I found that white working- and middle-class students were mostly like George: they were some of the firmest believers in the school. Why, then, the racial division of this negotiation of contradiction? How was it that non-white students were more likely to see the school as "bullshit" and non-elite white students to be some of its staunchest supporters? If my explanation of Carla's position is correct, and non-white students must manage the contradiction between the frame of a meritocracy and the reality of durable inequality, why is it that middle-

and working-class white students do not confront this contradiction and see the school as being "bullshit"?

I believe the answer is racial. Race is still enormously important within the elite. This runs directly counter to the work of William Julius Wilson, who has argued that

> [t]he life chances of individual blacks have more to do with their economic class position than with their day-to-day encounters with whites.... [W]hereas old barriers bore the pervasive features of racial oppression, the new barriers indicate an important and emerging form of class subordination....
>
> [The] problems of subordination for certain segments of the black population and the experiences of social advancement for others are more directly associated with economic class [than racial oppression] in the modern industrial period.[7]

Wilson sees a division among blacks in the United States between underclass blacks who are concentrated in urban neighborhoods of poverty, and middle- and upper-class blacks who are (finally) able to realize some of the promises of equality. As a result of this division, he argues, the significance of race is in decline; instead, class is what matters. While Wilson looked primarily at the poor and middle classes, looking at the elite I find something quite different: race does indeed matter. I offer two explanations for why and how.

First, non-white students are often seen by their peers as the carriers of legitimate popular culture. In listening to students discuss popular music, it became clear that non-whites were seen as arbiters of taste. At dances, time and again white students would often dance with and mimic the movements of non-white students; white students rarely, if ever, did this with one another. At my seated meal table, if the group was homogenous, white students would claim to be from "New York" or "Chicago," even if they were from a suburb; when non-white students were present they reported being from "just outside" the city or mentioned the town itself. The assumption, I assume, was that the non-white students were more legitimately "urban"; though suburban white students wanted to believe that they were "from the city"—and even claimed to be among other white students—they were hesitant to make such claims before the more authentic, non-white city dwellers (not all non-white students were from the city, but they were commonly assumed to be). These moments of authority and legitimacy were granted in arenas that students respected—music, dancing, the authenticity of what was assumed to be the hood. Yet at the same time they negated that which makes St. Paul's students distinct: their exceptionality. In being seen as the legitimate and authentic carriers of popular culture, non-whites were given power, but ironically such power cut against the expression of privilege. This is because such power came from their ties to the ordinary, everyday aspects of social life, shared by most in the nation, and not the exceptional qualities that would be found among the elite. And rather than have a facility across social context (from rap to classical music), students interacted with non-white students as if their authority and ease were in a particular realm: that of popular culture.

Second, and more important, black students have a mark far more obvious than taste in wine or knowledge acquired on European travels: their bodies themselves. While class distinctions may be able to "disappear" or, better, be imagined away in interactions, race cannot. While some may claim that Americans are less and less likely to "see" race—an argument more convincing now that a black man has become president of our nation—we also know that Americans are incredibly good at recognizing the most subtle racial distinctions.

I consistently answer the question "Where are you from?" incorrectly. I begin to tell of the story of where I have lived, but soon it becomes clear that this is not really the question. Something about me reveals that I am not completely white. The asker wants to know "what" I am but also knows that perhaps there is something inappropriate in such a question. I answer the question incorrectly in part to challenge the asker to say what he or she means, and in part because I sometimes forget people are not interested in the fact that I was born in New York but instead in where my parents were born. In these moments I must move from my narrative of place to a narrative of lineage. With me, and with everyone else, race is visibly present at the moment of every interaction. Americans have worked hard to make many distinctions between people "disappear," but race does not. Among the elite, who today are working especially hard to make distinctions appear to disappear, race stands out as a reminder that this work is not always easy and that the quest to elide all traces of difference is not always possible.

If these are reasons why race matters among the elite, why is it that class does not seem to matter? I believe that class matters quite a lot, but in our particular American moment it is easier for the elite to ignore. In the last chapter, I suggested that one of the problems for non-elite white students was that they "really" believed in the institution; their excessive faith in the institution caused a degree of reverence rather than ease. The same point continues here with George. In a way, then, poorer white students manage a different kind of contradiction than do non-white students but a contradiction nonetheless, and their belief in the institution is not necessarily an advantage. Whereas black students confront the ways in which the school organization is one among many and that the expression of privilege is just as much "bullshit" as any other, working-class students like George continually told me that what they were learning was the way the world works.

Both poorer students and non-white students acknowledge that there are multiple versions of how the world works; the difference is that poorer students are more willing to accede their own version of the world, whereas non-white students are less willing to give up their world to adopt the Paulie perspective. If we look back to what he says, George implies that he places less value in "where he comes from" than Carla does. The difference is perhaps not surprising: "black pride" has become a rich, cultivated way of life in the last fifty years; "poor pride" hasn't really caught on. The lack of a sustained class movement in the United States, compared to the civil and women's rights movements, means that the saliency of a class identity is less resilient in the lives of the poorer boys and girls at St. Paul's.

Yet this greater openness of the last half century, as well as the self-awareness and self-pride that have come with the various "rights" movements, has thrown a wrench into St. Paul's vision of remolding their youth. The basic assumption of the lessons I have charted in the last two chapters is that the students will be willing to submit to them—that they are happy to be remade into a "Paulie" and thus enjoy all the privileges that come along with being a part of this club. But once you find pride and advantage in your own innate identity—as a black person or, as we shall see in the next chapter, as a woman—then giving up your old self, submitting to a Paulie vision of the world, may not seem so desirable.

Success at St. Paul's requires learning the school's lessons, and these demand that students remake themselves. Most are happy to do so. With the exception of the Chase Abbotts, who are few, wealthy students are already eager to cast off their reliance on their family name, money, or status. Such old inheritances are problematic in today's world. And as their "new" home at an elite institution like St. Paul's continues to provide advantages to them and be a comfortable space for them to occupy, giving up their sense of origin is not a problem. Poorer white students seem similarly happy to give up their sense of class because they feel that St. Paul's is teaching them how the world works, and that what they are learning is more valuable than anything they can learn at home. As class is not a particularly salient identity in America, to give it up does not require an enormous sense of loss. Non-white students—and as we shall see, many women—are unwilling to so easily forego their hard-fought selves in order to embody the St. Paul's model. Carla laments the ways that the school wants her to change. Those who take pride in their past before St. Paul's face the greatest difficulties at the school; their unwillingness to shed their former salient experiences in favor of their new "elite" one makes them less able to embody the ease of privilege.

The work of Pierre Bourdieu can be oversimplified by the popular adage "The more things change, the more they stay the same." Many of the topics of this chapter are utterly banal. The first lesson St. Paul's inscribes in students is something they already know: how to eat a meal. In beginning with this most basic of tasks the school highlights the ways in which students entering the school do not know the most basic of things. They must be taught from the beginning. The aim is not to belittle. Instead, teaching these mundane practices highlights the importance of experience at the school. What came before—wealth, title, position, preparation—does not matter. What matters are your actions and talents.

The content of many of these lessons is not just knowledge but also comfort. The examples of meals are particularly instructive. All high school students know how to eat a meal. Most students who come to St. Paul's know how to eat a formal meal. Yet they are unable to do so successfully in their first months at the school. Boys and girls buy new clothes, borrow from each other's wardrobes, get new haircuts. And still possession is not enough; owning a Savile Row shirt does not make the man. Practice is the key. And only with experience can you achieve ease, the true mark of the privilege that is essential to being an elite. Thus we have the great trick of ease: ease requires hard, systematic work, yet the result should be "natural" and effortless. Just as hierarchies were obscured in the last chapter, the hard work for privilege is obscured (naturalized through ease) in this one. Carla helps us question this naturalness.

In conversations with non-white students about their lives before St. Paul's, I was startled by one consistency: they did not frame themselves as exceptions—as the smartest kids in their school. In fact, they often spoke of others like them from home, other boys and girls who were equivalent to them, who perhaps deserved to be at St. Paul's just as much. Wealthy white students, by contrast, never talked about others who were not at St. Paul's. They believed they had gotten into St. Paul's because of their hard work and merit; they already believed that they were exceptional. There-fore, they didn't need to concern themselves with those who hadn't gotten in. These students accepted the St. Paul's vision of the world as the way life is. And in that acceptance, they achieved ease. They slipped into their new identities as Paulies.

Carla, however, could never quite find that ease. Instead, her peers and teachers spoke of the ways in which interactions with her felt formal, dis-tant, or forced. She knew where she was from, and while she learned how to translate, she wasn't willing to forsake her pre-Paulie self altogether. She couldn't stand that St. Paul's pretends to be universal ("the way the world works") when it is in fact contingent. And though she never said so explic-itly, I think she couldn't stand that while the school cultivates the values of a meritocracy, it does not ask the most difficult question of all: why, if the world has changed so much, has who we are changed so little?

Gender and the
Performance of Privilege

The whole social structure is present at the heart of the interaction,
in the form of schemes of perception and appreciation inscribed in the
bodies of the interacting agents.
—PIERRE BOURDIEU

It is a profoundly erroneous truism, repeated by all copybooks and by
eminent people when they are making speeches, that we should cultivate the
habit of thinking about what we are doing. The precise opposite is the case.
Civilization advances by extending the numbers of important operations
which we can perform without thinking about them. Operations of thought
are like cavalry charges in battle—they are strictly limited in number,
they require fresh horses, and must only be made at decisive moments.
—ALFRED NORTH WHITEHEAD

Mary Fisher almost always appeared quite frantic, even lost. Everyone was
eager to tell you how busy they were, yet other students took care to display their control and management of their endless obligations. Mary simply seemed overwhelmed. Her life was not a disaster, at least not compared
to the occasional students who neglected to bathe regularly or do their
laundry. Yet she seemed on the edge of a precipice. Whereas other students
could be seen casually walking around campus, a light backpack tossed
over their shoulder or a notebook and a couple of books in one hand,
Mary seemed instead to dart through campus, leaning forward into the
unknown. If she stood up straight, it appeared the weight of her bulging
L.L. Bean backpack might throw her backward onto the ground. While
returning from tennis practice with David, one of the players on the team
I was coaching, we saw Mary on one of her rushes across campus into the
library. "There she goes!" David said with a smile.

"What do you mean?" I asked him.

"That's all you ever say—'What do you mean?'"

"You haven't thought about it?"

David looked at me, frustrated with having to answer what seemed like my thousandth question. "This is the first time."

I didn't let him off. "Well?"

"I don't know. I really like Mary. But there's something about it. Like she's different. I mean, she doesn't get *that much* more done than anyone else. She doesn't do better. Here we are walking. And there she goes, quickly waddling through campus." As he said this, he did an almost perfect imitation of her distinctive walk across campus. I could not help but burst into laughter. But quickly remembering my role as teacher, I said, firmly, "Okay!" in the hope that he would stop, and I could compose myself.

"Whatever. You're laughing."

"It was wrong of me to. So she doesn't fit in?"

"No, it's not that. Well, kinda. I guess it's just that she doesn't get it."

I wondered out loud, "What doesn't she get?"

Sick of my questions, David ended our conversation, "I don't know. Isn't that your job to figure out?"

After talking with David I realized I was far from alone in noticing that there was something about Mary. I had never seen her in a classroom, and so I asked a few teachers about her. "She's a good student," her humanities teacher told me, "quite strong, actually. She always gets her work done. But God, sometimes she just seems so high-strung. Like she's going to break. I can almost feel her vibrate." The phrase reminded me of small dogs that almost seem to shiver with nerves, an unfortunately accurate analogy. Mary never did snap; she held it together and survived both St. Paul's and her own tendencies. Why then did so many of us notice her and wonder about her? Mary epitomized the code I spoke about in chapter 2, the ever-valued staple of a Paulie: relentless hard work. And yet she went about it all wrong. Her display of this code, and what made her such a curious puzzle to other members of the community, betrayed an extreme lack of comfort. She succeeded, but she did so without ease.

When studying behavior, we tend to focus on cognitive explanations. As social scientists gather information about people, we are most often interested in what is going on in their minds: we survey humans, asking them what they think; we interview them, and dutifully attempt to give a sense

of their ever-important inner mind. Even when we gather data from observations of what people do, we ask, "What are the motivations behind these
actions? How does this help us think through what is *really* going on in
the heads of these actors?" Rational actor theory—an approach developed
by economists—is the most exquisite example of this very common way
of thinking. Actors are walking calculators, quantifying their desires and
weighing them against constraints, quickly reasoning their way through
the world.

But what happens if we consider what happens from our neck to our
toes? Perhaps the body is not a mere input mechanism for information that
the brain then makes sense of. Instead, the body itself can be the site of
inquiry. I follow the lead of others here. Michel Foucault argued that "the
body is also directly involved in a political field, power relations have an
immediate hold upon it; they invest it, market it, train it, torture it, force
it to carry out tasks, to perform ceremonies, to emit signs." Foucault thinks
of this as "the political technology of the body," where the effects of such
a technology can be attributed to "dispositions, manoeuvres, tactics, techniques, functionings."[1] In short, our bodies are expressions of the larger
power relations of society, and each act of the body works to express itself
relative to its own position within these power relations. In a similar vein,
taking issue with the Freudian social psychological accounts of how we
learn about the world and act within it, Bourdieu argues that social injunctions are not things we "learn" in the mind—they are imprinted not upon
some unobservable "super-ego" but on a corporeal "memory pad." Our
experiences of the world are inscribed upon the body: "We learn bodily.
The social order inscribes itself in bodies through this permanent confron-
tation, which may be more or less dramatic but is always marked by affec-
tivity and, more precisely, by affective transactions with the environment.
. . . The most serious social injunctions are addressed not to the intellect,
but to the body, treated as a 'memory pad.'"[2] Our social knowledge is not
simply some cognitive framework we are taught but a corporeal inscription. By observing the body within the world we can see far more than the
simple physicality of any one actor; instead we can see "the whole structure
. . . at the heart of the interaction."[3]

A crucial part of being an elite, as we have seen, is displaying the right
corporeal marks of belonging. My focus on the body is not some laborious
scholastic imposition, an exercise in theory to try to display a ponderous

erudition. Quite the opposite: becoming a part of St. Paul's is very much a corporeal process. Students learn to interact in particular ways, in effect embodying their privilege. As we shall see, students inscribe the logic of St. Paul's upon both their own bodies and the bodies of their peers. The basic insight is that to understand the elite we must understand their corporeal disciplining and the interactional "marks" that result from this discipline. And again, the trick of such disciplining and marks is that this social inscription appears as the natural, distinctive, particular quality of each individual student instead of a social product that helps further durability of inequality. With this in mind, let us return to David's challenge to me and see if we can figure out what, exactly, it is that Mary doesn't get.

Corporeal Misrecognition

I knew Mary reasonably well. She was the advisee of a friend and played in the club soccer league I had coached. One afternoon, between the end of classes and before sports began, I ran into her in the Schoolhouse. "Hi, Mr. Khan!" Mary greeted me. Though often frantic, Mary was almost always amiable. At this moment she seemed slightly more relaxed. In fact, she was practically strolling through the halls. "You look well, Mary," I replied, "like you've had a good day."

"It's Friday!"

"You don't have classes tomorrow?"[4]

"Just one!" Mary exclaimed with a smile and a clear sense of relief. "The others got canceled."

"That's nice. Looks like a weight has been lifted!"

"Oh! I still have so much to do this weekend," she said, as a hint of worry returned to her face. "But tonight I think I'm going to watch a movie."

"You should." I tried to sound like a tender, compassionate advisor—a tone many of my colleagues had mastered after years of teaching. But it came out flat.

"I don't know, I'll pay for it later."

"No one dies saying, 'I wish I'd worked more!'"

Mary looked at me skeptically, noting that I was the last person left in the building on a Friday afternoon. "You're one to talk! Plus, I mean, I bet a lot of people die wishing they'd had a better life. How else are you going to get one? We've gotta work for it."

"That's true. A movie isn't going to kill you, though."

Clearly sick of me, but still always polite, Mary headed to the door. "Yeah. Thanks, Mr. Khan!"

My praise of Mary was intentional. But it is also clear that I was unconsciously trying to inculcate some sort of ease within Mary, acknowledging any shred of the relaxation that seems to elude Mary so much of the time. When I attempt to undermine the importance of work—"No one dies saying, 'I wish I'd worked more!'"—Mary scolds me for it, reminding me that I seem to be always in my office and that success in life is a product of hard work. This "work talk" was similar to countless other conversations I had with students, faculty, and staff at the school. Mary was not that different from other students, and she clearly was not unhappy at the school. And as David indicated, her fellow students seemed to like her. So perhaps I had misread Mary. Was I overemphasizing the importance of embodying ease?

Early one evening a few days later, I was sitting in the library reading. At certain times of the day the library is quiet. It sits right next to one of the lakes on campus, and as you look out many of the windows, it feels less like a building and more like a boat, floating atop the lake in the middle of the wilderness. Students began to pile into the library and I prepared to leave; soon it would be filled with activity and I wanted to relax. Yet one group set up quickly on the table next to me, preparing to dig into a science project. Mary was part of the group. It took some time for the group to start—they were initially more interested in catching up on gossip than working. Mary became more and more agitated. She began with casual interruptions, but her classmates continued to ignore her, silently handing her the assignment, the data, or looking at her and then returning to their conversations. Close to rage after several minutes of being dismissed, Mary finally threatened to leave.

"I have a lot of work to do! If we're not going to do this I've got to go. We can find another time to meet."

"Okaaaay," Tom said, clearly annoyed, and similarly condescending, as if he were dealing with a pestering younger sibling.

"I know. It's just . . . well, . . ." Mary stumbled. She was being demeaned; she was nervous, and she did not know how to recover.

"Yeah, you have a lot to do. We all do." Susan, a third member of the group, tried to smooth over the situation. But Tom was not finished.

"What's going to happen, Mary?"

"What?" Her voice quivered. I thought she might start crying.

"Oh, no! We didn't start on time!" He mocked.

Mary began to regain her nerve. "I've got a lot to do tonight. . . ."

But Tom was still hoping to torment her. "I don't?"

"We all do. But I really want to get to work on this."

"I don't?" Tom tried again.

Susan had had enough of the bickering at this point. She started to take the books out of her bag. "It's not going to take that long."

"I heard that it took Brett, Jenny, and Colin six hours," said Mary. She seemed to gloat at being right that they should have started long ago.

"What? Six hours?" Tom said incredulously. "They haven't even started."

"Yes they have!"

"Well I guess you'll have to work for twelve, won't you!" Tom mocked. "Gotta work more than everyone else, right!"

Susan ignored them. "Let's divide it up."

"Too bad you're with us, Mary. You'll have to check our work! You'll just have to work harder, won't you." Tom laughed, noticing that I was watching him, and tried to play his cruelness off as a joke. Mary joined Tom in his laughter, if for no other reason than discomfort. As she began to say something, Susan cut her off before she could start. "Okay. Come on, let's get started."

Mary believed in the meritocratic frame. She had earlier exclaimed to me: "I bet a lot of people die wishing they'd had a better life. How else are you going to get one? *We've gotta work for it.*" For most Paulies, hard work was a mode of understanding—vital, for sure, but an idea that could be used when convenient and exchanged for others—but for Mary it was a way in which she organized her life. I began to see Mary's running around campus slightly differently after her interaction with Tom. She embodied not only the notion "work hard, get ahead" but an even more uncool manifestation: that working hard was the *only* way to get ahead.

The difference between Mary and the other students was that though everyone talked about how much they had to do, Mary *showed* it—in her bulging backpack, in her adamant stride, in her constant reminders to work. Most other students produced a kind of indifference to what they described as a seemingly insurmountable pile of work. For Mary, you felt that the pile was on top of her. As we all know, in many high schools across the nation Mary's treatment would be utterly typical. Some of us may even see more than a bit of ourselves in Mary. In the typical American high school, students who embody work, who "vibrate" with the tension of being a conscientious adolescent, are sanctioned by their peers and made outcasts. At St. Paul's, however, as at a few other academically insistent schools, a different culture reigns. Students all emphasize how hard they work; they even "compete" with one another, comparing how much they have to do. Working hard and excelling are commonplace; being extraordinary is simply what you do. The highest-performing students are often the most popular. While the ostracization of Mary would not be surprising at most schools, in one where the utmost value is placed on work and achievement, it is.

But as David said, she didn't get it. Though everyone claimed an enormous amount of work, they displayed an ease or indifference to it. The work didn't matter. The difficulty of getting it done was not displayed. Instead, achievements seemed to almost passively "happen"—as if the students themselves hadn't done it or that doing it was not really very hard for them. What Tom did was seize on Mary's *real* belief in and manifestation of hard work and torture her about it. Hard work was a frame, as we've seen, that students mobilized to code their advancement within hierarchies, but this frame did involve an attendant corporeal display of effort. Their displays were meant to be just the opposite: full of ease. Why did these students get ahead? Because hard work comes easy—they are naturals.

The next afternoon I saw Mary back in the library, burdened by her usual anxiety, every muscle seemingly clenched in her body. As I prepared to leave, I approached her table, in part because I was worried that the previous day's interaction with Tom had hurt her. As she looked up at me, she had none of the casual feeling that she did a few Fridays before, as she walked out of the Schoolhouse and debated watching a movie with friends. "Hi, Mr. Khan," she said, attempting to feel warm. But she couldn't accomplish it. I wasn't surprised. I could see the stress in her face. "I've got to get this science report done. We split it up, but it sounds different in different places! And Mr. Tuttle cares about the writing, not just the results." When I replied, "I'm sure you'll do a great job on it," she quickly responded, "I hope so. That's what I'm working on!"

Mary does not work that much harder than other students on campus. Lots of students spend as much time as Mary working in the library and their rooms. This is particularly true of girls. David points this out when he says, "She doesn't get that much more done than anyone else." But other students do not manifest this work as a part of their identity at the school. Mary would later tell me, "I'm always worried that I'm falling behind." Kids like Tom manipulate this fear to make her realize she doesn't have the mark of belonging.

This display is gendered. To put it simply, girls have to work harder than boys. Study after study has concluded that girls across the nation have better grades than boys and perform better in college; in no small part this is because they are working harder.[5] But elite colleges are gendered institutions that strive for an equal male-female ratio, even though the girls are stronger candidates. Girls at St. Paul's must work harder than boys to find a space within the "girls' pool" of college applicants.[6] Having to work harder makes it harder for girls to display the requisite St. Paul's ease.

It was not simply ease that Mary did not display. Unlike most girls on campus, Mary looked practical. She wore comfortable fleeces and pants. Her clothes were, for the most part, utility items. And her burdened walk around campus, beneath the weight of her bag, did not display any kind of sexuality. This was particularly notable in light of what other girls on campus looked like; unlike Mary, most girls on campus actively mobilized their sexuality.

Embodied Ease

"Learning how to dress" is not simply learning what to wear but also disciplining one's body into how to wear it. We can think of culture as a resource—a kind of "capital" that like money has a value. But culture isn't just what we *cognitively* know about the world—say, mastery of a wine list or about where to buy the nicest shirts. One must learn to look the part—to (inter)act in ways that *mark* belonging. Unlike cognitive knowledge, which is fairly easy to disseminate and display (and difficult to exclude in a more open society), such corporeal knowledge is hard to embody or mimic because it relies on experience.

Girls' dress was often the subject of controversy during my time at St. Paul's, and at no time was it more contentious than during seated meals. During these meals boys must wear a jacket and tie. Girls must dress in a similarly formal way—but as there is no "standard" outfit like a jacket and tie, they have much more flexibility in their dress. The girls find this flexibility to be very ambiguous, and it makes it quite difficult to figure out "appropriate" dress. Boys constantly complain that girls can wear just about anything they want and that therefore the dress code isn't fair. Girls complain that their options for attire are actually quite limited. As Lee, a Latina from New York, said to me, "I either dress like I'm going to the prom, like I'm working the corner, or like I'm a forty-five-year-old business exec. I'm none of those things."

But the main complaint over seated meal comes from the faculty. The complaint is that girls wear far too little clothing to the meals. Just before I arrived at St. Paul's, the administration changed the rules for girls' dress: they are now required to cover their shoulders, resulting in what was called the "no bare shoulders rule." This fairly minor rule was the subject of major headaches for faculty and continual acts of protest by the girls. In particular, young and single male faculty know that they must enforce the "no bare shoulders rule," but many are uncomfortable saying anything to girls about their physical appearance. To tell a girl to go back to her house and change her outfit is to openly recognize the bodies, and thus the sexuality, of these girls. And such an acknowledgment, for many male faculty members, crosses a line and reveals a tension that they would rather not recognize. Senior girls are eighteen years old, and there are several male faculty who are barely out of college. Girls will often test this tension and push the line of appropriateness. One student, for example, came to a meeting with me after seated meal dressed in what was effectively a slip. And at my seated meal table girls often showed up wearing similar outfits.

During the first weeks of school, my demands that girls leave the table and change were almost always met with resistance. The girls' most common reply was that they lived at least a ten-minute walk away. And in the twenty minutes the trip would take them, they would miss a meal. This reply was a trump card. Faculty constantly worried that students weren't eating well—and worse, that the girls in particular did not eat enough. To send a girl home without a meal was something most faculty members were unwilling to do. So as the year progressed, like most of my colleagues,

I pointed out the inappropriateness of their attire, quietly suggested they go and change, but never required anyone to leave the table. As a result, little changed. The girls continued to wear what they wanted, and if continually pressed, they'd often start dinner with a shawl that would casually fall off their shoulders as dinner progressed. The adults continued to pretend not to notice and then lamented the abundance of displayed flesh in every faculty meeting.

It was no accident that girls challenged the bare shoulders rule, and their tension demonstrated the crucial place of embodied ease at St. Paul's and the central role that clothes played in that experience. On the one hand, it attempted to take away one of the primary vehicles through which they expressed challenges to faculty power. By making faculty uncomfortable, by making the faculty aware that they were (almost) women with bodies like other women in their lives—that they were not children but adults—and by making the faculty aware that we were not infallible, and that at least some of us had inappropriate urges, desires, and thoughts, the girls were able to use their sexuality to subvert authority at the school.

On the other hand, some of the girls saw this rule change—correctly, I think—as yet another concession that girls had to make because men couldn't be expected to control themselves. The girls at St. Paul's are asked to manage a contradiction: they must learn to wear formal clothing with ease—clothing that for women is often revealing—while at the same time they are made to feel as if there is something wrong with that expression, something dangerous or inappropriate about it. How can you feel at ease when you are given the simultaneous feeling that what you are doing is inappropriate?

Seated meal was not simply about *what* to wear but also an opportunity for girls to display their bodies. While the discomfort of and challenges to faculty were important, these were not the central aims of the displays. Girls used these meals to engage in a kind of conversation with one another. Some sought to impress boys seated at their tables whom they were interested in. But more often than not, when I talked to girls about why they dress the way they do at seated meal, most never mentioned boys. "I mean, I never get a chance to dress up. And it's something fun to do. You should see the dorm before seated!" Emily was clearly excited to tell me about a scene I could never see. "Girls running around, borrowing dresses, makeup, a shawl, a necklace, anything. It's the most fun I ever have in the dorm. Sometimes it's the best part of my week! We're all there, getting ready for the same thing. . . . And it makes us feel, well . . . I don't know. But it gives me a chance to dress a way I normally can't. And I like it. And sometimes Lindsay or Carroll will have a new dress or something. And it's cool to see them in it. Or to try it on myself and see how it looks on me. I guess it's weird that I'm telling you this. You probably don't care. But Lindsay's mom just sent her this new dress and she wore it last week. But this week she gave it to me, 'cause it looked great. Lindsay even said it looked better on me!"

The ritual of dressing is not—or not just—for boys. As Emily tells me, "you probably don't care." She assumes I don't care not just because she understands that I am oblivious to fashion or because I am a teacher but also because dressing is a way that girls communicate specifically with one another about where they belong in the school. When asked about dressing up for seated meal, the first thing Emily talks to me about is her experiences in her girls' house. Emily was not unique in her emphasis. Many girls never mentioned boys at all when talking about their clothing choices. The use of clothing and the displays of bodies are part of the articulation and negotiation of their positions. They are not just negotiating a hierarchy, a system that creates stratification and difference. They are also organizing relationships with one another and creating meaning in everyday life—we will see this all the more clearly in a moment. The bodily performance of dressing up is an eagerly anticipated—and at times gut-wrenching and anxiety-producing—part of the everyday life of these privileged girls.

This sheds further light on the protests of girls to the "no bare shoulders" seated meal rule—to put it simply, the rule limits girls' capacity for self-expression. The wearing of clothing, the displays of bodies, and the use of sexuality are the central organizing principles for the daily lives of girls at St. Paul's (and, I'm assuming, at every other high school in the country). We should not forget how Emily describes these events: despite the views of faculty members, dressing up is not harmful but "fun." Girls are also playful with their sexuality; as Emily said to me later in this same conversation, "Someone has to make that whole thing [seated meal] interesting; I do it with my dress." The dresses that make the meal interesting are not those that are particularly special; despite the wealth at St. Paul's, there is no haute couture here. Instead, they are those that highlight the bodies of girls. Recalling what Lee said about the perils of figuring out what to wear—"I either dress like I'm going to the prom, like I'm working the corner, or like I'm a forty-five-year-old business exec. I'm none of those things"—we see more than just the constraints of formal dress. We see a Latina girl whose upbringing in working-class New York presents twin challenges: knowing *what* to wear and knowing *how* to wear it. The student who came to visit me wearing what I described as a "slip" could have been seen, in a different world, as "working the corner." However, she wore her dress with a kind of authority. She was able to carry herself in a way that indicated she was doing something quite different: expressing herself to other girls at the school and embodying the privilege of a girl from St. Paul's. One of the many privileges of being such a girl is that you will not be mistaken for a prostitute, no matter how revealing your dress.[7]

Knowing how to act appropriately is not the same as actually doing so. If we think about the examples from this and the last chapter—from boys looking as if they are wearing their fathers' suits to girls displaying and disciplining their bodies as both expressions and challenges—we see that integration into the school is not just "knowing" or learning a set of rules. It requires a bodily discipline, a persistent practice, until you can "pull it off" with apparent ease. But sometimes this pulling it off comes with a price. The disciplining of bodies is not always an easy or pleasant process. And for girls in particular the lessons of ease with one's sexuality can cut directly against the possibilities of the expression of privilege.

Belonging through Sexuality

From their first day on campus, students at St. Paul's quickly learn a new vocabulary, a new way of relating to one another, and a new way of understanding themselves. We have seen numerous examples of the school's lessons and rituals that all seek to reinvent the students into Paulies. But another key means of this conversion is through hazing rituals. In the 1990s hazing was quite common in boys' houses. Known as the "Newb Olympics," young boys would be subjected to varying degrees of abuse (and various abusive events)—being awakened in the middle of the night, water-drinking competitions, boxing, tortuous mental exercises, forced midnight runs in the cold, beatings, and, on extremely rare occasions, sexual abuse.

These hazing events were most frequent in the opening days of school and decreased through the year—with occasional eruptions. Throughout the 1990s, hazing was mostly a "boys' thing," especially anything physical. But certain Olympic events went far beyond physical beatings into the realm of psychological abuse, and girls were known to engage in their own forms of ritualistic abuse—from circling areas of fat on girls' bodies to forcing new girls to be silent for extended periods of time.

In the late 1990s the school began to pursue and punish such rituals in boys' houses; the administration adopted a mostly consistent no tolerance policy where hazing would result in expulsion. This response was addressed almost solely at boys and only in terms of activities within dormitories. Other forms of hazing—particularly on sports teams and by girls—were mostly ignored. Not surprisingly, hazing rituals remained a part of the school.

On the second night of my year at St. Paul's, almost all houses held a "newb night." Far from banning these rituals, the faculty actually gave tacit sanction to them but set limits on what could happen. Occurring late at night, after faculty have left the house for the evening and retreated to the comfort of their homes, what transpired in each house varied enormously. Yet universally, I was told that its purpose was "to welcome the new students to campus" and "to give them a student introduction to the school." For the most part faculty recognize the importance of a student introduction to the school. As the social rules for student interaction are complex, becoming aware of them quickly is important for a smooth transition to boarding school life.

In my own house the seniors negotiated with me and the other faculty advisors about what, roughly, they would say, how they would say it, and what they would do. Once satisfied with what was going to happen, we agreed to disappear from the house while the event took place. We challenged the students to be responsible and carry the authority of upperclassmen rather than simply infantilizing them with rules. Faculty often relied on student authority both to teach new students and to mediate student conflicts when they emerge. There are countless petty conflicts within houses, and seniors take a leading role in dealing with most of them. This teaches them to lead. For teachers, allowing students to mediate some of their own challenges both teaches them to be responsible and helps reduce the headaches of constantly patrolling students. Given the recent legacy of expelling boys for hazing, we had a relatively easy time making sure our boys were respectful and restrained in their rituals.

The boys recognized the importance of this self-management, relishing the authority provided them. Even within our strictures, they believed that they would provide the real introduction to St. Paul's—an introduction that we teachers were incapable of giving, since we didn't really know how the school worked. Our boys talked to the new students about things they wouldn't talk about in front of us—how to avoid getting in trouble, what to do if you get in trouble, how romantic and physical relationships can be managed (sex is not permitted on campus), and some of the important social events of the calendar (particularly dances) to be attentive to. They also explained to new students that they should never knock on each other's door; they should always just walk in (rooms have no locks at St. Paul's). Though this might cause some embarrassment at times, it was seen as essential. The reason was simple: if someone knocked, it meant the person was a teacher. And if you were doing anything you shouldn't be, this would quickly alert you to who was on the other side of the door. This lesson was the hardest for most new students to learn.

The older girls also relished their authority but approached it in a very different way. When I asked girls about what they did during these events, they offered a wide variety of topics: they talk about boys, faculty, sex, themselves, what to expect at school, and how to develop a good reputation and avoid a "bad" one, and they just try to get to know one another. Yet when pushed, many of the girls revealed that the broad undercurrent of these events is sex. As we saw from the dressing up for seated meal, sexuality is an important form of expression in the lives of girls at St. Paul's. And while adults are more likely than they once were to provide sex education to girls, this education often denies that girls are sexual actors themselves. We think of adolescent boys as highly sexual, blindly driven by their sexual desires. The sexuality of girls is something we tend to think less about—other than to worry about how they are objects of boys' desires. The enormous importance of sexuality to their everyday lives, and the fact that such sexuality is not actively talked about by the adults in their lives, leads to something that should not surprise us. Girls take it upon themselves to figure out and teach each other about sexuality.

What happens in girls' newb nights varies widely. The events are often harmless. There is a lot of gossiping about the reputation of different dorms and different sports teams. New girls are warned about being preyed upon by older boys—some boys are singled out as being particularly predatory. Before they spend too much time with any boy, new girls are told, they should talk to the seniors in the dorm to learn his reputation. A lot of attention is paid to an early dance. "Screw," as it is called by the students, is a dance where seniors set up dates for all the new students in the house. The students take this dance incredibly seriously, as the sexual desirability of girls is determined by their value on the "screw" marketplace. If a desirable older boy is interested in a new girl, this means a lot for her status and the status of her dorm. If not, the girls and the house suffer. The double meaning of the dance's name is purposeful—both that one might get "screwed" by having a bad (undesirable) date and that the dance might set up a sexual relationship. The older girls take on the role of older sisters. They do the good and bad: at turns suggesting they will both take care of the new girls and torment them. Overweight girls can often be relentlessly teased. As a result eating disorders are enormously common at St. Paul's, and there are almost no overweight students on campus. At the newb nights, the girls who look "experienced" are pumped for information about their previous sexual exploits and are both praised and demeaned by the older girls. Several houses play games where the seniors pass around a bag of small candies to the new girls and have them take some. Only after the new girls have taken the candies are they told that they have to reveal something about themselves for each piece taken. In some houses, it was made explicit that this meant things they've done with boys. The activity served the double purpose of drawing out information about sexual pasts and disciplining girls into recognizing the problems of having too much candy. Those with a big pile had a lot to reveal on their first night.

During my year, however, one newb night was truly different. In the middle of the night, the senior girls of Barclay House stripped out of their normal clothing until they were barely clothed, put on wigs and body and face paint, and awakened each of the house's new girls. First, they locked the new girls in a closet. Then they forced them to put on adult diapers; as it was explained to the new girls, "Wear these because you're the babies of the school." The new girls were then brought into the seniors' rooms to play a sexually explicit game of "never have I ever" (where they were asked to admit what sexual acts they had performed). Senior boys were called and the new girls were prodded into sexual conversation with them. The new girls were given new, sexually laden nicknames, such as "backdoor Becky." The girls played a game of deep throat with bananas—simulating oral sex and competing to see who could put the banana the farthest down her throat.

Within a few days rumors circulated around the school about these incidents, and within a week the dean's office was working hard to figure out what had happened at Barclay's and other "newb nights" across campus. Disciplinary action was considered in four of the ten girls' dormitories, though in the end, it was taken in two. The events at Barclay were by far the most extreme of that year (and, according to recent alumnae, the most extreme ever heard of at St. Paul's). As rumors spread, so did shock among faculty, the administration, parents, and alumni. The *Concord Monitor* wrote several pieces about the "sex scandal" at St. Paul's, and readers were particularly critical of the school when the dean of students was quoted as saying, "These kids were wonderful kids who made a mistake here. No one was hurt. We think we're handling this situation in a sensitive way to protect these kids." Ultimately, the administration suspended five senior girls from the offending house for a semester. In another house, Emerson, where the events were far less severe, seniors were suspended for two weeks. Students, for the most part, were shocked less by the events and more by the school's reaction. New students who participated in the events in Emerson even came to the defense of the seniors. In a letter to the police, the new students claimed to have enjoyed the evening.

"We thought this night was a great way to get to know the seniors, as our leaders, and don't think that anything should have been done differently," the new students wrote. "Please take the fact that all of us decided to participate and did it comfortably into your disciplinary decision." The new students told of "voluntarily" going into Emerson's basement, laughing at their new nicknames, and enjoying a game of "never have I ever." "We were given candy and had a choice of whipped cream and a banana and a devil dog. Again, all of the new students wanted to participate and eat their food, meaning that no one was forced."

During the discovery process students were alarmingly honest about what had happened. The older girls thought that the events were not only appropriate but a legitimate welcoming of new students to the school.

Some even emphasized the necessary nature of this kind of introduction, arguing that it was for the good of the new students so that they could learn "how the school works." The language of "welcoming" and "necessity" was hotly contested by faculty, just as it was systematically invoked by students. In many cases, they believed their actions to be tacitly sanctioned by the faculty and administration.

"They knew about it," Stacey, an African American girl involved in one of the milder "newb nights," told me. "I mean, we talked about it with the faculty in our house. Faculty agreed to leave so we could talk to students, so we could welcome them. I mean, there are things that they need to know that you can't say in front of faculty."

I was skeptical. Having learned about what had happened in Barclay, I asked what students needed to know.

"Oh, you know. Come on, Mr. Khan," Stacey laughed. She looked at me, knowingly. "You were here. I mean, your first year matters here! You know, how you do things."

But I made her spell it out. "Like friends? Boyfriends? Classes? What are we talking about?"

"Oh, come on!" she laughed. "All that, I guess. Like how to do Screw, or dating. I mean, you set up a lot of your life your first year. And you want to do it right. You want to do well, but you want to make sure you make good friends and do it the right way. And dorms, well, they have reputations. Like you're in Hamilton." Stacey smiled at me, almost condescendingly. She knew, as I did, that my house had a reputation for being a "dork" house. "I mean, those guys are nice. But they're, . . ." She tried to be tactful about the house I was advising in. "Well, not a lot of girls go there. And you need to know stuff like that."

At this point, I pushed Stacey. I was frustrated by what happened on campus and felt she was avoiding the severity of what had happened in Barclay. "But as far as I can tell, that wasn't all that happened at newb nights."

"Well, in most places it was." She immediately stopped laughing, and the smile fell from her face. "I don't know about Barclay. But even there . . . I mean, well, it wasn't like . . . it just wasn't. I mean, a lot of it was about that stuff." She was clearly becoming more agitated. "And everyone knew about it. Roberts [the head of house in Barclay] knew about it! I mean, they talked to him. He talked to them. And then everyone pretended like that didn't happen!"

Stacey was right, to a degree. The students who had engaged in ritual sexual abuse had talked to their head of house about having a separate get-together without faculty. The head of house agreed that it was a good idea. At this point, the agreement ends. Oliver Roberts maintains he made clear that the atmosphere was to be respectful. As he tells it, he told them, "Don't do anything you couldn't tell your grandmother about." This "grandmother standard" was continually emphasized by faculty in justifying their tacit sanctioning of these events. And it was used by the administration to argue that while the "welcoming event"—their more tame term for "newb night"—was not banned, there were clear guidelines about what would be acceptable.

The female students—both those who had and hadn't been involved—made two somewhat contradictory claims. On the one hand, some claimed to never have heard the "grandmother standard" from any faculty member. On the other hand, they argued that what they did, while perhaps a little over the line, was not just acceptable but necessary. It was the only mechanism to teach new students about what St. Paul's was "really" like. As one senior girl put it, "We were doing things that had to be learned about school but you couldn't teach." The rest was a struggle between students and faculty. Students continued to refer to their events as "welcoming ceremonies"; faculty, by contrast, called them "hazing" and appealed to the "grandmother standard" as evidence that students would not, in fact, be proud to tell others about what they had done.[8] And so students were extremely frustrated. They thought of what they were doing quite differently from how faculty did. And further, that faculty knew about what was going on and only recently acted so negatively (and strongly) to the events was to many outrageous. From the students' perspective, if faculty disagreed with the "newb nights," they should have said something long ago. As one student told me, "I mean, really. It's been happening for years!"

There was the common denominator of sex and sexuality as a pathway to belonging and "welcoming" for girls. What senior girls quickly sought to instruct and inscribe in new girls—what was seen as necessary for understanding "real" life at St. Paul's—was a lesson in student approaches to

sex and sexuality. The ritualistic hazing practice emphasized for new girls
the importance of sexuality, just as the weekly dressing up in dorms taught
a similar lesson whereby girls learned to organize, articulate, and negotiate their positions with one another. This inscription was a corporeal one.
What the hazing did was inscribe on the bodies of girls their position
within the school. The event was certainly a form of psychological abuse.
But the kinds of things done—games of deep throat, dressing up, being
confined in a closet, and so forth—are primarily a form of corporeal discipline and inscription. In "teaching" the new girls about the school, older
girls did not *tell* them about what was important. Rather, these lessons
were literally inscribed upon the bodies of these new girls; as we'll see, the
body and the myriad ways it can perform have crucial implications for the
elite and for the gender of the elite.

Boys, for the most part, felt alienated from what had happened. The
word among boys was, "If you haze someone, you get kicked out." "Hazing" was interpreted as physical beating. The older boys were often mean
or condescending to the new boys. But they almost never touched them.
In fact, boys systematically avoided physical contact with one another. In
my year at St. Paul's there was only one fight on campus. Compared to
other high schools, and given that these teenage boys are living so closely
with one another, this is rather astonishing. This "fight" happened in the
spring between two friends on the hockey team. One of the boys, Craig,
had had a sexual encounter with the other's sister. The brother, James, was
very upset and arranged to meet Craig at one of the school fields to re-
solve the matter. James attempted to push Craig into a fight, shoving and
shaking him. But Craig continually refused, keeping his hands down and
repeating, "I'm not going to fight you." The encounter ended as James
pushed Craig to the ground and walked away. This scene between two of
the most physical hockey players at the school is rather astonishing for
its lack of significant physical violence. Yet it becomes less so when we
consider the character of St. Paul's. Put simply, "fights" are almost never
physical at St. Paul's; even those that are don't involve the kind of blatant
violence one would typically associate with such interactions. Fights result not in beatings but in ignoring one another and attempting to make
the other boy feel isolated. We can't ignore the class elements of these
boys' self-control of physical strength and the realigning of power on a
non-physical basis.

Despite—or perhaps because of—the relative rarity of violence, the administration took it very seriously. As one of the deans described the adoption of the no tolerance policy in the late 1990s, "When we started kicking boys out for hazing, they quickly learned. They're not going to forget that for a long time. They're not going to do it. And not just hazing. None of that physical macho bullshit." The dean's disregard for such "bullshit" exemplifies the St. Paul's mentality—that violence is idiotic, counterproductive to elite success, and, though no one would ever say this, reeks of the lower classes. This is not to suggest that boys are exempt from corporeal discipline and inscription. Rather, inscriptions do not happen through physical violence—and part of the inscription is the rejection of such physicality. Yet because of the strong prohibition on such violence, boys felt largely confused by and alienated from the hazing crisis. Knowing that I worked within a dean's office and was constantly asking questions, the boys tried to get information from me about what had *really* happened in the girls' dorms. The rumors were fantastical (and as it turned out, so were parts of the real events). The image of half-naked girls prowling their dorms late at night playing sexually explicit games was too much for most of them to keep out of their minds.

Despite the public face of shock and disappointment, many faculty quietly voiced that they weren't that surprised by what had transpired at Barclay. Beyond the earshot of the press and anxious parents, many of the faculty commiserated that the girls on campus were in fact meaner than the boys. It seemed to faculty that girls could wake up one morning, finding that many of their friends had decided to ignore them. This cruelty often reached its peak in the spring, when housing for the next year was decided. Students can request whom they want to live with and where. Groups of students work the system so that friends can live in dorms together. Each spring some girls find that their friends have lied to them— that they have not listed them on the housing request form. They discover that their former friends will be living together somewhere and that they have been abandoned. The faculty were not at all surprised by *who* had been responsible for the hazing in Barclay. "These girls should never have been living together," one teacher said to me. "They're mean. Just awful." He blamed the administration of the school. "They knew that but they weren't going to do anything about it. They don't want to make decisions that are unpopular with the kids."

What surprised me was that for the most part, the faculty were blind to the parallels between newb night and the school's official activities. St. Paul's, after all, is built upon ritual. The school's own abundance of such events—though lacking body paint or diapers—give shape to the school day, the school year, and, indeed, each student's entire trajectory at the school. Every faculty and administration member enforces the importance of ritualistic events, which impose hierarchy and emphasize what is "truly important" about a St. Paul's education. The "taking one's place" in the Chapel symbolically marks the importance of hierarchy to the everyday life of the community. Similarly, everything from formal meals to the senior couches to the boat docks on one of the campus lakes that the seniors have reserved for themselves are ceremonial challenges, moments that dot each student's consciousness and help prod each student into figuring out how to act.

All kinds of student activities take their cue from these official rituals. These consecrated times and spaces and ceremonies are readapted to give shape and meaning to the "second" life of the school: the student life. Most rituals created by students are simply seen as part of the school's fabric; they are taken for granted as an inevitable, foundational part of the St. Paul's experience. So should we truly be surprised when a few of these rituals cross the boundaries of what we (or our grandmothers) consider appropriate? Like so many of the official events, the rituals created by the senior girls at Barclay imposed hierarchy and reinforced one's position—in this case, their own dominance and the newbs' subordinate status within the house's hierarchy of social relations. What the senior girls didn't anticipate, however, was that the explicit sexuality of their ceremonies would provoke such anxiety. These seniors knew that learning how to use your body— how to discipline it, how to show it off, how to figure out your emerging sexuality—was a crucial part of the St. Paul's experience. What they didn't realize was how deeply uncomfortable the rest of us were with that fact.

All of these examples point to the ways in which students struggle to belong at the school: how they look for spaces where they fit, how they work on one another to define what it means to fit, what they symbolically mark as important for fitting in, how they orient one another to become a Paulie. These rituals also reveal that students cannot fit in just anywhere. Rather, they must take their place within existing status systems. The rituals described above exemplify the myriad ways in which the systems of the school (and of elite life) are inscribed onto the bodies of students. New students learn that they are at the bottom of the status hierarchy. They learn to embody this position in part through the disciplining acts of hazing and corporeal control. To return to an earlier argument, as students embody this subordinate position, they learn to occupy the bottom rungs on the school's ladder of dense relations. Essential to the arc of one's time at St. Paul's is figuring out how to navigate the different rungs of the hierarchy, until you ascend to the top and successfully inscribe the subordinate position on others. The goal is for such navigation to become natural so that you can converse with janitors and CEOs alike, so that you can be an elite with ease, living a life of ascension.

What the Barclay girls "got wrong" was that their acts of hazing were too extreme; they constructed too great of a chasm between those at the top and those at the bottom. The distance within the hierarchy was too large. The ritualistic sexual abuse suggested that perhaps the hierarchy could not be negotiated; those at the top were too distant and dominant. This lesson was unacceptable (as, of course, were the acts).

The Performativity of Privilege

The Barclay's hazing—and, to a lesser degree, many other newb night proceedings—had a remarkably theatrical quality, replete with everything from makeup to props, from character names to simulated acts. We might look further at the ways in which relations at the school are not simply learned but performed. Judith Butler, among others, has argued that we should think of social categories not simply as existing "things" but instead as a kind of performance. Such a focus on performativity complicates our understanding of how people interact and suggests that "both motives and actions very often originate not from within but from the situation in which individuals find themselves."[9] We must look further than simply the imposition of norms or rules upon actors, which they then adopt. Instead, we need to focus on how the actors themselves produce particular relations within life's many contexts.[10]

Butler asserts that such performances serve to create an implied interiority to what are actually social categories of distinction: performances, once well practiced, make the socially constructed seem natural. Particularly relevant to our discussion is gender. Butler argues that we are all constantly performing gender, and in doing so we create the illusion that this social construct is actually a real, innate, or natural quality within us.

> Gender ought not to be construed as a stable identity or locus of agency from which various acts follow; rather, gender is an identity tenuously constituted in time, instituted in an exterior space through a *stylized repetition of acts*. The effect of gender is produced through the way in which bodily gestures, movements, and styles of various kinds constitute the illusion of an abiding gendered self.
> . . . Significantly, if gender is instituted through acts which are internally discontinuous, then the *appearance of substance* is precisely that, a constructed identity, a performative accomplishment which the mundane social audience, including the actors themselves, come to believe and to perform in the mode of belief.[11]

We have seen this stylized repetition of acts in St. Paul's students with regard to both gender and the numerous other aspects of self. Through repetition these students gain experience and produce an embodiment of privilege that is not "work" but instead appears a naturalized, innately easy quality. This naturalized privilege, like Butler's gender, obscures the ways in which privilege is a product of an advantaged social position (attending a $40,000-a-year high school, for one). This aids in both preventing others from displaying the marks of the elite, insofar as the ease is quite difficult to produce, while suggesting that those who are not marked by privilege simply "don't have what it takes."

We can extend these insights to think about relations among the elite. Being an elite is not a mere possession or something "within" an actor (skills, talents, and human capital); it is an embodied performative act enabled by both possessions and the inscriptions that accompany experiences within elite institutions (schools, clubs, families, networks, etc.). Our bodily tastes, dispositions, and tendencies are not simply something we're born with; they are things that are produced through our experiences in the world. Not only do they occur in our minds, but they are things we enact repeatedly so that soon these performances look less and less like an artificial role we're playing—a role that might advantage us—and instead look more and more like just who we naturally are.

As part of its response to the hazing crisis, the school had a series of discussions in houses about sex and sexuality. The results were at times even more discomforting than the original incidents at Barclay. In one of these discussions a senior girl who was well respected in the community said, "Well, it's like the greatest gift you can give someone. I mean, it's one of the most selfless things you can do." She is talking, here, about performing oral sex on a boy. Using one's sexuality as a "selfless gift" was brought up, in different variations, again and again by the female students. And St. Paul's is not unique in this. Milton Academy—an elite preparatory school similar to St. Paul's—was rocked by its own sex scandal the year I was at St. Paul's. In this case, a girl performed oral sex on her boyfriend and four other boys in the school gym. She did this "as a birthday present for him." The discussion at St. Paul's took place in reference to this incident at Milton.

Thinking of one's sexuality as a "selfless gift" or as a present to be given highlights the contradictions for girls between their sexuality and privilege. Whereas privilege is manifested through many of the relations we have seen before—"intimate respect," autonomy, authority, self-management, ease, and the realization of interests—girls' sexuality is often manifested through the selfless giving of oneself to another. The performance of girls' sexuality and the performance of privilege often lead to deep contradictions that cannot be easily resolved. Whereas girls talked openly about sex and sexuality in their houses, and often about how sex was a gift, the talk in boys' dorms was notably different. These discussions varied depending on whether or not the boys were in relationships or single, but there was one commonality to all the talk: boys described their sexual urges as natural or hormonal. And there was no mention of gift-giving.

"Well, you know, I mean, we're going through these changes," Dan said. Early in his time at the school, you would see Dan with a different girl on his arm at every dance or coming by his room almost every week. Now, as a sixth former, he felt supremely confident in his sexuality. "And you just feel different now. I mean, third form to here—wow! That was a change."

"Yeah! I mean, it's like this stage," Jim eagerly followed Dan.

Steve burst out laughing. A particularly mischievous fourth former, he could barely get out his joke: "And there's a reason you all knock on our doors before you come into our rooms." The room erupted with laughter. Steve often joked that the reason we knocked on student doors was because we didn't want to walk in on the boys masturbating—something teenage boys were thought to take every opportunity to do.

Dan fashioned himself to be beyond such juvenile concerns. "But really. I mean, it's hard." As Steve began laughing again, even louder, at this last word, Dan shot him a cruel stare. The room was almost instantly quiet. Continuing to talk about his own sexual exploration, Dan looked at one of the younger students who particularly idolized him. "This is the kind of stuff we're supposed to be doing. It's just that time. Well . . . it's different now that I'm dating Katie, but before that sex was all I could think about."

Later I pushed Dan on what he meant. I wondered if Katie simply satisfied his sexual urges or transformed them. "She made me think about it all differently. I mean, our relationship is really important to me. It's not just about physical stuff. I mean, she taught me, well, not really to control, but I guess what was important. So she's helped me get through this whole crazy stage." This naturalization of male sexual urges is a form of male entitlement. Girls are seen as more in control of their sexuality and thus have the capacity to rein in a boy's sexuality through a relationship. As we moved to a more concrete discussion of girls, the boys spoke very differently and less openly and freely. Nevertheless, what emerged was revealing about how gender identities were performed at St. Paul's. In the view of many boys, girls were thought of as the holders of sexual power, power they could manipulate, exploit, control, and reform.

"You see the way they dress for seated!" Steve almost screamed. "I mean, come on!"

"Like, it's like they egg you on. And they get away with murder. I mean, if I dressed like that . . ." Andrew could not finish his thought. He next words were drowned out by boys mocking him for suggesting that he might go to seated meal in a little black dress. "No! Seriously! You know what I mean. I mean, like, they get away with murder. They dress in a way to get attention."

"And you give it to them!"

"You would too if they gave it back!" Andrew defended himself.

"At least it makes seated meal more fun!"

"Yeah, the only problem is I always end up taking the tray," Steve lamented about always doing this least desirable job at the end of seated meal: lugging the dishes away. He turned to one of the advisors in the house, "You remember this. You asked Susan to take the tray and I said I would instead. I just did that 'cause . . . um . . . well . . . I didn't want to. But I totally was going to!"

Girls are seen as manipulating boys into doing things they don't want to do. Yet this "manipulation" is not the only thing girls do. As Dan suggests, having a girlfriend changed him. Katie moved him away from his natural urges to "something different." This reformatory potential is talked about not only by the boys but also by the faculty. While coaching the tennis team I had a difficult time with one of my players; he was unfocused and on a path toward trouble. A faculty member who knew him well said to me, "The best thing that could happen to Brian would be if he got a girlfriend. He had one in the fall and was *much better*. She really kept him honest." The standard view was that boys had an uncontrollable sexuality, which led to all kinds of problems; girls—thankfully—could either manipulate or reform them.

This presents a double bind for girls. After the hazing scandal and the events at Milton Academy, the school seriously worried about the health of sexual relations at the school, especially for the girls. From this perspective, girls suffered because of what one reverend called "the new sexual norms" of casual sex (especially oral sex) and expression through sexuality. Girls were expected to perform sexual acts on boys, encouraged to exploit their own sexuality, present their sexuality as a "gift," and constantly express themselves as sexual beings. Yet on the other hand, no one talks about boys suffering at the hands of their own sexuality. For teenage boys, sexual urges are a natural problem—the consequence of a developmental stage—that apparently renders the boys unable to control themselves. In short, by describing boys' sexuality as natural and hormonal, for the most part boys abdicate responsibility for any sexual relations. Girls are seen as able to control both their sexuality and the sexuality of boys. And so, paradoxically, girls are both the victims of unhealthy sexual relations, yet the only ones capable of controlling these relations. In the stories they tell about themselves, and that are told about them, these girls are victims of a situation they control.

This paradoxical situation is a way of utilizing discourses of liberation for women in such a way that makes them problematic and aberrant. This double-bind confirms our current cultural constructions, which cast girls as having more agency and being less reliant on the opposite sex, but it

also mobilizes these constructions to blame them. So female sexuality becomes salient while boys' naturalized sexuality remains in the background.
Agency over one's own sexuality, a focal point of the women's movement,
has been distorted until it now places limits on their full equality within
social relations.[12] In terms of their performative, corporeal displays, girls
are placed in a more self-conscious managerial position; boys, by contrast,
are able to fall back on the notion that they are just acting "natural." Boys,
in their sexuality, can rely on a type of sexual ease that is largely unavailable
to the girls at the school.

The result is a significant gap between the sexes. Girls display performative acts that contradict the ways that privilege is supposed to be performed; in other words, there is a tension between being a girl and being
an elite. Girls must regulate their sexuality, they must act self-consciously
in order to control both themselves and the unapologetic impulses of boys.
But such regulation is the opposite of ease, the opposite of the elite goal
of making hard work look like no work at all. Further, while the sexuality
of girls is central to their relationships with one another, the expression
of such sexuality is often met with disappointment by the faculty at the
school. The "no bare shoulders" rule is one example, and faculty reactions
to girls' dress at dances, where their lack of clothing is lamented and the
source of countless conversations, is another. The girls learn to wear formal,
revealing clothing with ease and yet feel guilty and inappropriate for doing
so. The expression of sexuality at the school demands that girls engage in
performative acts that cut against the proper expression of privilege.

Opting Out

Lynn, an eleventh grader from a wealthy background, had been in a close
relationship with another girl, Susan, for two months when we sat down
to talk. She was surprisingly willing to discuss her new, semipublic life with
another girl. "I mean, it's been a change. I'm sorry to put it like this, but
with all the shit I don't have to put up with now, it's been great. People
look at me now, all weird, when I hold Susan's hand on the path. And that
used to really bother me. But now I almost do it so they can see me, so
they know that I've changed. I'm not part of those stupid games anymore.
I think I'm happier. No. I *know* I am."

Lynn doesn't identify as a lesbian, but through her somewhat ambiguous relationship she has transformed herself and her life at the school. As we chat she wears a pair of baggy fatigues and a St. Paul's sweatshirt. Her top suggests that she hasn't fully rejected the school—although few will be surprised to know that Paulie girls don't wear fatigues too often. She sits comfortably in my office and looks at me forcefully as we talk. She doesn't worry about her "reputation" as a lesbian, except when she thinks about her parents. "My mom totally freaked when someone told her this crazy story about me and Susan!" she exclaimed. "I feel bad for her, and I kinda just told her that we were really good friends. But that's what sucks about being from Connecticut. Lots of people know my family. I mean, they talk to others from home. That makes it hard for my life outside here."

While thinking about her life outside the school makes Lynn agitated, inside the school she is relatively unfazed. She talks about a shift in her dorm life—how fewer girls come into her room now and how one in particular doesn't like to be in the bathroom at the same time as her—but for the most part she doesn't seem to notice that much of a difference since she's started her relationship with Susan.

Many other students treat Lynn as a social outcast. Students don't just find her weird, they find her presence on campus somewhat questionable. When I once told a group of students that I had been talking with her they responded, "What are you doing talking to her?" Another chimed in, "Yeah, I thought you were here to study *St. Paul's*." The reason Lynn is treated as not being a Paulie is not simply her sexuality. During my year at the school, the president of the student body, Gene, came out as gay. He was one of the most respected students on campus, and if anything his coming out seemed to increase, not decrease, his popularity. However, in the ways in which he carried himself, Gene did not otherwise challenge the school. He walked, talked, dressed, and acted like a Paulie. Lynn, by contrast, did not. She performed her identity quite differently, in a way that challenged the rather homogenous way of being a girl—or even just a student—at St. Paul's. In choosing to opt out of "those stupid games," Lynn effectively (and perhaps unwittingly) struck a blow to the foundation of the Paulie identity: she revealed the illusion behind the seemingly "natural" dress and performance of her peers. She demonstrated that their seeming ease was not innate but a conscious decision—a decision much like her own to opt out.

When I ask Lynn what she means by "those stupid games," she has a lot to say—about getting ready for every public interaction, about constantly worrying about what she looks like, and, most important, about worrying what others think. Now she feels, for the most part, free of those concerns.

"God! I feel like I have so much more time now. Getting ready for chapel, or seated, or a dance, or even for intervis [visiting a boys' dormitory] used to take me so long! Even when I just rolled out of bed, like when I didn't have time to change before chapel, I'd still work on my hair and face for a long time," she said, laughing at her old self. "Sometimes I'd even change my top—not into something nice but into a different pajama top if I thought it looked better. Then I'd run to chapel. That's crazy! The worst part is, none of it was ever for me. I don't know who I did it for, but it was never because I wanted to."

As much as Lynn emphasizes that she is liberated from the status regime of sexuality, she cannot help but talk relentlessly about how she looks to others and compare her life to the time when she actually played "those stupid games." Almost everything she talks with me about is in relation to those games. Whether it is how students now look at her clothing and hand-holding or her life in her dorm, Lynn's benchmark is the view of other girls. And while she seemed to suggest initially that she acts in new ways because she now actually wants to, when I proceed to ask about how she now dresses, her answer is very different. "I think it's funny. Like, I make lots of people uncomfortable. They see me and they think about how I'm dressed, but they also think about how they're dressed. I mean, I *make* *them* think about it with this!" She said, grabbing her fatigues. "I think about that when I get dressed in the morning."

Lynn's refusal to play "those stupid games" does not enable her to reinvent herself in any way she wants. Rather, even her acts of resistance are in dialogue with the sexuality regime that she seeks to reject. So while Lynn refuses the legitimacy of the ways in which other girls are organized, in defining herself in opposition to this organization she further consecrates the organization. Though she does not play "those stupid games" of getting dressed up for boys and girls or working within the dominant sexuality regime, she still plays the overall game. She corporeally inscribes her resistance (sitting "like a boy") and engages in performative displays that are in dialogue with the performances of other girls. As Lynn sees it, she forces students to consider how their displays of ease are not simply an expression of their innate self but performances themselves. And though she is willing to admit that her new clothing and attitude is a performance as well, she doesn't seem to be aware of how tied she is to the school's vision of how to embody privilege.[13]

Boys similarly resist the processes that seek to integrate them into a cookie-cutter mold of a Paulie. But their possibilities of resistance are greater. While girls like Lynn resist from *within* the sexual stratification system of girls, we shall see how boys can "opt out" of this stratification system for another.

Eric Kim was liked by just about every faculty member. He worked hard; he was smart; he seemed to "do the right thing" in almost every situation; he was pleasant to interact with and was generally kind to other students—new and old. Though he worked incredibly hard and took his work very seriously, Eric manifested none of the signs of tension and stress that Mary did. Though busy, he appeared both comfortable and in control. Students respected his hard work, appreciated his friendliness, and perhaps even admired the way in which he navigated his way through St. Paul's. But he was not extremely popular. Eric did not have an attractive girlfriend; he didn't have a girlfriend at all. Popular kids did not invite him to join them on vacation weekends away from school. In fact, his peers did not visit his room very often or go with him to town for dinner. In his work ethic and physical carriage he embodied much of what I have identified as the "ideal" St. Paul's student; yet there was something missing.

When girls did come to visit Eric, they did not interact with him as they did boys they were attracted to. Another boy in Eric's dorm, Jonny, was frequently visited by girls (whom he was alternately dating or "scoring"). These visits tended to be purposeless. As girls visited dorms they were expected to tell faculty members why they were there. The girls who visited Jonny would often say a variant of, "Hello, Mr. Khan. I wanted to see if Jonny was around. . . . Um, is he in his room?" By contrast, when girls would come by to see Eric—which happened with far less frequency— they would almost always indicate a reason for their visit: "Mr. Khan, I need to talk to Eric about our calculus homework; is he here?" Jonny's visitors, of course, couldn't reveal to me that they were hoping to make out with him, or more. Nevertheless, there was little doubt why girls visited Eric: to do calculus, not to hang out with him.

In one interesting exception, an attractive and popular girl, Kate, clearly liked Eric. She visited him regularly to "go over homework." During one lunch I was chatting with their teacher and mentioned her visits, noting that Eric must be really good at math. He was happy to correct me.

"Actually, Shamus, Kate is at least as good as Eric, maybe even more talented. But she doesn't work as hard," Parker told me.

"Really? Why does she keep coming over to do her homework with him?"

A veteran teacher, Parker laughed at me. "You still don't get these kids yet! Why do you *think* she's coming over?"

I couldn't believe it. Was it possible that the two of them were together?

"Of course not."

"Well, then?" I asked, annoyed.

"Well, they probably like each other. But it just wouldn't work here. I mean, she's with someone like James," Parker instructed. James was one of the more popular, attractive boys on campus. Parker couldn't resist a joke at my and Kate's expense: "For this week at least."

"Oh!" I exclaimed. My worry, and perhaps my disappointment that Kate and Eric who seemed so fond of each other would never be, clearly showed on my face.

"High school is tough," Parker told me, matter-of-factly. "Tougher here."

After this conversation with Parker I noted that again and again, as Kate came to see Eric she said variations of "I'm here to work on calculus." This marked to me, to Eric, to others in the common space, and even to Kate herself that she came to see Eric *because of work*, not because of Eric.

When I asked Eric about Kate's visits, he was not revealing. "We work well together. It's nice to find that. I don't work really well with lots of people. But we seem to have found a way to get more done together." Here and elsewhere it seems that Eric resists being judged by the same standards as other boys. He did not tell me that he liked Kate, as he clearly did, but could do nothing about it because other boys beat him out for her affections. And so he opted out of competing with other boys on the basis of Kate's sexual attraction to him. But Eric's "resistance" to a hierarchy that would not favor him does not look like Lynn's; in fact, it does not look like resistance at all. It looks like a sidestep, which is for the most part what it was. Eric simply chose not to compete on the terrain of athletic ability and attractiveness. Eric was a competent athlete and far from unattractive. But he was an excellent student and a hard worker. He played to these strengths. When I asked Eric about why he didn't hang out with or do the kinds of things some of the more "popular" kids did, he told me, "You know, Mr. Khan, when you have an Asian mom things are different. I mean, I better work hard or else! She'd kill me. She has always pushed me. And for a while that was it; now I push myself."

But I found Eric's diagnosis largely unsatisfactory. There were kids who did just as well as Eric who did not self-present as hardworking. Some very popular kids, in fact, spent as much time working as Eric did. But they didn't frame themselves to the community in this way, as Eric had. The difference was that in the school's stratification of excellence, Eric would be near the top; in the hierarchies of attractiveness, sexual prowess, or athletic ability he would be in the middle. So he simply opted out of competing on the dominant terrain of attractiveness and sexuality and opted into competing on the basis of his academic excellence. That Eric could compete on a different terrain required the existence of such a terrain, one that didn't exist for Lynn or Mary. And as the visits by a high-status girl like Kate indicated, doing so had the kinds of rewards that I never observed for a student like Lynn. This point should not be taken too strongly. It is not that boys have it so much easier or that their opting out is more effective. In fact the multiple stratification systems of boys are themselves stratified (which is to say that athletics and attractiveness are paramount among them). But the existence of other systems that boys can situate themselves in allows for a different form of resistance that is not as destructive or confrontational.

If we recall Mary, we might wonder why Eric is allowed to be "successful" in his insistence on hard work and excellence, whereas Mary is not. Eric's motto could certainly be "I better work hard or else!"; Mary believes in something very similar: "We've gotta work for it." So what explains the gulf between Eric and Mary? Two things. First, as we have discussed, there is a gendered difference in the range of expressions available to boys and girls. Girls are dominated by sexuality; boys have more options. And so Eric had options that were largely absent for Mary. Second, and in relation to the theme of this chapter overall, Eric employs the frame of hard work and excellence, but he also employs the corporeal display of "naturalness." Whereas Mary darted through campus, crushed by the weight of her bag, Eric made it seem as if working hard was what he had been born to do—it came easy, or naturally, to him. And so his performative display fit with the ideal Paulie stance. For Mary, displaying her hard work was a challenge in part because doing so meant not fitting into another available way of being in the school but instead positioning herself in opposition to the dominant expressional form of sexuality. Eric could be at ease because his activity was acceptable for boys; Mary seemed as if she might snap because she did not enjoy such a possibility.

We can appreciate Eric's options, and Mary's bind, when we consider Steven Amory. Steven was by no means an excellent student; in fact, he was a very mediocre one. He was also a mediocre athlete. And he had a disheveled look to him—like he had been sleeping in his clothes for a few days or that he'd picked them out, eyes closed, from a pile on his floor. This is not to say that he was dirty or even that he made no effort; rather, he seemed to make an effort *not* to fit the mold. And still, unlike Lynn, Steven was well liked by almost all the students and faculty. This was because he was an artist (or presented himself as such). Steven played the guitar and wrote poetry; he was in plays and displayed his paintings each term in the school's art shows. He was not driven crazy by the everyday academic pressures, and neither did he yield to the pressures of "looking good" each day. Steven was eclectic. Something different. And both students and faculty respected this—to a degree.

Steven was seen as acting differently than others—as having different priorities. As other students were talking about preparing over a break for an upcoming assignment and the SATs, Steven chimed in, "I just can't do that kind of stuff. I'm not bad at it. But what does it get you? Yeah, maybe into Harvard. But then what? Law school?" Steven waited for effect but knew no one would answer him. "And then you're working like crazy. Like my dad. He doesn't even know how to live. Or he forgets what it's like to be a normal person. A person at all. I'm not going there. I'm finding what I like, not doing whatever it takes for me to be 'successful'—whatever hat means."

Steven had opted out of the hard work ethic of St. Paul's. Yet really, he had not. What he had opted out of was talking about work and doing "conventional" modes of hard work. Steven's schedule was just as full as other students'. He took just as many classes. His evenings were busy, whether in the art studio or play rehearsals.

But he didn't "make the rounds" of dormitories, visiting girls and boys. He didn't participate actively in formal dances. And when he did go, he dressed "oddly." Other students noted this difference. Upon returning from a dance, the boys in my dormitory were eager to talk about him.

"Man, Steven is frealky," Alex said, using old Paulie lingo to mean he was weird and likely smoked pot. "Did you see what he wore tonight?"

His roommate, Manny, couldn't wait to join in. "Oh my God. Yes. What *was* that?"

"I don't know. But whatever he's on I want some!"

Intrigued, I asked them what they were talking about. Turning to me, Manny suggested there was no way I could understand. "You *had* to see it, Mr. Khan. He was wearing these *crazy* pants."

"I bet he made them himself."

"I hope he did," Ryan joined. "Unless they were made by blind children and he got them at a charity auction."

"Nice." Manny noted my confusion, and tried to paint a picture of his clothing. "No, but seriously. They were like patches of clothes that we'd thrown away. And they were all puffy and then narrow and then puffy. Like MC Hammer pants. Only weirder."

"Try uglier," said Alex. "And his shirt wasn't much better."

Ryan, one of the more conservative students on campus who rarely left his room without an impeccably pressed Brooks Brothers shirt, said with a degree of contempt, "That dude is weird."

Manny, slightly more Bohemian and in defense of such weirdness, objected, "But brilliant. His art is crazy good."

"Yeah. I probably won't be able to afford it one day," said Alex.

Ryan was still not impressed. "If it looked like those pants I don't know why you'd want it."

"Someone will."

Steven, according to these students, is both eccentric and brilliant. From my perspective, he may have been eccentric, but as many of you have already guessed, the art was by no means brilliant. This is not to take away from his talents, only to say that he was a skilled teenager and, despite the reviews of the St. Paul's critics, not a genius. But within the community he was seen as the pinnacle of artistic expression: someone who was "weird" but whose weirdness was not a liability. In part this is because students at St. Paul's consistently overestimate just how talented the population of students is. Those at the top of each hierarchy are assumed to be not simply the best in the school but near the best there is. Whether it is music or squash, math or hockey, science or creative writing, the students who rise to the top within the school are read as being at or on their way to the top in life. So Steven is heralded by these students; they are eager to point out that even though he is "weird" he is also "brilliant," and his work will eventually sell for so much even his schoolmates won't be able to afford it. Since, in the stories of his peers, Steven is destined for art-world fame, his status at St. Paul's is not at all surprising. Though he evades some of the standard displays of a Paulie—namely feverish hard work and a carefully attended social life—he is a "natural" at the most important category of all, what all St. Paul's students want and often believe themselves to be: an exceptional human being.

This is not to say that Steven is enormously popular. But his transgressions away from the normal of attractiveness and athleticism, like Eric's, were not nearly as negatively responded to as Lynn's. And the issue is not simply one of sexuality. When the president of the student body came out to the school during a chapel speech he received the longest standing ovation I heard while at St. Paul's. Other gay boys were similarly accepted. The difference, then, lies in the fact that boys *can* opt out. They can be the smart guy. Or the weird artistic guy. Some are "funny," others play the lovable dork. Others can even be the "gay dude." Boys are given options to act differently or to play a different game altogether. And when they play that game, they are also offered different means to express excellence. In "opting out" of the sexuality regime, Lynn did not have other options for expression. And so her opting out was a direct challenge to the regime itself. This challenge highlighted the ways in which the bodily displays of girls were not "natural" but performances, just like her own. The boys, by contrast, were able to participate in other expressional displays that did not challenge—but instead worked within—the school's dominant performance of natural ease. Eric's expression of academic excellence was simply a natural expression of who he was. Steven's artistic persona was similarly a presentation of self; it required work—he was often in the art building most of the day, painting or drawing or practicing guitar. But this work was carried off as ease because it was *who he was*.

All students perform in one way or another. But the crucial measure of their success is whether they undertake the right performance for that particular context—in this case, the elite training that takes place at St. Paul's.

Mary believed the meritocratic frame. Yet Mary failed to understand the proper way to perform such hard work. The difference between Mary and the other students was that though everyone talked about how much they had to do, Mary's cardinal sin was that she *showed* it. Most other students produced a kind of indifference to what they described as a seemingly insurmountable pile of work. Mary had the frame of hard work right; however, in her own corporeal display of this frame, she misrecognized how to embody privilege: she did not show ease. Yet we must be careful here not to read Mary's lack of ease as some kind of failure on her part. The dominance of sexuality as the hierarchical regime for girls also limited Mary's capacity to "properly" embody the relations of St. Paul's.

As we have seen, girls face contradictions that boys do not. There is a tension between being a girl and being an elite. Girls' sexuality requires a self-conscious regulation; it is a part of them they can, and must, control, which gets in the way of the crucial performance of natural ease. So the school's own expectations about sexuality demand that girls perform in ways that cut against the expression of privilege. Obviously, for some girls this was less of a problem. For very attractive, popular girls, these contradictions were less pronounced, as the hierarchy was set up to reward their qualities. But for most girls on campus, the tensions were palpable. The massive disparity in depression—which girls are many times more likely to suffer—and the fact that the students who had to leave the school because of mental stresses were almost all girls testify to these challenges.

Even trying to opt out is not a simple task. Through her ambiguous relationship, Lynn sought to remove herself from the "stupid games" of sex and sexuality on campus. Yet Lynn's refusal to play "those stupid games" did not give her license to reinvent herself in any way she wants. Rather, even her acts of resistance are in dialogue with the sexuality regime that she seeks to reject.[14] By contrast, Eric and Steven also opt out of the essential features of attractiveness, athleticism, and sexuality. But their opting out did not jeopardize the ultimate goal; they found other self-expressions that did not challenge—but instead worked within—the dominant corporeal-performative display of natural ease. Boys had options that were unavailable to Lynn and Mary. Further, their ability to think of their sexuality as a natural biological stage and not something to be negotiated with other girls and used to manage the sexuality of boys—as girls learned—allowed boys a natural ease that few girls could enjoy.

Over the last half century, the elite have had to adjust to and even adopt many of the ways of life that are common across the nation. In many ways elites look more and more like the rest of us. Such is a consequence of the enormous social and cultural upheavals of the 1960s; equality is a commonly accepted—if not always commonly practiced—goal. But there has been a curious and unexpected result of our quest for equality: if the elite look like us, their everyday appearance suggests that the elite are who they are because of their own innate, individual distinctions and not because of any categorical advantages they have. In short, the "commonness" of the elite is both a consequence of the democratizing demands of the past fifty years and a mechanism to obscure the still very real categorical distinctions that help maintain American inequality.

In a world where distinctions between classes and peoples seem to be vanishing, the appearance of the elite becomes a crucial marker, an invisible sign of status. One of St. Paul's basic though unspoken purposes is to teach the new elite how to embody their privilege. Over and over life at St. Paul's offers a series of lessons that inscribe privilege on the bodies of each student; through corporeal acts of everyday life, students figure out how to manifest the natural ease that is the foundation of the new elite. As students achieve this ease, they further—often without any conscious awareness—the "trick" of privilege: obscuring the relations that allow for its realization. Teaching the ease of privilege—the naturalness of wealth and power—is thus a fundamental role of elite institutions like St. Paul's.

Many of us have become savvy enough—or jaded enough—about the workings of power to recognize the fundamental inequalities of our world. But what I don't think we often appreciate is how deeply embedded the structure of culture and society is in our own bodies. If we think of culture as a resource, we should think of it not just as a cognitive one but as an interactive one. Thinking of culture as interactive (or relational) reveals something about the naturalized corporeal marks of culture. These marks are not just individual properties, something an actor "has"; they also have to be recognized by others in our web of relationships to be valuable. This is to say that capital can only be spent if others recognize its value in you.

5

Learning *Beowulf* and *Jaws*

Education is an admirable thing, but it is as well to remember
from time to time that nothing that is worth knowing can be taught.
—OSCAR WILDE

Just don't take any class where you have to read *Beowulf*.
—WOODY ALLEN

We can now retell the transformation of elites from chapter 1. Elites knew who they were as a group, and they knew who wasn't one of them. They were a "class" who protected their interests. They had a distinct culture that they isolated from others and used to distinguish themselves. But today elites are far more "omnivorous," culturally constituting themselves quite freely across social boundaries or distinctions. They no longer define themselves by what they exclude, but rather their power now comes from including everything.[1] What marks elites as elites is not a singular point of view or purpose but rather their capacity to pick, choose, combine, and consume a wide gamut of the social strata. The "highbrow snob"[2] is almost dead. In its place is a cosmopolitan elite that freely consumes high and low culture, and everything in between.[3] The new adolescent elite listen to classical and to rap; they eat at fine restaurants and at diners. They are at ease everywhere in the world. We even seem to demand this omnivorousness pluralism of our elite. We don't want a patrician president; we want a man who knows how to act around the queen of England but is just as comfortable sitting in a lawn chair holding a beer summit.

Today's elites share not just a cultural propensity to be omnivorous but also a capacity to do and appreciate many things. They have the time and resources to explore broadly, cultivating not a class character but an individual one. Further, this picking and choosing is not just in how elites approach the world of culture and tastes but also in how they constitute themselves—their group is no longer narrow and exclusive but wide and varied. From this perspective, the distinction between the elite and the marginalized is that it is now the marginalized whose tastes are limited; they are closed-minded, they exclude anything that is unknown.

This is not to say that the distinctions between social classes are disappearing; rather, the class divide is appearing differently. As pressures to open the elite have increased in the last fifty years, so have the cultural practices of the elite. Elites have incorporated some of the cultural attributes and tastes of those they had previously excluded. Yet this new practice—omnivorous consumption—is itself a symbolic marker. Omnivorous consumption develops within elites a sense of indifference, or an ease of position. They are comfortable almost anywhere. It is as if the new elite are saying, "Look! We are not some exclusive club. If anything, we are the *most* democratized of all groups. We are as comfortable with rap as opera. We can dine finely or at a truck stop. We accept all!" Such an attitude makes it appear that privilege is obtained through democratic *practices,* not aristocratic exclusion. But these practices, this omnivorousness, become their own mark of distinction. Following the classical sociologist Max Weber, I think of privilege as a "mark"—something that the privileged display to one another and to the disadvantaged.[4] And through the display of these marks, the privileged seem to say, in response to the disadvantaged, "It is your own closed-mindedness, your own choices to not take advantage of this new open world, your own lack of interest that explain your position and not durable inequalities."

The Audacity of Capacity

Let us return to Concord, New Hampshire, to see omnivorous behavior in action. As we near the end of our story, we finally get to the reason why we go to school in the first place: to learn. That we are talking about learning last is not entirely unironic; as we shall see, learning is often the last thing on the minds of St. Paul's students. But it is an examination of knowledge that gets us to the heart of how the elite are created and how they think about themselves and their own relationship to the broader world. Here we shall examine St. Paul's approach to learning, what and how the students actually learn, and ultimately how learning shapes their engagement with the world.

The St. Paul's curriculum is not like that of most high schools. Rather than take English, history, and social sciences, students take one course, humanities, which combines all of these areas. In addition, most students progress through the mathematics curriculum all the way to calculus, and there are even several advanced courses beyond it (including linear algebra and advanced math seminars); most students also take at least one upper-level science class. Students at St. Paul's have the opportunity to study many languages: Chinese, Japanese, French, Spanish, German, Latin, and Greek. And students may do considerable coursework in music, ballet, theater, and art. Seminar courses are available in every academic division. Each student takes five classes in the each of the school year's three terms—and many students take more. The humanities, math, science, and language courses stretch through the whole year. But as students advance, more and more "elective" options are available to them. In the humanities division, there are over fifty courses available, from Contemporary Irish Literature and History to Daughters of Eve: Women's Experiences in Religion. There are seminars on Shakespeare and on Toni Morrison, and ones titled "Globalization and the 21st Century" and "Middle Eastern Voices." But the classics are not all that are taught. Students can also take a course titled "The Rise of the Graphic Novel." In the sciences students can learn about artificial intelligence, robotics engineering, and galactic astronomy; in the arts there are seminars on European and American art and courses from music composition to furniture design. This curriculum works to set Paulies apart from the average high school student. The school's academic program is different, its capacity is greater, and what is required to meet its academic needs far surpasses what is needed for most schools. The program helps instill in students a sense of their tremendous abilities and options in life.

St. Paul's often touts its academic program as the best in the nation. In its advertising literature, the school boasts that it has "the highest level of scholarship" and that its "students stand at the top of their peer group in terms of academic preparation." And according to eager administrators and lackadaisical adolescents alike, the centerpiece of St. Paul's academic program is undoubtedly the humanities. The humanities program introduces students to the history, literature, and thought of different moments in world history. The humanities division describes its own project as an interdisciplinary, multivocal investigation of "great questions."

The humanities faculty teaches the habits of mind that nurture curiosity and welcome exchange of ideas among students. The three-
year interdisciplinary core program employs a "great questions" approach. ... The program is primarily an integration of literature and
history but also includes religious studies, art history, philosophy,
and politics. This integration allows students to understand literature and historical events within a cultural context and to interact
with "texts," for example, a work of art, theological treatise, short
story, or movie. ... Humanities teachers place a priority on development of skills related to rigorous classroom discussion of course
content, scholarly research, and critical reading and reasoning. Students write in different genres, such as analytical papers, personal
narratives, art interpretations, and creative work.

This program, significantly, does not teach students to know "things." The
emphasis is not on memorizing historical events, for example. Instead it is
on cultivating "habits of mind," which encourage a particular way of relating both to the world and to each other.

The first course that students take at St. Paul's is Humanities III. It
is often a radical shift from how students are used to learning in middle
school. Students read everything from Homer to the Qu'ran, from Sopho-
cles to Chaucer. And they are asked to "think big," to answer impossible
questions. The course is centered around such questions as "What is love?"
"What is virtue?" "How does religion shape the world?" "What is history?"
"Who is the other?" and "What is myth?" The program aims to introduce
third formers to no less than the "central ideas in the Western tradition."

The Humanities III course follows central ideas in the Western
tradition through literature, religion, and history. Chronologically,
the course begins with the Greeks and ends with medieval Europe.
Students read poetry, drama, and prose from both literary and historical perspectives, and they learn to recognize universal themes
while making connections between ancient and modern texts, or
between texts and film, visual art, or music.... Students become independent researchers by learning how to analyze a source critically,
take careful notes, and apply them to focused research and writing
assignments.

Students are shocked by this course. This is not simply because the course material is challenging; it is because the course asks them to think differently about the world. As Danielle, a black ninth grader, said to me, "You know, the humanities thing was like totally different for me. I mean, well, it was more than about what you need to know for the test. I was used to that. But now it was like, well, it was like *anything* could be on the test. I mean, *anything*. 'What is virtue?' Man, that's deep. We never had to think like that before. Not in school at least."

St. Paul's students arrive at school at the beginning of their adolescence with the expectation placed upon them that they can learn "the central ideas in the Western tradition." They are expected to figure out how to navigate a wide variety of texts in a variety of ways, from poetry to drama to prose, through literary and historical perspectives, identifying universal themes throughout each. They are asked to think about these ideas in their historical context and to make transhistorical connections between the ancient and the modern. And through this they are asked to continually think through the heady themes of reason, evolution of culture, virtue, heroism, and the divine. Students are asked to make the impossible possible, and they are encouraged to believe that the grand sweep of the world is knowable to them.

In their fifth form year, this audacity reaches its apex. Humanities V is an introduction to Europe, from the Renaissance through World War I. It is an attempt to trace the development of Western civilization's massive project of the Enlightenment. I quote at length from the course description, as no simple summary can do justice to the presumption and hopeful expectation of this course.

> Students encounter in Humanities V a rich interdisciplinary study of European civilization from the beginnings of the Renaissance to the First World War, integrating literary, visual, musical, historical, philosophical, and religious themes that help develop perspectives useful to understanding the complexities of the twenty-first century. The course begins by introducing the medieval worldview as a launching point from which to begin a serious study of the Italian Renaissance. Close attention is given to investigating the emergence of humanism, as expressed in examples as varied as the letters of Petrarch, the sonnets of Shakespeare, or the visual realism in the

arts via techniques like *chiaroscuro* and vanishing point perspective in Masaccio's work. The impact of Florentine Neo-Platonism in Renaissance culture is discussed, and the artists of the glorious High Renaissance—especially Raphael, da Vinci, and Michelangelo—are analyzed with an eye towards their compositional structure as well as content. The focus then shifts to the Protestant Reformation and its impact on Elizabethan England in general and Shakespeare's plays in particular—one of which is the culminating text of the term.

The Winter Term's emphasis moves to the development of the Enlightenment inheritance, including the philosophical and cultural forces that generated the French Revolution. Integral to this is an examination of the insights and impact of the Scientific Revolution with its emphasis on rationalism and the skeptical critique of traditional religious piety by the *philosophes*. During this time students are also asked to select and investigate a topic of their choosing related to the Humanities V curriculum and to write an original 8- to 10-page thesis-oriented research paper thereon.... The Winter Term culminates in a study of the emergence of Romanticism, a movement that crystallized the novel as a form and generated some of the most memorable music in the Western canon. While Jane Austen and the Romantic poets are given special study, students also become acquainted with Romantic artists like Goya, whose work is contrasted with that of neo-classic artists like David.

In the Spring Term students look closely at the impact of the Industrial Revolution on the twin towering achievements of the nineteenth century: the liberal democratic reforms that shaped the republican aspirations of the Enlightenment and the growth of nationalism in Europe, which unleashed the horror of the First World War. Marx's classic pamphlet *The Communist Manifesto* and Ibsen's controversial play *A Doll's House* are studied as social critiques, and Conrad's slender but powerful novella *Heart of Darkness* is analyzed to reveal a multifaceted approach to the issues surrounding European imperialism. Special attention is given throughout the year to the development of student voices, both in class discussion and on the page through a variety of creative writing and speaking assignments....

These years in European history reflect periods of great creativity and change during which the arts flourished and humankind developed a new self-consciousness. Moreover, many of the important intellectual, cultural, and political forces governing the modern world emerged during this time, furnishing us with rich and, at times, troubling legacies. The Humanities V course offers students a sense of some of the best and worst elements of the world that we inhabit.

All this in the thirty weeks of a single academic year; all of this from sixteen- and seventeen-year-olds. This is the last of the required courses in the humanities division and the culmination of the school's scholastic vision. At the completion of Humanities V, as one teacher put it, "a student's introduction to Western civilization is complete. There is still much to learn. But what students learn is then their choice."

The enormity of this program is both thrilling and terrifying. The thought of knowing all of that, of being swept up and carried through the tide of history, is tantalizing. It is also the product of St. Paul's hubris. How can any one person possibly teach everything listed above? As I prepared to teach my own class at the school, I soon found out that I was asking the wrong question. Of course the expectations were ridiculous. No high schooler could ever learn all that the course offers. The more important question, I eventually realized, is much harder to answer: what does it mean to present material in this way to teenagers?

Perhaps the point is not really to *know* anything. The advantage that St. Paul's instills in its students is not a hierarchy of knowledge. As we have seen, knowledge is no longer the exclusive domain of the elite. And these days, information flows so freely that to use it to exclude others is increasingly challenging. By contrast, the important *decisions* required for those who lead are not based on knowing more but instead are founded in habits of mind. St. Paul's teaches that everything can be accomplished through these habits, even while still in high school. What strikes me as presumptuous, even shocking, about this vision of the world is taken for granted by pretty much every teenager at St. Paul's.

Though I marveled at how impossible it seemed to teach students all these things, the school itself seems largely unconcerned about this. Indeed, St. Paul's approach seems closer to Plato's outline of education in *Re-*

public. Building upon his famous cave metaphor, Plato tells us, "Education isn't what some people declare it to be, namely, putting knowledge into souls that lack it, like putting sight into blind eyes. ... The power to learn is present in everyone's soul . . . that sight is there but it isn't turned the right way."[5] In short, education is not teaching students things they don't know. Rather, it is about teaching them how to think their way through the world (in Plato's terms, how to "turn toward the light"). These habits of mind are quite different from facts or learning "things." To ask students to develop habits of mind is to ask them not to know things *about* the world but instead how to *relate to* the world. In Plato's view, the knowledge is already *in* them: the trick is to find ways to release it.

What was the War of the Roses? When was the French Revolution? What were the major factors that precipitated it? Who was involved? What did the political organization of the Greek Republic look like? These are questions that students, upon completing their training in the humanities division, cannot answer. These courses don't focus on the events of history or culture but use them to ask "bigger" and often more abstract questions: What is myth? Who is the other? To whom do we owe our obligations? The result of these two styles of learning is two very different approaches to the world. The former set of questions, which expects students to memorize facts and tangible details, will be recognizable to anyone who had a more "traditional" education. The difficulty with these questions is that one can be wrong in answering them. The latter, by contrast, are the result of a more "progressive" pedagogical model that cultivates habits: these questions don't have a wrong answer. They reveal not knowledge but styles of knowing. Such questions are concerned not with the details but with the intangible realm of our world, with interpretation and point of view. Right and wrong do not apply. As we shall see, this intangibility allows for a new form of exclusivity—privilege—that is not what one knows but how one knows. And such habits are what are taught at places like St. Paul's.

"I don't actually know much," an alumnus told me after he finished his freshman year at Harvard. "I mean, well, I don't know how to put it. When I'm in classes all these kids next to me know a lot more than I do. Like about what actually happened in the Civil War. Or what France did in World War II. I don't know any of that stuff. But I know something they don't. It's not facts or anything. It's how to think. That's what I learned in humanities."

"What do you mean, 'how to think'?" I asked.

"I mean, I learned how to think bigger. Like everyone else at Harvard knew about the Civil War. I didn't. But I knew how to make sense of what they knew about the Civil War and apply it. So they knew a lot about particular things. I knew how to think about everything."

The emphasis of the St. Paul's curriculum is not on "what you know" but on "how you know it." Teaching ways of knowing rather than teaching the facts themselves, St. Paul's is able to endow its students with marks of the elite—ways of thinking or relating to the world—that ultimately help make up privilege. As the exclusionary practices of old have become unsustainable, something new has emerged from within the elite.

Think again for a moment about what it would take to teach Humanities III, for example, and what you would have to believe about the capacity of high school students to decide to teach it to them. First, from the perspective of your faculty, you would have to have confidence in their capacity to traverse literature and history, art and philosophy, sociology, economics, and religion. How many of your high school teachers could do this? How many would be comfortable teaching the Qu'ran alongside Chaucer? I do not wish to claim that the teachers at St. Paul's are not up to the task. Rather, I found their ability far greater than I would have expected. My point is that the school believes that such things *are* knowable by individuals. We can expect them of a high school teacher. We can expect the astonishing.

Similarly, young students can be expected to grasp such material. When I expressed shock at the Humanities III curriculum—that we were supposed to teach "the central ideas in the Western tradition" to fourteen-year-olds—I was told by a particularly aloof senior faculty member, "Actually, it's the perfect age. We get them while they're still very young. Very green, in fact. You've taught college. You know how hard it is to get students to think about things. What would your department say if you were to teach a course on 'What is truth?' They'd tell you to do something *useful*. But these kids are still struggling to figure it out. And so we get them right then. They're thinking about these things in their own lives. And we can have them think about them in relation to Plato."

Another teacher summed it up a little more bluntly: "Our students are not *normal* students." Just as you can expect astonishing things from your faculty, so can you of your students. The audacity of St. Paul's vision of pedagogy requires that everyone believes that the students are something special—not just the teachers but the students themselves. For these students the world is not a closed space; possibilities are not conditional. Everything is doable. Constraints are largely absent. Such a vision of the world allows for a felicity of reference to the Western world, a kind of comfort with the big ideas. Just as the students cultivate an ease, as we have seen, in how they present themselves and perform their roles, so too do the teachers cultivate in students an ease in how they think. Students at St. Paul's learn to "think big," as if it is the most natural thing in the world.

Early in the winter term I was asked to give a talk to a group of humanities students on the dissolution of the British monasteries. It was a project I had worked on as a research assistant while in graduate school. Upon completion of the lecture a student approached me and ask if I might give him the "relevant literature"; he believed that with his research project he could "make a contribution" to the subject. My reply was defensive and less than courteous: "Contributions to the literature do not come in ten-page research papers by eleventh graders. People dedicate their lives to projects like this." The student seemed stunned. Afterward I felt guilty but nevertheless couldn't help wondering if anyone had ever questioned his abilities before.

Then, as I observed a humanities class later that week, it was my turn to be stunned. The teacher was coaching his students to think of their work in the same grand terms—as contributing to the general knowledge on a topic. During the winter and spring, a few teachers mentioned to their classes that I might be someone to speak with as I knew what it meant to do a major research project. Several students earnestly approached me with research proposals. The students really wanted to think of their projects as contributions to the world's knowledge. Their sincerity was stunning. I had been disciplined to believe that only with rigorous and arduous training, and years of advanced education, could one uncover something valuable about the complexity of historical and social processes. St. Paul's students learned something quite different: that as sixteen-year-olds spending a few weeks on a paper, they could make a contribution too.

Just as they believe they can contribute to the specific knowledge in a particular area, students also learn to consume from an enormous variety of sources. They learn to work and "interact" with art, literature, and history, from the popular to the scholarly, and have a huge range of materials at their disposal. For example, one of the major assignments in Humanities III is to compare *Beowulf* to Steven Spielberg's *Jaws*. Students are asked to think about the ways in which *Beowulf* is a monster that man must confront, just as Jaws is a monster that prowls the waters of humanity (and perhaps even our own internal waters). The goal is not to endow the students with a kind of highbrow elite knowledge. Rather, they are taught to move with ease through the broad range of culture, to move with felicity from the elite to the popular. They learn to be cultural egalitarians. The lesson to students is that you can talk about *Jaws* in the same way you can talk about *Beowulf*. Both become cultural resources to draw upon. And most important, the world is available to you—from high literature to horror films. There are not things that are "off limits"—limits are not structured by the relations of the world around you; they are in you. Students are not to stand above the mundane, perhaps lowbrow horror flick. Instead they are taught the importance of engaging with all aspects of culture, of treating the high and the low with respect and serious engagement. As our future elite, these students are taught not to create fences and moats but instead to relentlessly engage with the varied world around them.

The consequences of the St. Paul's philosophy can be seen all over campus, evident even in how students carry themselves. Students have the sense that they could do it. The world is a space to be navigated and negotiated, not a set of arrangements or a list of rules that are imposed upon you. The students are taught that they are special, and they begin to realize this specialness. This is a kind of self-fulfilling prophecy—thinking everything is possible just might make it so.[6] But there is a deeply social character to this self-fulfillment. The classical sociologist Emile Durkheim speaks of "acts of consecration" as the ways in which we tend to imbibe very small differences with tremendous importance and power. Though the "religion of liberalism" might consecrate those who are most able, it is in fact a particular social arrangement that has made those who are merely "able" into something sacred.

Think for a moment of someone famous. It would be difficult to explain that person's fame or specialness by his or her personal qualities. These qualities are rarely that different from those of others. Instead, we all work to consecrate such people, to make them almost sacred and to help make them into who they are. We make Madonna "Madonna" by consecrating her. To "consecrate something is to put it in contact with a source of religious energy," and such energy is the experience of being so special. Yet that which is consecrated is not inherently sacred.

> [I]n the present day just as much as in the past, we see society constantly creating sacred things out of ordinary ones. If it happens to fall in love with a man and if it thinks it has found in him the principal aspirations that move it, as well as the means of satisfying them, this man will be raised above the others and, as it were, deified. Opinion will invest him with a majesty exactly analogous to that protecting the gods. And the fact that it is society alone which is the author of these varieties of apotheosis, is evident since it frequently chances to consecrate men thus who have no right to it from their own merit.[7]

As we have seen throughout our story, St. Paul's students believe that they are exceptional. They would take umbrage at Durkheim's notion that their mere able qualities can be elevated to the sacred or that meritorious talents are not internal qualities but social constructions. And yet in telling the story of how an institution trains elites, I am firmly telling a Durkheimian story of how elite culture works through the elevation of a small group not by their individual characters but by a social process of schooling. Students experience consecration each day on campus through the teachers that give themselves to the students. These privileged students are *made* into elites by the interactions that consecrate them, by the consistent, generous feedings they receive of their own capacity and promise.

The audacity of this system is shocking and ingenious. Asking big questions seems profound, but you cannot be wrong. The point is to develop a voice, and interpretation, and a way of articulating it. While most schools across the nation are busy disciplining students into taking regular tests—tests that evaluate cities, districts, schools, teachers, and students—St. Paul's is making such concreteness irrelevant. It's not about knowing those things for these kids. It's about this vague, intangible way of knowing that becomes embodied ease. And rather than using standard benchmarks against which to measure students, St. Paul's is cultivating individual characters that are later used to explain their success.

The Myth of the Exceptional

Jason Anderson arrived on campus as the caricature of a geek. He had thick glasses that seemed identical to the ones I first wore to St. Paul's twelve years earlier. He had a large, round face peppered in acne. His pinched lips revealed his braces. He carried his heavy body with great, clumsy effort. And his nasally voice instantly revealed that Jason would never be the object of widespread sexual desire. He had the kind of endearing awkwardness that only a teenager can have—one that just a few years later he would grow out of. In short, I was incredibly fond of him. Perhaps more surprising, however, is that I was not alone. Most students also respected and really liked Jason. This was in part because Jason was easy to get along with and generally amiable. It was also because he was in a house that looked out for and protected him. But even further, Jason was incredibly good at math. As a ninth grader, he enrolled in one of the highest-level math courses available. And, surrounded by nearly all seniors, he excelled. Seniors would even visit his room for help—something incredibly rare for a third former.

Students did not believe that, if they tried hard enough, they could become as good at math as Jason. Their presumption was not limitless. They appreciated his excellence, his talent that exceeded their own. Seniors even spoke of his future career as a mathematician.

"Do you know Anderson?" Ken said.

"Yes, why?" I replied.

"That kid is crazy. Taking Braden's class as a newb!"

"Seriously. I mean, he's going to win the Nobel Prize or something," David chimed in.

"Dumb ass," Ken quickly corrected David. "There is no math prize. He'll get the Fields Medal."

Chastened, David still concurred. "Whatever. He's unbelievable."

Jason's excellence was widely known and touted among the other students. These students even knew what prize Jason was likely to win— the highest honor in mathematics, given out every four years to a mathematician under forty. This kind of assumption—that the best student in each particular subject at St. Paul's was probably the best person in the world—was widespread. When a student, Jimmy Chen, played Pablo

Saraste's *Zigeunerweisen* (a devilishly hard violin piece) in chapel, another student asked me, knowing that I played the violin, if it were true that Jimmy could leave St. Paul's to be an international soloist. When I said that Jimmy was nowhere near that good, I was met with a combination of skepticism and disappointment.

I coached the squash team. Our top player, Will, was a truly outstanding player in our league, particularly as a freshman. Yet again I was asked on several occasions if he would win the Junior Olympics. When I explained that though Will was very good for an American player, American players were comparatively terrible at squash, I again was met with disappointment. The same myth was repeated over and over again: Jason or Jimmy or Jason (or Steven, the artist we met earlier) was the best at St. Paul's and therefore must be a talent of international caliber.[8]

I do not seek here to deflate the quality of students at St. Paul's. Jason was a special math student that few high schools would have been able to keep stimulated for four years. Will was on a path to being one of the best squash players in the country. And to even make it through *Zigeunerweisen* requires a special talent on the violin. But being very good, as we all know, is very different from being the best. To imagine that the best mathematician at your school will win the Fields Medal, that your squash player will win the Olympics, that your violinist could embark upon an international solo career, or that your artist will soon be selling paintings that few can afford goes beyond claims of the extraordinary into the unbelievable. There is, no doubt, a certain teenage mentality to this. They assume that the world around them is the whole world. But it went deeper than this, as these narratives were often accepted and even reified by the school. It was not simply that the students thought of themselves as having a sense of potential—that the world was theirs to contribute to. They recognized simultaneously that certain people had extraordinary talents, skills that far exceeded their own. But at St. Paul's, the students believed that they were *surrounded by* such talents; as a result, that which was extraordinary became a part of their ordinary reality. So even if students did not think that they themselves could excel at anything and everything, there was a sense of the everyday quality—even the banality—of the exceptional.

Teachers were sensitive to the kind of arrogance that such an approach to life could breed. Further, they worried about the psychological toll that the constant expectation of excellence, from social to academic to athletic, could have on students. Such pressure particularly bothered my closest friend at the school, admissions officer Scott Bohan. He pointed out what he saw in chapel, day in and day out. During a moment of frustration, Scott vented, "What happens in chapel? Someone gives a speech or musical performance. And what do we do? We jump to our feet, giving an ovation for just how unbelievable it was. And then it's announcement after announcement of how amazing these kids are. The debate team won this. Anderson won a math prize. Everyone in our Latin and Greek classes got highest honors on some exam. The cross-country team won its tournament and Kelley broke the course record. No one ever fails here. No one is ever ordinary . . . no, I don't mean that, I mean that no one is allowed to be normal. What does that teach them?"

Scott graduated from St. Paul's two years ahead of me. He thinks of himself as "normal." He was a good, hardworking student. Like me, he attended an excellent liberal arts college. During our regular evening faculty basketball games at St. Paul's Scott would joke about how he "sucks." And he laughs about how as a three-year-old, his son is "already getting to be smarter than me." Scott's "ordinary" or "normal" persona operates in stark contrast to the self-presentation of the students, and even to many of the faculty.

Two parts of the myth of the exceptional frustrated Scott. The first was that everything at the school was deemed truly extraordinary. At least once a week we stood in chapel to cheer extraordinary speeches or performances. Every day came a long list of students' extraordinary achievements. Yet in contrast, Scott asked, which alums are doing extraordinary things? Though there was the occasional senator or artist, they were few. "I mean, if everyone is so unbelievable, where are they going? What happens to them after they leave?" The most common notable trait of the alumni is that many are very wealthy. However, wealth is explicitly *not* the kind of extraordinary achievement lauded at St. Paul's. Quite the opposite. The school did not claim that the students were exceptional because they were rich—a classic position of the entitled. It claimed they were immensely talented and worked hard. And yet the dearth of artists or athletes, of Nobel Laureates or Fields medalists, suggests, as Scott indicates, something different.

Scott's second frustration was that the students weren't allowed to be "just normal kids." There were constant and relentless pressures to think of yourself as more than that—as being anything but normal. From Scott's perspective, this marginalized a lot of students in the school. Or worse, the vision of the world as nothing but potential to be realized could be oppressive and overwhelming, rather than freeing. Though the exceptional was expected, the cold reality is that for just about everyone it is never really a possibility. Scott's response to this was to emphasize his "ordinariness" with the students, attempting to make normal a viable and visible option for students.

In fact, when students found out that Scott was one of my closest friends they were often incredulous. I had a reputation among the students for being "brilliant." The students' perceptions of me were a perfect demonstration of the everyday extraordinariness taken for granted at St. Paul's. It was rumored that I had been one of the best college squash players in the nation (untrue) and that I was, in the words of one student, "one of the finest violinists of my generation" (also untrue). A rumor circulated about my extraordinary wealth—that I was the heir to the Aga Khan fortune (a particularly powerful Muslim dynasty). Every so often a student would peek into my office to view what was thought to be an "important" tapestry on my wall and an original Dali painting (the former was a rug my father had bought years ago in Pakistan, probably for less than $5; the latter, a print). Students and fellow faculty informed me that they had discussed it, and it was clear that I was destined for a MacArthur Grant (the "genius" prize). Such a laundry list reveals the extremes of the school's belief in their own extraordinariness, which in my case required some very determined, even desperate searching for extraordinary stories. But these false beliefs also reveal something about the students'—and the school's—own sense of self-importance. I was simultaneously an heir to a billion-dollar fortune, a world-class violinist, a former squash player of international quality, and a genius, and yet with all these possibilities what I chose to do was be a teacher at St. Paul's.

Scott was not alone in confronting this myth of the extraordinary. Teachers were often very critical of students in the hope of making them recognize their limits. Yet when parents pay a lot for school, they expect that there will be results; those results are almost always indicated by college admission. As the college admission process has become more competitive, grades have steadily risen. Just like at other elite schools, at St. Paul's receiving an A is closer to average performance than it is exceptional work. This extension and expansion of excellence can be seen most dramatically at the end of the school year, when award ceremonies take several hours and nearly every student at the school walks across the stage at least once to be recognized for his or her achievements. These range from being the best student in chemistry to attending all your classes to simply not getting any Cs on your transcript that year. It seems that whatever attempts are made by individual teachers to confront the myth of the extraordinary have had minimal effect. Everyday there are more and more examples of just how wonderful the school is.[9] At least once a year, for one reason or another, almost every student is asked to parade in front of the entire school community and is showered with applause for his or her achievements.

Exceptional Disappointments

Berkeley Latimore is a short, stocky, mustached teacher in the humanities. With a doctorate in history, "Dr. Latimore," or "Daddy Lat" as he is called behind his back, is respected by his students and his teaching appreciated by his peers. His southern drawl reveals an amiable character. His small stature makes him endearing, like an older distant relative.

Late in the winter term Berkeley's classes were discussing a work of Charles Dickens. At this point in the school year students are largely worn down. The winter in New Hampshire is long and cold. It is also the most demanding time of the academic year. One morning, I sat in the corner and watched the students slowly enter the class, many of them late. Alex, a bright but mischievous boy from California, complains bitterly about the continuing cold. Meanwhile, Stacey, a gregarious girl from outside of New York City, seems to have countless layers to remove and is in no hurry to get them off. In this moment, Berkeley indulges his students. At other times I have seen him and other teachers scold their students about being on time and ready for class. Yet Berkeley seems to have decided that at this late point in the term the students are simply tired and should be given some leeway. The class conversation is halting, a little painful to observe. Clearly the exhausted students have no interest in impressing their visitor. But Berkeley slowly opens them up, and the discussion begins to warm.

Pointing the class to a section of the text, reading some of it aloud, and covering other bits with a quick summary, Berkeley asks the class, "So what is Dickens doing here in this passage?" After a period of awkward silence, one just long enough that I begin to think that few of them have actually done the reading, Emily begins, "Well, it's sort of a morality tale. . . ."

Hearing this, David quickly jumps in, interrupting Emily. "Yeah. Like *Everyman*," he exclaims, referring to the sixteenth-century morality play. I was shocked that David knew of the work, until it dawned on me that the students must have read it in class; they had, two years earlier.

"How so?" Berkeley inquires. When it becomes clear that David has no further contribution to make, Berkeley turns his eyes toward the rest of the class.

Trying to pick up on the thread, and end the painful silence, Stephanie slowly tries to work out the idea. "Well, it tells a story of what you should and shouldn't do. Good people and bad people. People change, but there's a clear moral world."

I can see Berkeley's frustration at this point. "Okay. But it really isn't that simple. . . . This is a Bildungsroman—a novel of self-cultivation. This is what Dickens is doing. It's not just a strict story of morality, it's about how one develops such a—"

Before he can finish his thought, David almost erupts out of his seat, blurting, "Kinda like Dostoyevsky!"

Taken aback, Berkeley asks, "How do you mean?"

David looks down to his desk. His pale skin begins to redden. He looks back up, searching his teacher's face for help, in desperation. The other students in the class look away from David and their teacher, some awkwardly making eye contact with one another, and then quickly breaking it to avoid the embarrassment of the moment.

"Well, I guess you could read *Crime and Punishment* as a play on the idea." Berkeley gracefully moves away from Dostoyevsky and returns to the idea of a Bildungsroman, explaining the term and why it is germane to the conversation. David again interrupts, to exclaim, "Yeah!" as if he had known Berkeley was headed in this direction all along. Berkeley ignores the second outburst and continues with class.

Berkeley does here what countless teachers have done before him: save a student from complete embarrassment. As we have seen, the pedagogical philosophy of St. Paul's prides itself on teaching grand ideas and weaving innumerable texts into a big-picture vision of Western culture. The students quickly learn to do the same. The results, however, are mixed at best—audacity has its price. Making compelling connections takes a deep understanding of the texts involved, as well as their surrounding contexts. The beauty and the absurdity of St. Paul's is that it cultivates the assumption that students can and should be making these connections, all the time, whether or not they know what they're talking about.

David was later described to me by one of his teachers as "very young for his age." He is incredibly energetic, bordering on hyperactive. Among his peers he's liked, but friendships are hindered by his somewhat unpredictable, spastic demeanor. His wiry frame and fidgety movements reveal an unbridled, undisciplined personality that made interacting with David both charming and unnerving. When David dropped his Dostoyevsky reference I immediately wondered, "Could David possibly have read Dostoyevsky?" I asked Berkeley this at the end of class. His response was the same as my intuition: "Absolutely not." Weeks later, when I asked David about it, he did not remember the incident. He chuckled, telling me, "I don't know. Sometimes I just say things. I've heard of him [Dostoyevsky] before. Maybe I saw a movie?"

David's casual connection happens relentlessly in the school. The curriculum is set up to demand that students make connections across disciplinary lines. They are taught philosophy, history, English, art history, sociology, political science, and economics in the same class. Similarly, in math classes teachers talk about how the ideas they are learning are connected (or used) in the work they are doing, or have done, in science. Arts classes, too, are structured in dialogue with the happenings of humanities. If this sounds like an educational system ideally set up for training dilettantes, I don't think that caricature is far off. The classes I observed abounded in variations on the interaction described above. The conversation of the day wasn't great for learning Dickens but certainly would make for good cocktail conversation. Yet as my year at St. Paul's continued, I would come to know a more complicated truth.

In the spring semester I taught an elective class to two sixth formers, August and Lee, on moral philosophy. The course was not a part of the regular curriculum. But in addition to the countless electives, students can request that teachers teach independent studies on topics of interest. From their experience in Humanities V these two seniors became interested in questions of modern moral thought. I had been observing classes for two semesters by this time and was somewhat skeptical of their proposal. They wanted to read Spinoza, Kant, and Nietzsche. I thought this too demanding of the students and worried that it stretched the limits of my own philosophical understanding. However, August and Lee pushed me hard. They had their former humanities teacher talk to me. He told me that they were "two of the finest philosophical minds at the school." This description was more amusing than illuminating, but it helped incline me to teach the course. In part I wanted to see just how sophisticated students at St. Paul's could be and if their training allowed them to meet the high scholastic level I was continually told the students could reach.

In preparing for the course I first asked the students what they knew. They told me that they had a fairly firm grasp of Kant and were well versed in the ideas behind Enlightenment philosophy. I was impressed and wondered whether my mostly cynical view of what I had observed in classes thus far—where such knowledge seemed very unlikely—was incorrect. I designed a course that began with Descartes and ended with a novel by Jean Genet. The students were asked to read the following:

- Descartes: *Meditations on First Philosophy*
- Hume: *An Enquiry Concerning Human Understanding*
- Spinoza: *Ethics*
- Kant: *Groundwork of the Metaphysics of Morals*
- Wilde: *The Picture of Dorian Gray*
- Mill: *On Liberty* and *Utilitarianism*
- Nietzsche: *On the Genealogy of Morality*
- Genet: *Our Lady of the Flowers*

These works were to be covered in a ten-week term. My arrogant naïveté should be clear to every reader. I believed that, though challenging, this would be a doable course. I had become part of St. Paul's, a teacher par excellence, believing in and instilling the sense of the extraordinary possibility in my students.

I began the first day of the seminar asking August and Lee to tell me about the basic principles of the Enlightenment. They were unable to generate any ideas that one might even loosely connect with Enlightenment developments. Given the curriculum of the Humanities V course that they had completed the previous year and the glowing recommendation from their past teacher, I was shocked. In fairness to the two students, they were expecting a fun, interesting class for their final semester at school and had not thought about any of these ideas since the previous spring. I think they were just as shocked by my hard-nosed approach as I was by their blank stares.

But I felt I had been duped. Here was evidence that the school's emphasis on "habits of mind" ultimately translated into clever but insubstantial ways of relating each text to something else, of talking around ideas rather than engaging with them. They did not know anything concrete about the Enlightenment. They knew how to talk as if they did (and fool me in the process, which perhaps is more important than knowing anything). When I later inquired why I had been asked to teach Spinoza, of all people— a notoriously difficult writer and hardly a "common" philosopher who might be known by a high schooler—I received a smiling, wry, and infuriating answer: "I saw his name once; I always liked that name. That's how I picked it." I was fooled because rather than display any competence, August and Lee asked for something innovative. They wanted to combine novels, operas, and paintings with philosophy, talking about ideas of morality not just in the context of theorizing but in the arts and literature. I was carried away by the exciting possibility and, in this excitement, never uncovered that there was little behind this talk.

Despite our rough start, August and Lee surprised me. Though their thinking lacked the kind of sophistication I had foolishly expected, for the most part they got it. This was because they specialized. Lee related philosophical ideas to characters in her fiction, and August worked on following small bits of arguments and mapping out their formal logic. Nothing particularly profound happened in the class, but I soon realized I should not have expected it to. Like my colleagues around me, I had become caught up in the myth of the exceptional, with the idea that somehow these kids should be something more than they were—high school students. They were eighteen. Just as other students were not going to win the Olympics or the Fields Medal or make a debut at Carnegie Hall, neither were these high school seniors "the finest philosophical minds" anywhere. They were high school students, very able adolescents but nothing more. Their normality was actually a relief. The myth of the exceptional is not all exciting potential; it can also be a great burden—a weight that suggests you should be something more than you are.

In attempting to find places where they are extraordinary, students like August and Lee explored arenas where they were "better" than others. We

have seen these specialties already: Jason was known around campus because he was great at math; Jimmy was recognized by fellow students because they had all watched him play the violin. Freshmen could be seen
working to find a niche. Some played guitar; others would try out for
plays, join a comedy group, or look for something at the school where
they were special. It could be nearly anything: leading an astronomy club,
building model rockets, defensive play in hockey, creative writing, philosophical thinking, painting, playing video games.[10] This specialization gave
students a place to excel and took on special importance as they began the
college admissions process.

Getting into College: Fuzzy Math

St. Paul's has almost one hundred formal organizations and far more informal ones. With only five hundred students, this effectively meant that
nearly every student could run one of these groups (particularly by their
senior year); similarly, the breadth of the academic offerings gave students
options for excelling within the different academic divisions of the school.
Through these nearly countless areas the school is structured so that every
student can find a space to be one of the best at something.

There are advantages to being both broad and specialized. These are
most palpable during the college admissions process. When I was looking at boarding schools as a thirteen-year-old, I visited Groton, a school
much like St. Paul's in its status as an outstanding high school and home
to the social elite of our nation. As we walked the grounds, my tour guide
at Groton smugly told me, "The headmaster here used to gather together
the senior class and hand them three sheets of paper. On the top of one
was written 'Harvard,' another 'Yale,' the third, 'Princeton.' These pieces
of paper were circulated among the senior class; each boy would write
his name on one of the lists. This is how they were accepted into college.
It's different now, but not that much." This story was not true, of course,
but it represents the elite notion of what it used to mean to go to a boarding school.

A similar story existed at St. Paul's. I was told by an alumnus that as
late as the 1980s, Harvard would come to St. Paul's to interview students
(importantly, Harvard came to them). "We used to put the Harvard ad-

missions folks up at Scudder [a house on campus]. We'd fill the place up with booze. They'd interview our kids and make decisions that weekend. We always had someone in the room when they made their decisions." I could never confirm this story—I suspect it is part reality but mostly fantasy. Regardless, this is the lore of elite boarding schools. They are seen as inextricably linked to our nation's finest universities—and with all of the prestige and promise of the good life that follows from a Harvard or Yale or Princeton degree.

The notion that boarding schools have an advocate in the room continues today. In advocating for their students, St. Paul's exploits their numerous "extraordinary" students to help get them in at rates that are the envy (or illicit the ire) of other schools. I would best describe the interaction between schools like St. Paul's and elite colleges as a negotiation. As college admissions processes have become more and more competitive, so have colleges become more and more competitive with one another for cherished rankings. Elite schools have played upon this competitiveness to get a leg up. It may not be as simple as the Groton story. But the effect is largely the same.

Imagine that you're a Harvard admissions officer. One of the key aspects of your school's ranking is your yield—the percentage of students you accept that actually attend your university. The higher your yield, the lower your acceptance rate, and the higher your ranking. Yet when you look at outstanding students—and there are many of them—you have a challenge. These outstanding students will also be outstanding to Princeton, Yale, Stanford, and everywhere else. How do you know the ones you pick will attend your school? You can't quite trust applicants, as they are all likely to tell you how much they want to go to your school. And if students you accept go somewhere else, there's not much you can do. But you can get better information—information you want—from their high school. And you can reward that school for good information and sanction it for bad information.

Now imagine that you're St. Paul's. You want to get as many kids into Harvard, Yale, Princeton, Stanford, and other top schools as possible. Unlike many high schools, you have lots of students who stand a good chance of getting in. But there's a problem: some of these students are slightly better than others. These students will likely get into more than one school—but they can only attend one. And this will lower the chances of your "second-best" students getting into top schools. So what do you do? You talk to your students about where they really want to go. And then you talk to colleges. This requires a staff of college counselors that most schools could only dream of—an office of four people working on behalf of a graduating class of about 140 students. Their job is to know each student intimately—their talents and trade-offs, and, most important, where they want to go.

Let's say I work as a college counselor at St. Paul's, and I have two very strong students—Susan and Billy. Susan is going to get in everywhere; she is the best of the best. Billy might get into some top colleges, but he is less of a guarantee. Billy really wants to go to Yale. Susan really wants to go to Harvard. What do I do? I call Harvard. As we talk about the kids I have applying, I tell them how great Susan is. I make sure they know they should accept her. This conveys to Harvard that if accepted, Susan will go. I may even say this explicitly. Depending on the strength of our relationship, I might even get Harvard to tell me they are going to accept her.

Then I call Yale. I work on Yale for Billy. I tell them how great he is. If Yale asks about Susan, I tell them, "You really want Billy." Yale realizes what I am saying: that Susan will not go to Yale—I may even explicitly tell them she is going to Harvard. One of the delicate challenges is to make Yale not feel like they are getting a second-best student. In a moment we will see the solution to this challenge: at your school you have many "best" students. Susan may be the best at some things, but Billy is the best at others. Knowing Billy well, I might emphasize how he is truly a "Yale man"— the kind of student they want. Susan, by contrast, has more of a "Harvard character." Through this conversation, Yale accepts Billy.

With these unofficial negotiations, as the St. Paul's admissions officer I have just turned one Ivy League admission into two. I've doubled the number of kids that St. Paul's will send to the Ivy League. For Harvard and Yale, I've helped them increase their yield. This game only works if the college counselor at the high school has lots of students to trade on, knows them well, and has long-term relationships with the colleges (and is thus known to be reliable), and if the colleges in question have an interest in taking such phone calls. In short, this game works perfectly between the elite high schools and elite universities, where lots of desirable students are up for grabs and where the matching of students and schools is valuable.

I have asked you to "imagine" this situation because I could not get college counselors or admissions officers to verify the veracity of this process. Nor could I watch these discussions, nor would anyone go "on record" with me about them. This scenario would, no doubt, be adamantly denied by all involved.[11] Let me be clear about what I can tell you. Elite high schools are actively working their phones. One college counselor at an elite boarding school told me, "I fear the day Harvard stops taking our phone calls. I'm not sure what we'd do. And you know, they don't have to take them."

Today as in the past, elite colleges still listen to elite high schools. During a meeting I had at St. Paul's, the rector barged in with a letter in his hand. It was from an Ivy League school, informing a student that her early admission decision had been deferred. The rector angrily shook the letter at my colleague, exclaiming, "We need to do something about this. *Now.*" The translation was simple: get on the phone to the school and work on convincing them to take her. The reader might be particularly surprised to learn that this girl was one of those who lived in Barclay House and was suspended for a semester for hazing other girls. Still, she was worth fighting for; the close relationship between St. Paul's and this Ivy League school would be exploited on her behalf. This should make clear that it is not just the quality of the students that gets them into college but the quality of the relationship between elite high schools and colleges. Colleges do not always make the kinds of decisions that St. Paul's would like—sometimes counselors would complain that they were making the wrong ones—but regardless, information was flowing, relationships were being exploited, and elites were helping themselves to advantages.

This is not to say that students are unimportant, that they can just sit back and let the system work for them. Returning to my example, Susan and Billy both have something important to do. It may seem ridiculous to point this out, but by definition only 5 percent of any one class can be in the top 5 percent. Even the best of high schools cannot convince top colleges that they should accept students who are not at the top of their graduating classes. How, then, do these schools make most of their class in the top 5 percent? There seems to be an impossible math going on here. How is it that the bottom 50 percent of these high school classes are still getting into outstanding colleges?

The first thing to note is that the bottom 50 percent of a St. Paul's class is very strong. The year I taught at St. Paul's the average SAT scores were

1390/1600. That's slightly below the average score of the Harvard fresh-man class (1470). But more important, the seemingly impossible math becomes possible when we realize that there are lots of 5 percents. We typically think of the top of a class as being an academic category. This may be particularly true for most high school students who are ranked. But St. Paul's refuses to rank its students. And its grading system (high honors, honors, high pass, pass, and fail) does not allow for the construction of a grade point average, as grades are categories, not numbers. These im-pediments to a single scale upon which students from St. Paul's are evalu-ated are telling. The trick is to create as many scales as possible. So while academics are one dimension upon which to compare students, there are many others we could look at. There are sports, arts of many varieties, even community service—a whole host of arenas for success. If you can get almost all of your students above a basic performance bar where they will be attractive to colleges—high enough grades and board scores—and then create lots of places for them to do well, then suddenly you have lots of "best" students.

The great game of college admissions gives us a different way to read what is happening with the schooling of students at places like St. Paul's. No matter how good, academically, their students are, the top 5–10 per-cent will always only be 5–10 percent of the student body. But if all of your students can have qualifications equivalent to the top 10 percent of most other high schools, and if they have something else special—they can really row, or play the oboe or squash, or are promising violinists or painters or mathematicians, or they write interesting fiction, or even if you can argue that they have an interesting philosophical mind—then suddenly your students become that much more interesting to colleges. You have lots of top 5 percents, and most of your students fit in somewhere at the top. Your students are about as good as others everywhere, and they have something that makes them special. This combination makes them interesting to col-leges, which want to stock their incoming classes with students who are well qualified but also interesting.

In his own ethnography of the inner workings of an elite liberal arts college, Mitchell Stevens finds that colleges are not looking to pick one kind of student again and again—say, outstanding academic performers.[12] Instead, they are looking to pick a group of students whose individual stories each say something interesting, from the kid who is from a potato farming family in rural Idaho to the one who climbed Kilimanjaro last summer. These different students allow colleges to talk about just how diverse, fascinating, and qualified their classes are.

Though we might think that this rejection of a single academic standard is something that helps boost diversity, historically the practice had a more nefarious origin. Jerome Karabel's work on admissions to Harvard, Yale, and Princeton shows how these schools chose to give up on pure academic performance as standards for admission and instead focus on something more varied, ambiguous, and amorphous as "character."[13] Looking at the personal writings of admissions officers, college deans, and presidents, Karabel found that the move away from academic standards to character was motivated by a deep anti-Semitism. In the early twentieth century, across the East Coast the children of Jewish migrants were academically thriving and their success was allowing them access to the most prominent schools in the nation. The schools that had served as training grounds for established, wealthy Protestant families largely despised the increasing presence of Jews and sought to find ways to exclude them. The solution, settled upon by Harvard, Yale, and Princeton, was to begin to deemphasize academic credentials and focus instead on the personal traits that tended to be found among WASPs.

Gradually, "a good or interesting character" was introduced to the college admissions process. The Ivy League's strategy was largely successful. As such "interesting characters" tended to be defined by what WASPs liked to do (and tended to do) and for non-WASPs these character traits were costly to acquire, these schools had found a way to exclude the advancing members of society and protect the powerful. As Stevens shows, today schools across the nation continue to focus on character. And what was once rooted in exclusion is now mobilized to celebrate the triumph of diversity in the higher levels of educational institutions. It would be intellectually dishonest to deny that elite schools are far more diverse than they once were. But we must also think of the ways selection based on "character" continues to help students from elite schools as they are given more opportunities to develop "interesting characters" through the wide range of activities that are a central part of their everyday schooling.

Resources really matter. You can only create many areas for your students to succeed if you have the money to invest in getting them all above a basic bar and then still have some left over to pay for many areas wherein students cultivate diverse interests. On a budget of $8,000 per pupil, most high schools cannot create music, painting, photography, sculpture, and dance programs; they cannot have seemingly countless clubs for students to join, from literary, philosophical, and language societies to science teams that build robots and observe the heavens from their own observatory. Most high schools have trouble covering a basic curriculum. But on a budget of around $80,000 per pupil, St. Paul's can do so much more. Everyone can find a place to be the best at something, and everyone can develop a notable character. So when college counselors get on the phone, they have an interesting story to tell about almost every student—a story that colleges want to hear.

The Consequence of Audacity

Entering the fifth form students generally dread having Ivan Reim for humanities; he is said to be incredibly demanding and an extremely hard grader. He certainly is in the first term, when the grades he gives are lower than those of most of his colleagues and his comments on papers are very critical. However, in talking to students who had had him in previous years, the number of students who reported receiving the highest grade possible in his class struck me as shockingly high. Checking the year-end grade distribution for Reim's classes I found that nearly 80 percent of his students received high honors. He was one of the easiest teachers at the school. It was actually quite difficult not to get an A. Yet students believed they had beaten the odds. And faculty were similarly thrilled with their advisees. It was a "tremendous achievement" and, as one advisor put it, through learning and hard work, to "unlock the Reim chest."

This mutual self-deception hints at a curious paradox. Students openly discuss with one another that they are *not* doing the required readings for class. Faculty will often lament that "students are not working during the evening hours" when they are in the dorm watching students (and when students are supposed to be studying). And still both groups maintain the façade of the enormous academic challenges at the school that are only met through hard work and discipline. The question is, why? I believe that the façade is too valuable to let reality get in the way. Students and faculty work to *believe* that students are working hard, which is the linchpin to validating contemporary elite life: their abilities explain their achievements, and their achievements thus justify their elite positions.

The simplest way this happens is through the practices of "busyness"—walking around campus, meeting with friends, going to group meetings. These busy practices are certainly a kind of work. They are about building and maintaining relationships, involving oneself in groups, and developing a distinctive personal character. But they are not about sitting at a desk, performing tasks. They are far closer to the practices of management (both of the self and of relationships) than they are of classic scholastic activity. So let's be even more blunt: How hard do students work? Do they do what is required in their classes? The short answer is that most students do as little as possible to get by. At the same time they operate under the fiction that they are working quite hard, struggling even.

It is only a slight overstatement to say that I rarely saw a student reading during my year at St. Paul's. Given the amount of material students were expected to absorb, this was surprising. As an experiment, I decided to spend a week doing the work of an average fifth former at St. Paul's, based on a collection of syllabi. I found that I was reading for about two and a half hours each day. Other forms of work—from math problem sets to biology labs to practicing an instrument—took me well over another hour. During this week in my house, however, I never saw a student read for more than thirty minutes between 7:30 and 11:00 P.M.—the major "work hours" for students. Though they could have been reading at other moments during the day, their days are typically quite busy with classes and extracurriculars. And most are in bed by midnight. Perhaps all of these students were far faster workers than I? The much more likely explanation is the more dispiriting, and more obvious, one: the students were not doing all of their work.

And yet as I sat in on class after class, students seemed to know the material. Everything about their performance suggested that they were doing the work. Something didn't add up. I talked to students about this disparity and watched what the students in my own house did. Like many of us, they Googled. They relied on Wikipedia. To cover their copious amount of class reading, they primarily used online summaries of books to "prepare" for class. SparkNotes was the most commonly used site, but they relied on a wide variety of online summaries.[14] My initial reaction was outrage. I thought students were "cheating"—not just the academic spirit of the school but themselves. When I confronted students about this, they did not get angry or defensive; rather, they acted as if my own offense was quaint, and perhaps a little dishonest.

"Oh, come on, Mr. Khan!" Nick said to me, gleefully. "What am I going to do? Spend three hours reading *Beowulf*?"

His roommate, Graham, joined in. "Yeah! It doesn't make sense."

Frustrated, I replied forcefully, "That's the point. You work through it so that it *does* make sense." Still, I was unable to suppress something of a smile.

Graham was having none of it. He looked at me, incredulous, refusing to accept my feigned outrage. "Don't tell me *you* did all the reading when you were here."

"I read a hell of a lot."

"*Now,*" Graham replied, "but what about then?"

Realizing this was going nowhere, and perhaps getting a little too personal about my own experience at St. Paul's, Nick returned to his point. "Listen, you want me to know what was in *Beowulf*? Fine. I know what's in it now."

"That's not the point," I exclaimed. "The point is to help you think through the material. It's more than just knowing what happened."

"That's what papers are for."

"So, how do you write papers?" I wondered. "Do you do the reading then?"

Laughing at my insistence, Nick shook his head. "Of course not. But my papers are good. I do really well." He explained that using summaries guided him to the parts of the text he needed, and from those he was able to write papers that impressed his teachers. Expressing my disbelief, Graham joined Nick in laughing at me: "Believe it, baby!" There was an awful glee in his voice.

Again sensing my frustration, Nick returned to wondering. "No, but seriously, what's the difference?" And again joining him, Graham followed, "Yeah. I mean, I've actually done worse than when I did the reading."

Nick—who had been Graham's roommate for the last two years— looked at his friend quizzically: "When have you done the reading?"

"When I was a newb." Nick's skepticism was undeniable. Graham continued, "Really. But now I do a lot better. I might go back to the book after looking online. But it [online summaries] really helps me get what I'm supposed to get. Everyone does it."

The students I was talking to were the "dorky" students at the school—they were the ones that the other students thought did the *most* work. And yet even they thought it was standard to cut corners to get their work done. Boys were the more likely perpetrators, but girls were certainly not immune to such shortcuts. "Knowing" *Beowulf* was enough; it did not matter *how* you knew it or whether you knew it with any depth. In fact, learning it yourself was seen as an almost foolish way to master the material. And that one could do well on papers by preparing in the way that Nick and Graham did was taken as enough evidence that their mode of learning the material was satisfactory.

It was not only in humanities classes that I saw students taking shortcuts. Though they were supposed to be constantly practicing solving problems in their math courses, I found that students really only did work if they had to hand it in. The same was the case with language and science classes. I rarely saw students "studying" their science textbooks unless they had a test coming up or a lab report due. Even students who were good musicians tended not to practice regularly. Instead, the days before a concert or a performance evaluation were obvious because of the feverish sounds of students "cramming" with their instruments.

The dearth of engaged, sustained, in-depth work frustrated me. But Nick and Graham's responses eventually led me to be slightly more self-reflective. I thought of my own time at school. How would I answer Graham's question? I wondered. How, as a senior, did I do the twenty-five pages of creative writing assignments that were supposed to be done over the course of a semester? I wrote them in the twenty-four hours before the final assignment was due. I began to think of the ways I was assigned work as a graduate student, and in turn how I now assign work to my own undergraduate and graduate students: the assignments are often unreasonable, and students are not *really* expected to do them completely (or if they were, they could not be expected to do them well). Do I really think that my graduate students will be able to read a book of French social theory a week? Of course not. I teach Columbia's core curriculum, where students are introduced to "great books" of the Western canon. We fly though these texts so quickly that if pushed I don't believe I could defend the claim that students really learn them. Plato's *Republic* is the first text we read. It is some three hundred pages of complicated philosophical ideas. The recommended amount of time the college suggests we spend on this text? Two classes. Students are not really expected to learn *Republic* in one week. But after taking my class they can pretend they have.

If we think back to the history of how elite colleges accept high school students, we can recall how they have deemphasized academic excellence in favor of other factors ("character") so as to advantage students from already established backgrounds.[15] Though we academics often highly value grades and academic excellence, we must not forget that such a baseline for achievement is not universally shared. Indeed it is not what is instilled among the practices of the elite. As I have relentlessly emphasized, it is not simply knowing things that others don't. It's being at ease with a range of ideas and situations. Using SparkNotes is an extension of this.

My frustration with Graham and Nick slowly subsided; though petulant, they were also just being honest. My outrage was far more dishonest, or at least a form of denial. I have asked my students at Columbia about how they prepare for class; their responses indicate that students from St. Paul's are hardly unique in their academic practices. Graham and Nick had learned—just as I had while I was at St. Paul's—that the process did not matter as much as the result. The benchmark was whether your teacher liked your paper. One might assume that the result is students who are incredibly instrumental in their orientation to their work and, more important, to the world. Yet interestingly, I did not find this to be the case. Instead, most students endorsed the educational ideal of the school: they were learning "something greater" that would be essential to their future lives. This "something greater" was not knowledge about the world; it was a way to relate to it. Pushing my observations above, reading *Beowulf* does not matter. Or at least it does not matter that much. Anyone can read *Beowulf*. As barriers to knowledge have become more porous, particular forms of cultural knowledge have become less valuable. Knowing *Beowulf*, or Chaucer, or Shakespeare may have created a meaningful distinction a generation ago, when the symbolic boundaries around highbrow culture were still fairly solid. But today almost every teenager goes to high school, and every high school student reads Shakespeare. That students at elite schools like St. Paul's rely on widely available summaries of texts suggests that these symbolic boundaries have all but been given up on. As knowledge has become more democratized, it is no longer valuable for making distinctions within hierarchies, for distinguishing between the cultural haves and have-nots. Now, knowledge is not a means to distinguish oneself; instead students are almost indifferent to it. As Nick tells me, with smug satisfaction, "Listen, you want me to know what was in *Beowulf*? Fine. I know what's in it now."

The current humanities curriculum, as we have seen, actually deemphasizes particular knowledge. Teachers cannot be expected to know the history, philosophy, political thought, literature, poetry, art, and culture of several centuries with any depth. They cannot possibly convey to students what happened in all of these arenas. Instead, we as faculty cultivate a sense that these things are knowable and that one can relate to them not by knowing them inside and out but by making casual connections between them. We have to acknowledge that as teachers, indifference is also quite important. *Beowulf* can be treated like *Jaws*. This indifference is different from devaluing. In treating *Beowulf* like *Jaws*, the faculty equalizes the cultural plane, making students into cultural egalitarians. It is not that *Beowulf* does not matter—it does—but not so much as to be what is truly important. *Beowulf* is not used to exclude but instead to emphasize how the world is available, knowable, and at your disposal. This facility in the world is the truly important orientation, not knowing things that others don't.

The irony about this elite behavior is that it relies on what seems to be a great equalizing. The world of knowledge is being flattened, available to more people and less employed as a distinction by those at the top. Yet this equalization of knowledge has inequitable results, for how one uses, relates to, deploys, and integrates such knowledge varies. St. Paul's students do not use knowledge itself to make them different. We can all share the same knowledge in this democratized, meritocratic world. Yet the relationship to knowledge—indifference or ease, and how it is used—to make connections creates a recognizable mark of difference. For all the changes in the world, this elite mark remains, in everything from the clothes they wear to the music they listen to to the way the read *Beowulf* or watch *Jaws*. And this ease allows the new equality to help perpetuate the old inequality (while obscuring it).

Extraordinary Indifference

In addition to their classes, students also have abundant educational opportunities that include trips away from the school and visitors to the
school. The campus serves as a revolving door for an extraordinary list
of guests. Recent speakers have included authors Tobias Wolff and Rick
Moody, singer-songwriter Patty Larkin, the academic Ronald Takaki, poet
laureates Billy Collins and Robert Pinsky, poet Maya Angelou, musicians
Yo Yo Ma and Midori, conductor Ben Zander, FBI director Robert Muel-
ler, and politicians like John Kerry (the last two of whom are alumni).
These speakers do not simply arrive for a speech and then leave. They
almost always spend considerable time with students. Larkin led songwrit-
ing workshops with students; Takaki spent days with faculty and students
discussing multiculturalism on campus; Pinsky held poetry workshops
and gave a couple of readings; Wolff taught several creative fiction and
nonfiction courses; Yo Yo Ma held master classes.

What I found special about all of these events was their lack of specialness. When I was a student, Martin Luther King Jr.'s widow, Coretta Scott
King, visited the school on Martin Luther King Day. My parents asked if
they could come. At the time, I found the request incredibly odd. I was
embarrassed to ask the school about it. And as I walked with my parents to
the event, I could sense their extreme excitement to see Mrs. King speak.
To me it was merely another day of my school year. It was not clear to me
why my parents had made a special trip or why my father had taken a day
off work (a rare occurrence). Now I am embarrassed to admit this. But at
the time, seeing Coretta Scott King speak seemed mundane to me.[16]

The memory returned to me as I watched a seeming parade of notable
Americans come through St. Paul's in my year back on campus. While attempting to get my house seated so Tobias Wolff could begin his speech,
one student commented, "I really don't have time for this right now. I
have a lab due tomorrow." Another student audibly complained that Patty
Larkin was "some weird hippie" and spoke about the ways in which her
visit took him away from what he would otherwise be doing. This didn't
just happen on campus: an alumnus bought seats to Metropolitan Opera
performances in New York for students and paid for a plane to fly them
down on a Saturday. Students would leave early in the morning, arrive
in New York by midday, have lunch at the Met with participants in the

opera, watch the opera, and head home for the evening. As a student I participated in such an event, getting to see Pavarotti sing Verdi's "Ballo in Maschera."

There is a kind of banality of the extraordinary to all of these events. One can simply jump on a plane to catch a matinee at the Metropolitan Opera in New York, or go see a performance of the Boston Symphony when you are required to be somewhere else (in class), or have Robert Pinsky teach you how to write poetry, Rick Moody chat with you about developments of the modern novel, Yo Yo Ma play the cello for you in morning chapel, or Ronald Takaki help you work through issues of diversity in your community. At St. Paul's, these occurrences feel normal. And in some ways these campus visits are made more ordinary by the assumption that the community is already made up of internationally extraordinary people. These abundant opportunities for informal learning help reinforce the Paulie orientation to the world where seemingly everything is possible (and that you need not know things—experts can be brought in for such particular knowledge; your task is to put it all together). The orientation is not simply that one can expect astonishing things but that you can be almost indifferent to them. When one of America's great writers visits to speak with you, you can think of it as a mundane experience that takes you away from other mundane things, like writing a lab report.

These students, of course, are still young and they cannot be expected to appreciate every moment provided to them by St. Paul's. But the persistent indifference to extraordinary things is striking. When a student in my house, Steven, returned from a Met Opera performance, I excitedly asked him how it went. He provided me with a sober assessment of the mezzo-soprano's singing (something he must have overheard, as he knew nothing about opera) and commented that the Zeffirelli set was interesting. Another student, walking past our conversation, asked, "Oh, did you get to go on one of those Met things? Was it worth it?" To which Steven responded, "I guess." That was the last I heard of the event. Again, I understand that high schoolers can't be reasonably expected to be in rapture over an opera performance (and are unlikely to admit it if they were), but what is palpable here is the indifference. Indifference to flying to New York for the day, having lunch with internationally renowned musicians, watching them perform, and catching a flight home that evening. Even if that indifference is sometimes feigned, the performance is convincing.

The acquisition of cultural knowledge is not what St. Paul's students emphasize or display. As the above examples illustrate, St. Paul's literally showers its students with cultural knowledge. And yet the ways in which most students relate to such experiences is not to grasp the opportunity, to reach for it eagerly, to absorb it with curiosity, or to challenge it with an alternate perspective. Instead they learn to treat such instances ambivalently. One warm spring afternoon I passed a group of students throwing pebbles; I thought nothing of it until it occurred to me that they were throwing them at one of the many sculptures on campus. "What are you doing?!?" I screamed at them. "That's an Alexander Calder!" They looked up at me, somewhat shocked. They replied, "Oh, sorry," and turned in the other direction, throwing the rocks into the pond instead of at the sculpture by a major artist. They were largely unfazed. The Calder was simply one of many hunks of metal on one of many carefully manicured lawns outside one of many beautiful buildings.

St. Paul's students don't engage in cultural knowledge displays in order to distinguish themselves from others. In fact, those displays of knowledge—such as David's mention of Dostoyevsky in class, or the lecture on shirt thread counts, or Evan Williams's flaunting his "inside" knowledge to the other newbs—were for the most part failures. Their "cultural capital" was not that they knew something others didn't. Instead, their cultural capital was interactional: the way in which they related to culture (both high and low) and to each other. Their indifference is a particular manifestation of ease. Ease is the stance, the posture of the elite adolescent that I have tried to show time and again. Students aren't always indifferent; they care about their dress, and their hierarchies, and their status. But they do so always with ease. Yet the way to be at ease in classes and in relationship to high culture is to be indifferent to it all. You can throw rocks at priceless things and be annoyed by the distractions of notable Americans.

Work Hard, Fall Behind

As our exploration has hinted at, the myth of the extraordinary seems to have a favored recipient: white boys. This fact is not surprising, given that the elite has long been dominated by Anglo men, but it is discouraging given the realities of St. Paul's and the meritocracy that it tries to hard to foster. We have seen that girls at St. Paul's do better academically than boys; year after year, their grades are higher. They are like their sisters across America's high schools who are outperforming boys. However, at St. Paul's at least, girls win fewer awards. They did not perform or speak in chapel as regularly as boys did. They rarely hold positions of power within the student government. Only once has a girl been president of the school, though girls have been on campus since 1969. In fact, when I casually asked a series of students to identify the "best" student in different areas, boys were almost always named.[17] The best artist was a boy. The best athlete was a boy. The best student was a boy. Even breaking academics down by topic area, the best students in each were almost always boys. The exception was in physics, where the best student identified was a transgendered boy. Boys dominated the realm of the extraordinary, even though girls were doing better.

It generally shocked students when I pointed this out to them. In fact, without exception, they quickly named girls they thought could compete with or even beat the best boys. But I was primarily interested in who immediately came to mind for students. Further, with the exception of a black athlete who was occasionally named and an Asian musician, all of the boys talked about were white. Though extraordinary individuals were believed to be everywhere at St. Paul's, the specific people others pointed to as extraordinary were actually a very small group—an adolescent version of an "old boys club." When I mentioned this observation to faculty, most were quick to remind me of the many non-white students they have had who were "among the best" they have ever taught. I do not believe that St. Paul's is an explicitly racist or sexist place. However, there are clear racial and gender differences in the realization of privilege.

Returning to our previous theme, we now must complicate our vision of the student body's study habits. It would be inaccurate to say that none of the students do their work; there were several students during my year at St. Paul's who worked very hard. These students—both during my year there and in general—tend to be non-white and are more often than not girls. As I pointed out earlier, Asian students receive the highest grades at St. Paul's; black students receive the lowest. We may recall Devin, the black student from chapter 2, who told me, "I'm never going to be at a place like this again. Even if I go to Harvard, it won't be like this. This is my chance. And I'm making the most of it. You should know this by now. There's more to St. Paul's than grades." Devin worked very hard. Many of his black peers did as well; more often than not, and certainly more often than most of their white peers, they actually "did the work" required of them. But the results were not that they did better—in fact, they did much worse.

Devin adamantly maintained that he had read *Beowulf*. And if he had he certainly was working harder than those who were using SparkNotes. Unlike Nick and Graham, who expressed little problem "getting" *Beowulf*, in part because it was fed to them by a summary, Devin spoke to me about his struggle to understand the story. When I told him that others were not doing their reading, he told me, "I know. But that's their loss. I know that it's important to do it." Devin was getting the most out of his time at St. Paul's. This meant doing the work, even if he didn't get better grades as a result. It wasn't so much about the grades as it was learning from the experience. And the best way to do so was to do what you were officially supposed to. St. Paul's existed for him as a place in and of itself. But if we believe the argument I have been making in this book about the importance of ease, perhaps Devin is wrong to think that it is important to do his reading; perhaps the loss is his.

By contrast, several of the Asian students I spoke to shared none of the romantic notions about the importance of St. Paul's as a "place in itself." I heard nothing about "making the most of it" or that there was "more to St. Paul's than grades." Lily Wong grew up in Hong Kong. She was educated in English schools there; she was from an elite family. I enjoyed talking to Lily about her life at St. Paul's, and she dropped by my office with regularity. But as she sat in the chair across from me I always sensed a tension, like she knew she should be somewhere else. She might immediately remind the reader of Mary, from chapter 4. But Lily's tension was almost expected by other students, and she was forgiven for it in ways that Mary, who was white, was not. Students seemed to accept the increased pressures that Asian students seemed to manifest. Perhaps they knew how much harder it was for Asians to get into elite colleges.[18] Mary's exhibiting of work shows her to have more in common with Lily and Devin in the way she approaches the school than she does with her white peers. But as a white girl, she was made to feel particularly uncomfortable in ways that white students would never make Lily and Devin feel. No doubt this was because the white students were hesitant to be as cruel to non-white students as they were to their peers—the risk of being seen as racist was one they carefully avoided. Lily's tension didn't result in social discomfort. It seemed to make sense to everyone—and, I'm embarrassed to admit, even to me.

"There's so much pressure," Lily told me. "Not here. Well, [laughs] *definitely here*. But from home. I know I have to do well. My parents remind me every day. They e-mail me and call me. Sometimes I'm surprised that they haven't hired someone to stand over me and say it every day! [Laughs.] I mean, I know why I'm here. My parents want something special for me. And this is part of it. It's a step in my life. Part of the way there."

When I asked Lily what the next stop was, she laughed, "Hopefully, Harvard!" St. Paul's, to her, is not a place in and of itself. It is a stepping-stone on the way to an elite college and then to who knows what already-planned-for future successes in life. (Thankfully for her parents—and hopefully for her—she was accepted by Harvard.) In Lily's strategy, St. Paul's is part of a process; it exists within a much larger calculus about a long-term life plan. Devin's strategy doesn't have the same trajectory; St. Paul's is valued in and of itself. Whereas for Lily St. Paul's is an excellent stop in a life full of plans, for Devin St. Paul's is a unique experience unlikely to be offered ever again. There is some irony in these racialized differences, however, once we see them in relation to the subsequent opportunities available for both groups. It is very difficult for Asian students to enter into top colleges; the pool of candidates is exceptionally competitive. By contrast, it is not nearly as competitive for black students from a place like St. Paul's; the pool of candidates is comparatively weak (no doubt because the competition was played out in ever getting to St. Paul's).[19] Black students from St. Paul's do exceptionally well in the college admission process. They tend to come from a background of disadvantage and in graduating from St. Paul's have learned to negotiate higher institutions of privilege. Disadvantaged students from boarding schools allow colleges to tell a story they like to tell: they are educating not just the elite but also the truly disadvantaged. Yet unlike most students from disadvantaged backgrounds who are likely to struggle in a rich, elite college environment, students from boarding schools have already shown that they know how to make it through this kind of educational culture.

And so even though these two "ends" of the grade spectrum appear at first glance to be quite different—they perform differently and orient themselves to the school differently—both groups work relatively hard at the school and tend to do the work as it has been assigned to them. Black students, because they appreciate the unique opportunities of St. Paul's, typically seek to absorb as much as they can; Asian students work hard because of their family orientation to the school and their need to be competitive in an already very challenging college process.

Yet if the school's white majority is any indication, this orientation is, to a degree, getting it wrong. There is nothing inherently wrong with how Lily and Devin and like-minded students of color act at St. Paul's. Lily and Devin are not making bad choices—they just have different constraints than the majority of their white peers and therefore end up acting differently. The increased pressure of competition for girls and Asians, and the uniqueness and special quality of the experience for blacks and Latinos, means that they tend to act differently. Devin provides a strikingly different reading of the school than Carla, who saw it all as "bullshit." But for both the racialized problems of expressing privilege are ever-present. Devin's act of working doesn't allow him to seem indifferent; Carla's feeling that it was all bullshit leads others at school to seem like she is acting, that relationships with her are not easy but forced.

What is of note is that privilege is not as fully acquired by either Lily or Devin. As they sit in the rooms or the library, doing their work, doing what I thought Nick and Graham should have been doing, they are working against the ease of privilege and the indifference to work. The strategies of Lily and Devin cannot be thought of in a vacuum. The societal structure of the constraints that they and their families face leads to different strategies and different actions. How other students (and faculty) interact with them impacts what they do. We should be careful not to individualize culture in ways that suggest that these strategies are located within Lily or Devin. Instead they emerge within an interactive context, and what those on the other side of the interaction expect matters (be they institutions, parents, friends, or faculty). Privilege is racialized not because the privileged are racist or because people of color make the wrong decisions but because historical and interactive contexts lead to different choices. It "makes sense" for Devin and Lily to act as they do—but as they act in such ways they develop modes of understanding, orientation, and interaction that are contradictory with privilege and its attitude of ease.

The world around elites has transformed. Exclusionary practices are no longer viable or sustainable. Distinction has given way to equality. Omnivorousness is the strategy for being a new elite, and it is built upon an essential attitude toward the world: ease. Being an omnivore means not making distinctions: not having to, not wanting to, not needing to. It can even seem to be the most fundamental form of equality. *Jaws* and *Beowulf* are both cultural artifacts to be played with; they are equally worthy of our consideration. Though they are showered with remarkable opportunities, the elites at St. Paul's do not know more; they know differently. This different way of knowing is a mark possessed by an individual. The fact that some of us have this mark (and most of us don't) is not a product of inequality—we all have access to knowledge. But from the perspective of elites, their personal qualities and characters *produce* inequality within the necessary hierarchies that define our human lives.

The view of the world that students from St. Paul's come away with is one wherein the world is defined by its possibility, not its constraints. If we think of other ethnographic studies of schools—and for many, their own experience of school—the presence of rules, constraints, and punishments is paramount. These things, however, are almost completely absent from our story of St. Paul's. On campus, the world is presented as a kind of blank canvas, ready for students to seize. Thinking of the world as a space of possibility is consistent with a meritocratic frame: the world is yours; all that is required are hard work and talent. Students believe that they work extremely hard and they are exceptionally talented. While I would not characterize students as working hard—as they often do not really do their work—they are certainly busy. This busyness presents the appearance and feel of hard work. And yes, there is certainly a lot of talent at St. Paul's— though not of the meteoric variety that the students often believe about themselves and each other.

This vision of self and the world—both inculcated by the school and eagerly promoted by the students—has important ramifications. The attitude that the world is perpetually available—and that you are exceptionally capable—goes beyond the simple frame of meritocracy. The world and its innumerable possibilities is a space one can and should navigate with ease. As we have seen throughout our story, this ease is an essential Paulie posture, and it often manifests as an indifference to the remarkable opportunities granted them. These students see the extraordinary as everyday. Students can throw stones at a priceless sculpture. When thinking about a trip to the Met, the best answer they can give to whether or not it was enjoyable is "I guess." In their indifference, these students are, from their perspective, cultural egalitarians. They watch Jerry Springer, listen to hip-hop, go to the opera, and are equally comfortable dressed formally for seated meal and as "pimps" and "hos" at a school dance. They treat jumping on a plane to go to the Met Opera as an everyday affair, like walking to the local coffee shop to hear a new singer-songwriter.

If these newest members of the elite are cultural egalitarians, the natural question is, how is cultural hierarchy created and maintained? The standard story we have been told is that certain cultural markers are acquired and made exclusive by elites.[20] Thus, we think of opera as high culture and polo as a sport of the rich; the rest of us assume that those items of elite life are out of our grasp. I have no reason to doubt this story. Yet the rather ingenious trick is that whatever inequality still remains in our world can be blamed on those at the bottom—those who are *not* cultural egalitarians. Their closed-mindedness to the breadth of culture means they do not seize upon the fruits of our new, more equal world. The resulting image among the elite explains systematic inequality not as the product of conditions but instead as a product of people's doings. If the world is an open space of potential, why do some people fail? Because they don't seize the potential (available to all) within the world.

What St. Paul's is teaching is a style of *learning* that quickly becomes a style of *living*—with an emphasis on ways of relating and making connections rather than with a deep engagement with ideas and texts. It is no surprise, within this pedagogical model, that an indifference—not just toward *Beowulf* but toward much of life's opportunities—is the result. This ease of life is not just a mark of privilege. It is also a mark of protection. For if the elite truly embraced hard work, they could be outworked. Ease is both an obscure thing and hard for the rising classes to master. They must work hard to achieve, and it is nearly impossible for this hard work not to leave its mark on them. The advantaged have embraced the accoutrements of the open society with their omnivorousness. But through their marks of ease, they have found ways to limit advancement within such openness, protecting their positions.

Conclusion

The difference of natural talents in different men is, in reality,
much less than we are aware of; and the very different genius
which appears to distinguish men of different professions,
when grown up to maturity, is not upon many occasions so much
the cause, as the effect of the division of labor. The difference
between the most dissimilar characters, between a philosopher
and a common street porter, for example, seems to arise not so much
from nature, as from habit, custom, and education.
—ADAM SMITH

The same equality that allows every citizen to conceive lofty hopes
renders all the citizens less able to realize them; it circumscribes
their powers on every side, while it gives freer scope to their desires.
Not only are they themselves powerless, but they are met at every step
by immense obstacles, which they did not at first perceive. They have
swept away the privileges of some of their fellow creatures which stood
in their way, but they have opened the door to universal competition;
the barrier has changed shape rather than place.
—ALEXIS DE TOCQUEVILLE

What have we learned from this small, out-of-the-way place? St. Paul's is
a high school of just five hundred students, tucked away in the outskirts
of Concord, New Hampshire. If one is interested in the American experience, as I am, then this is not your typical spot to learn about it. And
even if we now know about St. Paul's, do we now know more about the
character of American inequality? I would like to think that we do. And
in particular we know something about elites: how they have adapted to
the changing landscape of the twenty-first century. I leave the reader with
some impressions that I have drawn from my time spent at St. Paul's. I will

resist the urge to suggest any programmatic changes we might try to realize as a nation. But I shall make some claims that are as brief as they are provocative. I will brazenly think beyond my case so as to make sense of what our new elite and our new inequality might mean for our new century.

The Rise of the Individual and the Death of Collectivist Politics

One of the ironic consequences of the collectivist movements of the 1960s has been the further triumph of the individual and the death of the collective. Groups gathered together—blacks, women, gays, immigrants—to argue that the properties that grouped them should not matter. It should be our own human capital that matters; we should all have opportunities based on our capacities, not on some characteristics ascribed to us.

The elite have largely adopted this stance. They have gone from seeing themselves as a coherent group, a class with particular histories and tastes, to a collection of the most talented and hardest working of our nation. They look more diverse, by which I mean that they now include members they formerly excluded. They have rejected moat and fence building around particular resources and qualities that might identify them as a class and have accepted the fundamentally American story of "work hard, get ahead." They think in terms of their individual traits, capacities, skills, talents, and qualities. They certainly know that these are all cultivated, but this cultivation is done through hard work, and access is granted through capacity rather than birthright. Recall the three lessons of privilege that I outlined in the introduction: (1) hierarchies are natural and can be used to one's advantage; (2) experiences matter more than innate or inherited qualities; and (3) the way to signal your elite status to others is through ease and openness in all social contexts. Inequality is ever-present, but elites now view it as fair. Hierarchies are enabling, not constraining. It is the inherent character of the individual that matters, not breeding, or skin color, or anything that smacks of an old-fashioned collectivity.

As the excluded have been included, we have assumed that the characteristics that served as principles for exclusion have dissolved in importance. Social commentators have heralded our new classless society; we congratulate ourselves on being "post-race." While our colleges appear to embrace these changes, some caution is warranted. Race still matters among the elite, just as it does across our nation.[1] Access is not the same as equality, and social inequalities still show a persistent importance of race and gender to one's life chances.

It bears repeating that as elite schools appear to have opened their doors, to a large degree they have not. There are more rich kids at top schools than there were twenty-five years ago and fewer poor ones. As we saw in earlier chapters, the lack of a language of and identification with class in our nation presents challenges to confronting our increasing class inequalities. The difference between rich and poor people can be understood very simply. Rich people have more money than poor people. And they use that money to buy advantages for themselves and their children. One of the places they do so is at St. Paul's School. And the trick of these advantages today is in their naturalization.

This is certainly not where we thought we would end up after the rights revolutions of the 1960s. Increased openness and increased inequality should not go hand in hand. The rise of the meritocracy seems a far more desirable world than the domination of aristocracy. And so too does openness feel more preferable than closure. How did we get to this place?

Our equating of diversity with equality is problematic. We do this in part because we lack class as a descriptive, resonant social category, and the political solidarity required to address its ill effects is largely absent. The new elite, who in the words of P. G. Wodehouse's Jeeves "are acute to the notion of class distinction," can integrate across the class scale, but there is embodied knowledge required to move up the scale that tends to keep others out. The irony of social integration absent class consciousness is that elites have been given the tools to more effectively remain elite and reinforce their status. This isn't necessarily solvable or even pernicious, but I hope to have shown that it is the case.

We are also here because of one of the key features of our American exceptionalism: individualism. Ours is a world of "me" rather than "we." Collectivism is far from a utopia: it is by definition exclusionary (there is an "us" and a "them") and it can limit innovations. But individualism is far too cherished in our nation. And when combined with meritocracy it has allowed for the justification of inequalities that should embarrass our nation. This attention to the individual has led us to ignore the conditions of our own making. We tend to think of our successes as our own work (we are less likely to do so for our failures) and our positions relative to our own qualities. This is certainly true. But it is important to note that our positions are part of our activity within a social context. We do not live in a flat world but in one with different conditions of possibility. These conditions are highly tied to ascriptive characteristics, creating durable inequalities.

When we combine race, class, and the decline of collectivist politics we are left to wonder seriously about the gains in educational institutions. Importantly, the weapons of the disadvantaged are in their numbers and organization. These are both only possible through collective identification and collective action. The triumph of individual man and the death of collective politics may make race go the way of class: to increasingly become a source of inequality but one whose capacity to challenge these durable inequalities is eroding. There is some evidence that this is the case. Most of the gains made in terms of both racial and class equality have ceased. During the moments of collectivist politics income inequality shrank, and the wage gap between black and white did as well. But since the 1980s we have not seen this trend continue. The triumph of the story of individual traits and capacities has been the death of collectivism and the solidification of racial and income inequality. Until we reclaim some of our social trust and solidarity I am not optimistic that these difficulties can be addressed.

The Trick of Privilege: The New Democratic Inequality

All of this is to say that the "new" inequality is the democratization of inequality. We might call it democratic inequality. The aristocratic marks of class, exclusion, and inheritance have been rejected; the democratic embrace of individuals having their own fair shake is nearly complete. Differences in outcomes are explained by the capacities of people; the elite have embraced differences among their roles while accepting and even consecrating the hierarchy between them and others. The difficulty with this move, what I have called the "trick" of privilege, is to make the hierarchy seem a natural rather than durable systematic process. My explanation here has drawn directly on the work of Pierre Bourdieu and deploys the ideas of embodiment and ease to show how such a naturalization of socially produced differences can occur.

Embodiment is a fancy word for a simple idea: we carry our experiences with us. Our time in the world becomes imprinted on our bodies themselves. Time in elite spaces matters, and by definition elite spaces are ones that are exclusive. The importance to embodiment is that once social experiences become embodied, they begin to seem natural. It's just how your carry yourself. We all have to act in some way; your embodiment is yours. The particular form of embodiment of the new elite is ease. This ease is enormously wide-ranging. As they have integrated those who have been excluded, the elite have adapted many of the cultural markers they previously shunned. And so the new elite are at ease in a wide range of areas.

An implication is that, perhaps, cultural hierarchies are not simply imposed from above by exclusive practices[2] but maintained from below. If elites are *generally* indifferent or (display ease) across cultural symbols, then the "specialness" of high cultural markers is maintained not only by elites through exclusive practices but also by non-elites who do not engage in practices marked as culturally elite. My own research only allows for this as a loose hypothesis. But if we think for a moment about, say, a concert, the price of a ticket to the Met Opera is no greater than the price of a ticket to see U2. Students from St. Paul's can be observed attending both. Students from Concord High School (almost) only attend the latter. And so we might ask where cultural exclusivity comes from—those who consume across culture or those who have stronger consumptive tendencies? This question is the one the new elite ask the world. And the answer is that they are open-minded and others are closed-minded.

Though the elite have been opened, and have opened themselves to the world, the world has not opened to all. Access is not the same as integration. But what is crucial is that no one is explicitly excluded.[3] The effect is to blame non-elites for their lack of interest. As we have seen, the result of this logic is damning. The distinction between elites and the rest of us appears to be a choice. It is cosmopolitanism that explains elite status to elites and closed-mindedness that explains those who choose not to participate. What matters are individual attributes and capacities, not durable inequalities. From this point of view, those who are not successful are not necessarily disadvantaged; they are simply those who have failed to seize the opportunities afforded by our new, open society.

Embodied ease is a physical manifestation of this openness, and it makes differences natural. Inequality becomes the product of who you are, not where you are from. Society has recessed in the minds of the elite as producing social problems. Society is to be as benign as possible—to sit in the background as we play out our lives on an even field. The world is flat, so the story goes. This is a delusion, a fable the elite tell to themselves and others in order to obscure their continued domination and inheritance. It bears repeating that one of the best indicators of your social position is that of your parents. I would like to think it is my wits that resulted in my job at an Ivy League university. But there is more to the story; my parents' wealth was able to buy me out of difficulties and create endowments. When less than a stellar student in middle school, tutors were hired. When wits weren't enough, I could fall back on my comfort within elite institutions—comfort purchased through a pricey education. These processes are more often than not obscured; elites, in embodying their costly experiences, simply seem to have what it takes.

The Democratic Conundrum

Privilege is not a uniform experience for the elite. There are contradictions for many students at the school. We can see this most clearly in the cases of blacks and girls. We might remember Carla, who thought the school was bullshit, or Mary, who was mercilessly teased for working hard, or Devin, who thought of St. Paul's as a once-in-a-lifetime opportunity, or Lee, who struggled to avoid dressing like she was at the prom, working the corner, or a business executive, or the girls of Barclay House for whom sexuality was a central part of a hazing ritual. There are contradictions to the experience of privilege and of race and gender for these students. All of the examples I just highlighted point to the ways in which social categories have real impacts on the experience of students at St. Paul's and to the fact that durable (categorical) inequalities can emerge from these contradictory experiences. For girls, the dominance of sexuality creates tensions with expressing ease; looking forward, such sexuality might limit success throughout the life course, especially when sexuality and youth are so tightly tied together. For black students, revering or rejecting the institution meant that time at the school is not as "natural"—it is either artificial bullshit or the kind of thing you'll never experience again.

As the languages of race, gender, and class are increasingly framed as academic liberal pandering or as old social categories whose usefulness has run their course, students begin to lose the tools to make sense of their experience, and challenging durable inequalities becomes more and more difficult. Not only does the success of some become naturalized, but the failure of others becomes internalized.

It is your own incapacities. Democratic inequality comes with a democratic conundrum. The new elites' suggestion that they "accept all" and that they do so within an increasingly open world makes the collectivism required for social transformations of any kind more challenging. And this leads to an odd, perhaps even ironic outcome: by becoming more democratic the elite have undercut the power of the weak within our nation.

The elite story about the triumph of the individual is just that; or better, it is a myth. Even though they are outperforming them in educational institutions, women still make less than men, blacks make less than whites, and students from St. Paul's get into better colleges than equivalent ones who attend non-elite schools. These "new elite" are less honest than their "old elite" ancestors, like Chase Abbott. I do not wish to suggest an invidiousness here. But in suggesting that it is their work and not their wealth, that it is their talents and not their lineage, elites function beneath a fiction. Would I prefer today's open yet obscuring elites to yesterday's closed and more transparent ones? Certainly. The changes in spaces like St. Paul's and its Ivy League counterparts have been profound and should leave any who value equality of opportunity optimistic. Meritocracy is a social arrangement like any other: it is a loose set of rules that can be adapted in order to obscure advantages, all the while justifying them on the basis of collective values.

And so my optimism is heavily tempered. If our economic trends continue, if the spoils produced by the many are increasingly claimed by the few, then the transformations among the elite may be durable. That is, we may have a diverse elite class. And this I imagine will no doubt be trotted out by the elite to suggest that ours is an open society where one can get a fair shake. But diversity does not mean mobility and it certainly does not mean equality. Ours is a more diverse elite within a more unequal world. The result of our democratic inequality is that the production of privilege will continue to reproduce inequality while implying that ours is a just world; the weapons of the weak are removed, and the blame for inequality is placed on the shoulders of those whom our democratic promise has failed.

METHODOLOGICAL AND THEORETICAL
REFLECTIONS

This book is a cultural study of inequality, employing a classic ethnographic method. This method means that the scholar embeds himself in the relations under study, spending long periods of time with research subjects. For me it meant getting a job at St. Paul's School, moving into an apartment on campus, coaching the tennis and squash teams, teaching, advising students in a dorm, and, most important, observing the daily life of the school. After my year at St. Paul's I returned many times and I sought out alumni to interview and discuss some of the things I'd learned. Collected, these observations and discussions make up my data.

The purpose of the ethnographic method is to provide an account of how people live their lives with one another in particular places. When I entered St. Paul's I was completely honest about my research project. I told the school my aim—"to understand the American elite"—and how I would achieve it—by living at the school, observing its workings, and talking to people. During my year of research I continually conveyed this purpose to the community. Such honesty is essential to ethnographic projects. This goes beyond the moral obligation to the people we are studying. Acting, obscuring, tricking, or hiding things from subjects works against the trust required to become part of the relations under study. No doubt some readers worry about this, both insofar as I am an alumnus of the school and that I continually embed myself in both the narrative and the lives of my subjects. How can I be an objective observer?

I cannot. But objectivity is often a false mask that researchers hide behind in order to assert their scientific authority. To stand outside people, looking in at their lives as if they were in some laboratory or snow globe, is to not understand them. During my first weeks at St. Paul's I had an incredibly hard time learning anything. People were mistrustful. Interactions were awkward. I had tried not to position myself anywhere in the school, feeling that being inside would leave large blind spots. But I found that from my attempts at an objective stance I could see almost nothing.

Luckily, I inadvertently positioned myself within the relations of the school. Early in the year, as we prepared for a faculty meeting to discuss the hazing crisis, a report was circulated by the school's lawyers to help us understand the research on hazing. The research was terrible; I sent an e-mail denouncing it, arguing that it should not be the basis of any policy. I soon received e-mails from fellow faculty members, joking that my firing was only a matter of time and that they would help me pack my things. I was surprised by the reaction and worried about the consequences. Though I was yelled at by the administration for undermining their lawyers, people soon began talking to me. They knew where I stood and this made connections possible. Though my relationship with the administration suffered somewhat, even they began to discuss things with me that they never had before. It was in becoming positioned that I could be a successful ethnographer, not in being somehow "outside" or "objective." This is not to say that I believe in a postmodern epistemology. I am a realist and an empiricist at heart. I simply feel that the study of human relations is necessarily an embedded one; to pretend otherwise obscures more than it illuminates.

We reveal and become ourselves among people we know. The task of the ethnographer can only be achieved through a deep embedding. Objectivity may be sacrificed, but it was never possible in the first place. Importantly, something far greater is gained: understanding. This is not to say that deep embedding is without challenges. For one, subjects become friends. You will tell your friend something you will not tell a researcher who is dutifully writing down everything at the end of the day. A responsible ethnographer will often have to remind his subjects that they are subjects—that that intimate and juicy detail that was just spilled might make its way into a book or an article. In this sense, the informed consent of research subjects is a process, not a onetime event. And through this process tensions can emerge, and feelings can be hurt. Friends are reminded that you are part of their life to study it and are not simply to be their friend. Students recall that their private moments might be subject to public revelation.

There are many things that never made it into this book because of this. As I reminded people of my role or later contacted them to fact-check my accounts of our interactions, there were occasions when I was asked not to include what I had seen or heard. I respected these requests. This does not mean that there are bits of information that would change everything I have written about, or even that I could forget these events. In fact I often actively remembered them and used them to form my argument. But I respected the trust that I had built with my subjects and the requests they made for my discretion.

In addition, I changed every student name and often details of their lives I felt were inconsequential (a student from Connecticut might actually be from New York or Massachusetts; a sophomore might be a junior; and so forth). The same is true for most faculty and staff. Initially I intended to obscure the name of the school. But I soon realized that this might prove impossible, as the details of the place and my own personal history would make the site clear. Midway through the year I asked for permission from head administrators to use the school's name, and it was granted. As I wrote the book I began to increasingly support Mitchell Duneier's assertion that anonymity is often a way to protect the researcher rather than the research subjects.[1] The strength of my obligation to "get it right" seems to have increased by revealing St. Paul's name. Protecting young students and people who work at the school simply seemed sensible.

I had some ideas I wanted to "test" during my ethnography, and I dedicated a lot of time to unstructured observations. I don't wish to place myself within any methodological school that claims ethnography is best when it tests theory[2] or when it simply observes relations unfettered by theoretical questions.[3] I employed a pragmatic hybrid of these two poles, feeling that ethnography is best when it gets the lives of people right, when it provides an accurate account of places or institutions, and when the argument is helpful for making sense of the world around us. Given my emphasis on embodiment, a feel for the place was essential. One could call this a kind of "carnal sociology"[4] or draw upon the same, far older idea among feminist epistemology that situated experience and standpoints matter.[5] Regardless, having "done it" myself—both as a student and as a faculty member of St. Paul's—helped me understand the life of the school.

Theoretically I have drawn on the long tradition of cultural sociology to write this book, as well as the resurgent field of elite sociology. My primary interlocutor in this project has been a man I was never fortunate enough to talk to about my ideas: Pierre Bourdieu. In my project's earliest stages

I imagined it as asking the kinds of questions Bourdieu does in *The State Nobility*, while employing an ethnographic method similar to Paul Willis's study of working-class English "lads" in *Learning to Labour*. The first title I imagined for the text was *Learning to Rule*. But a reproduction story that so dominates Bourdieu and Willis never seemed to quite fit. Instead my data led me to develop the idea of ease within the new elite.

My reading of Bourdieu kept guiding me to think of culture, but not in terms of culture as something that actors *had*. So the analogy of cultural capital as "money in your wallet" is somewhat misleading. Instead, I most often thought of culture in a relational way. My observations guided me to think of culture as a practice, not a possession. The interactional ease of privilege (negotiating hierarchies as ladders, not ceilings) is an example of this dynamic. Another way to think of this is that capital only "spends" when others accept it from you (they take your currency). I might work very hard to fit in at a NASCAR race. But without a lot more experience in that space it is unlikely that others would accept what I know about the sport. (I belong to a fantasy NASCAR league—something I joined with friends I made my second time around at St. Paul's—so I *know* about NASCAR, but I don't properly embody the practice.)

To think of culture as an interactive capacity is to highlight different aspects of the idea of cultural capital. The emphasis is on what actors *do*. That doing is either respected or rejected by others within an interaction. To understand culture, then, requires not just looking at the beliefs or ex-post explanations of actors but instead seeing them interact with others and institutions. We must see such beliefs and justifications enacted, otherwise we simply see the before and after of culture and not its moment of production in interaction itself. In this sense the ethnographic method deployed allows us to see culture in ways that surveys or interviews cannot.[6]

This book is possible because of others working on elites, and elite schooling in particular.[7] The insights from this literature have guided me to see how the institutional arrangement of schooling (and child rearing more generally) helps perpetuate inequalities. What I hope to have added to these voices is attention to embodied interactional dynamics, particularly the ease of negotiating hierarchies, and how the trick of such dynamics is the obscuring of durable inequalities.

My aim in doing a sociology of elites is to contribute to our understandings of inequality. The vast majority of research in this area is done on the poor—and for good reason. But in shining the light upon elites I hope to remind readers that poverty is not an aspect or property of poor people but a relationship that the poor are in with the rest of society. The same can be said of elites. Elites are elites not because of who they are but because of who they are in relation to other social actors and institutions. Elites are made. If this book helps show some of the ways how, then I feel it is a success.

ACKNOWLEDGMENTS

St. Paul's School opened its doors to me. It made a brave and bold move by allowing me to come and interrogate its inner working. The school gave me an office, a roof over my head, food to nourish me, and the freedom to roam. I hope they do not regret it. My portrait of the school is not always a flattering one. But I hope my respect for my alma mater is clear. The students deserve a particular debt of gratitude. Adolescence is not easy, but it is harder still when someone is there to write down what you're doing. I thank them for spending time with me, putting up with my questions, and pushing me in new directions when they thought I didn't understand their lives. The faculty and staff give themselves to the education of high school students—a calling I respect and admire. Their love and care for the students is something I hope comes through in the manuscript; it is a dedication I often marvel at. While at St. Paul's this second time I made many close friends who remain in my life. I hope they find something very familiar and at times surprising in this book.

The University of Wisconsin was my home for several years. The sociology department was an unlikely yet perfect incubator for this project. My work would never have been possible without the help and guidance of those who gave countless hours to help mold me as a young scholar. The faculty who took on this task are too numerous to name, but I wish to particularly acknowledge two intellectual homes: the Feminist Seminar and the Politics, Culture, and Society group. Also at Wisconsin were the graduate students who kept me intellectually stimulated and, importantly, happy. Special thanks go to Angela Barian, Jessica Brown, and Erik Schneiderhan. Long-term projects are trying. And Angela, Jessica, and Erik helped keep me sane and grounded. The love they extended to me helped me make it through. Bob Hauser and Harry Brighouse guided the project to completion; Patrick Barrett taught me what it means to be a compassionate and engaged scholar; Myra Marx Ferree took me under her wing and pushed me to my limits, yet with care; and Erik Wright's tireless dedication to and insights for his students still amaze me. Erik serves as a daily model of what I wish to be as an academic. A final word must be reserved for Mustafa Emirbayer. He had faith in this project and in me when few others did (including myself). This project began because of him. And, most important to me, a friendship emerged through it.

The Sociology Department at Columbia University took a chance on me. I arrived with little more than a set of half-formed ideas. Over the last two years my colleagues and graduate students have worked with me to give them shape. My department has provided me with a space to develop, and my colleagues have all been enormously generous in reading and commenting on my work. For this I am deeply in their debt.

Ideas from different chapters were presented at Columbia University, the University of Pennsylvania, Haverford College, New York University, Yale University, the University of Colorado at Boulder, and the University of Michigan at Ann Arbor. These audiences helped me push my thinking forward. My editor at Princeton University Press, Eric Schwartz, guided me through my first book. His insight and advice were invaluable to the final product. I will be forever grateful. David Lobenstine worked closely with me on articulating my ideas. He pushed me not to hide behind academic jargon. The result, I believe, is a far better (and more insightful) book. I am the beneficiary of the wonderful copyediting of Jenn Backer. I thank her for her careful hard work.

Maria Abascal, Karen Barkey, Rudi Batzell, Peter Bearman, Howard Becker, Claudio Benzecry, Yinon Cohen, Matt Desmond, Mitch Duneier, Mustafa Emirbayer, Dana Fisher, Herb Gans, Phil Gorski, Patrick Inglis, Colin Jerolmack, Michèle Lamont, Dan Navon, Pam Oliver, Aaron Patton, Jeremy Schulz, Richard Sennett, Harel Shapira, Carla Shedd, David Stark, Mitchell Stevens, Madiha Tahir, Diane Vaughan, Sudhir Venkatesh, and Josh Whitford all read either part or all of the penultimate draft of the book and provided invaluable comments. I hope the final result is a tribute to their work. Cooke Kelsey deserves a special note of appreciation. Cooke read and reread a very early draft of my work. His relentless pushback led me to spend an extra year on the manuscript. My work is much better for it.

Upon returning to New York I began playing music again. Together with Richard Sennett, Larry Wu, Susanna Prough, and Howard Bliwise I have waded through chamber music repertoire and countless bottles of wine. These Wednesday evenings are the highlight of my week and provide the kind of personal joy and fulfillment essential for sustaining me through my writing.

As he has with so many other students, Mark Gould introduced me to sociology. I became a sociologist because of Mark. His advice still echoes around my head as I write. I can't thank him enough for giving me the most valuable thing you can give a young mind: time. I still marvel at his commitment to his students.

During this project my vision began to fail. Dr. Farhad Hafezi of Zurich performed surgeries that helped me see again, and Dr. Stephen Trokel of New York has been tireless in his efforts to help restore my vision. I am particularly indebted to Dr. Trokel for his kindness, intelligence, insight, and patience. Without these two doctors, so much would be impossible.

The Johnson Street clan kept me spiritually and physically nourished throughout graduate school and continues to do so today. It started with Sunday night dinners together and turned into so much more. Through their love they showed me that life is not measured by work but by friendship. To Ben, Jonny, Sara, Grace, Tim, Mary, and all the others: my life is immeasurably better because you are a part of it.

Finally, to my family. Much of the time growing up it felt as if it were just the four of us here in this vast country—the rest of our family together on distant shores. I hope Omar and Divya know what they mean to me. And to Mum and Dad: for so many reasons, this book is yours.

NOTES

Introduction: Democratic Equality

1. See Massey and Denton 1998.

2. In his work on an elite boarding school, Ruben Gaztambide-Fernandez (2009) nicely elaborates this point.

3. I have taken this term from Charles Tilly, who argues that "Large, significant inequalities in advantages among human beings correspond mainly to categorical differences such as black/white, male/female, citizen/foreigner, or Muslim/Jew rather than to individual differences in attributes, propensities, or performances. ... Durable inequality among categories arises because people who control access to value-producing resources solve pressing organizational problems by means of categorical distinctions" (1999:6).

4. The data seem to firmly show that inequality matters and that it is bad for societies. See Jencks 2002; Wilkinson and Pickett 2009.

5. Bowen and Bok 2000:4.

6. Buchmann and DiPrete 2006.

7. The income of average American households increased from $40,261 to $50,303 (all numbers reported are in 2008 dollars). The richest 5 percent saw their incomes increase from $107,091 to $180,000; the richest 1 percent from $422,710 to $1,364,494; and the richest 0.1 percent from $1,447,543 to $7,126,395. These data are from the U.S. Census Bureau and Piketty and Saez 2003, available online at http://elsa.berkeley.edu/~saez/.

8. Delbanco 2007. The figures are from Bowen, Kurzweil, and Tobin 2005. The eleven institutions are Barnard, Columbia, Oberlin, Penn State, Princeton, Smith, Swarthmore, the University of Pennsylvania, Wellesley, Williams, and Yale.

9. Further, only 8 percent of Harvard's undergraduates receive Pell Grants (awarded to families with incomes of less than $40,000); the real middle income is vastly underrepresented at America's elite colleges. Fischer 2006.

10. Bowen, Kurzweil, and Tobin 2005:103.

11. This class composition of colleges has clear racial impacts. Though we tend to separate out such factors as class and race as analytically distinct, they are densely intertwined. The easiest way to see this is to simply look at the income of American families by race. The average income of the black family is about 62 percent of that of the average white family and almost half that of the average Asian family. Blacks and Hispanics are far poorer than the average American, and this poverty impacts their college chances and life prospects. This means that when speaking of the importance of class, race is a necessary part of the discussion. As William Bowen and his colleagues have noted, "the minority enrollment gap [in four-year colleges] is primarily a result of the fact that underrepresented minority students are more likely than other students to come from low-income families." Bowen, Kurzweil, and Tobin 2005:76.

12. A frequently cited paper by Stacy Dale and Alan Krueger (2002) is often credited in the press as showing that elite education does not matter—what matters is the capacity to get in. However, these reports are deceptive. In the models that journalists point to, Dale and Krueger control for such factors as the resources that schools devote to instruction and tuition cost. But both of these increase earnings significantly, and both are marks of elite schools. Further, in the study institutional quality is a product of SAT score, not prestige; yet prestige is a far better predictor of elite status than a student's average SAT score. Perhaps most simply, from Dale and Krueger's own study we find that men who attend the most competitive colleges (as evaluated by Barrons) earn 23 percent more than those who attend very competitive colleges. This is an enormous difference in wages. For critiques of the interpretations of the study, see http://www.overcomingbias.com/2009/03/college-prestige-matters.html. There are similarly clear advantages to attending an elite boarding school. See S. Levine 1980.

13. See Lemann 2000. Equality of conditions is not the same as equality of outcomes. It suggests that all members of society be given an equal chance of success. Some may achieve, and some may not. But such outcomes are a product of how the game is played, not how it is set up.

14. Ibid.

15. Tsay et al. 2003; Brim et al. 1969; Friedland and Alford 1991; Sen 1999.

16. See Young 1994; Lemann 2000.

17. It is important to note that the SAT is only a weak predictor of college grades in the first year, that performance on the test is highly correlated with demographic factors like family wealth and race, and that other indicators like class rank and high school grades are far better predictors of college performance.

18. Karabel 2006:267.

19. Ibid.

20. For a description of the methodology employed, see the methodological and theoretical reflections.

Chapter 1: The New Elite

1. Robert De Niro, dir., *The Good Shepherd* (2006).

2. An ascriptive group might be based on status (like being a member of the aristocracy), race, sex, or religion. Membership in groups is "assigned" by birth rather than achieved.

3. The term was originally coined by Tocqueville, noting how American political and religious institutions were qualitatively different from those of European societies. He emphasized high levels of social egalitarianism (due to the absence of feudal remnants and hence rigid social classes and status distinctions) and social mobility, the strength of religion, and the weakness of the central state. Karl Marx and Fredrick Engels, in their "Letters to Americans," later commented extensively on the exceptional character of the United States. Because it was the most democratic country and lacked feudal traditions and struggles, it had a distinctly modern and bourgeois culture with bourgeois prejudices strongly rooted in the working class. The analysis of American exceptionalism was revived in large part by Werner Sombart (1906). He echoed Tocqueville's analysis, arguing that America was freer and more egalitarian than Europe because there was no "stigma of being the class apart that almost all European workers have," due to America's democratic institutions and lack of rigid classes from a feudal legacy. Many other writers have come to similar conclusions, arguing that while the distribution of wealth in America has grown more unequal, consumption and the overall standard of living of the working class have continued to improve due to enormous economic growth. Thus class consciousness was inhibited due to a relatively high standard of living, egalitarian social relationships, and a belief in widespread opportunities for social mobility. Seymour Martin Lipset (1996) and Lipset and Gary Wolfe Marks (2001) have built on these and other analyses, ultimately emphasizing that America is a classically liberal society with widespread values of meritocracy within capitalism. Following Gramsci's analysis of "Americanism" (1971), this work focuses on American values and ideology that emphasize an individualistic religious tradition, anti-statism, and anti-authoritarianism, generating a libertarian and syndicalist—as opposed to state collectivist—disposition within the American labor movement. Americanism— anti-statism, laissez-faire, individualism, populism, and egalitarianism—served as an ideological substitute for socialism.

4. Indeed, by midcentury over half the peerage in France were descendants of the old nobility. We need only note that at the turn of the century there were but two republics in Europe: France (whose republican position was far from stable) and Switzerland.

5. Hobsbawm 1989.

6. Smith 1993.

7. Tocqueville [1831] 2003:646–47.

8. Smith 1993. As Rogers Smith has shown, Americans have worked within multiple traditions, embracing both liberal and exclusionary politics, often in the same moments. See also Smith 1997.

9. As an example, though the Van Rensselaer fortune of New York was initially built by mercantile wealth in the Dutch republic in the seventeenth century (Kiliaen van Rensselaer was a director of the Dutch West India Company), it was quickly based in the new world. The Van Rensselaer manor, Rensselaerswyck, was an astonishing 1,200 square miles. The last heir to this land, Stephen van Rensselaer, had landownings that made him one of the richest men in history (worth $88 billion in today's terms). And like many of the other Knickerbocker families of New York who held court over the social and economic life of the region (Stuyvesants, Schuylers, De Peysters, Van Winkles, Gansvoorts, Van Dams, Gerards, Vandewaters, Duyckincks, and Van Dykes), the wealth was heavily tied to both land and old titles such as Lords of Manors or Lords of Patroons. Such patroonships were established in the seventeenth century by early Dutch settling companies. With the industrial transformations of the Gilded Age and the associated increase in finance, these landed families lost much of their hold on the economy and society of the region.

10. Beckert 2003:294. It still stands today. And its lavish rooms remain a tribute to the opulence of the age.

11. Ibid., 295.

12. Beisel 1997.

13. L. Levine 1990; Bourdieu 1984; Bourdieu and Passeron 1977; Beisel 1997.

14. Thomas Arnold led the prestigious Rugby School in England from 1828 to 1841. He is credited with instituting a host of reforms at Rugby, which at the beginning of the nineteenth century had fallen into disrepair. Arnold was part of the "muscular Christianity" movement that was central to many educational reforms in the Victorian era. The basic principle of muscular Christianity was that moral and physical health were inseparable, and the ideal education constructed vigorously masculine men. Its earliest expression was in Rousseau's classic treatise, Emile (Rousseau 1979). Arnold attempted to bring these ideals of moral and physical education to life at Rugby and thereby helped transform both the school

and British education more generally. For more on Arnold, see Copley 2002. For more on muscular Christianity (particularly in its expression in America during the Gilded Age), see Putney 2001.

15. McLachlan 1970:150. See also Bamford 1967. Bamford's study does well to outline the moribund nature of public schools in the early to mid-1800s. As McLachlan demonstrates, it was truly the Swiss and German schools, and not the English, that served as a model for the American boarding school.

16. Heckscher 1996:6.

17. McLachlan 1970:151–52. Memories from these schools often tell of rather horrific experiences of sexual abuse, physical torment, and a kind of hard living that broke the spirits of many who would later reflect upon their past.

18. George Bancroft cofounded the Round Hill School in Northampton, Massachusetts. An experimental secondary school built upon the educational ideals of Swiss educator Johann Pestalozzi, Round Hill imagined students as having innate moral and spiritual abilities, and thus encouraged students to assume a high degree of personal responsibility (and freedom) for their intellectual growth. The school educated elite children—charging nearly three times what Harvard did at the time. And it quickly failed, closing within eleven years. The school was popular among American Transcendentalists, and some of its ideas proved enormously influential for subsequent schools, including St. Paul's. The view of children's innocence, of their capacity to grow through connections with natural beauty, was held firmly by St. Paul's founder, George Shattuck, himself a Round Hill graduate. Shattuck imagined a space embedded within "green fields and trees, streams and ponds ... flowers and minerals" (Shattuck to trustee, Ohrstrom Library, St. Paul's, Concord, NH). And he largely achieved this on St. Paul's campus. It was combining this romanticism with a religious education— one particularly near to clergyman Henry Coit's imagination—that made St. Paul's so successful.

19. Heckscher 1996:16.

20. Such influences were those of the poor, the migrant, and the Jew in the city. See Beisel 1997.

21. By the 1860s Harvard had mostly transformed to what we might today recognize as a university. Graduates were approximately twenty to twenty-one years old; in the 1820s they were around sixteen.

22. Girls, by contrast, were isolated in the home, both before and after marriage. Such isolation was protection. See Aries 1962. For boys these practices are now questioned as perhaps "feminizing" or "infantalizing" boys. See Sommers 2000; Sax 2007. These concerns have emerged in large part because boys now underperform girls at school. See Buchmann and DiPrete 2006; Buchmann, DiPrete, and McDaniel 2008.

23. Aries 1962:269–70.

24. Beisel 1997:6.

25. The seminal work on boarding schools is Cookson and Persell 1985.

26. Goffman 1961.

27. Cookson and Persell 1985:124.

28. Matthew Warren to alumni, Alumni Horae 41 (June 1960).

29. Piketty and Saez 2003. This might be understood as part of the financialization of the economy.

30. Brandeis [1914] 1995:27.

31. Mills 1956:18, italics added.

32. Baltzell 1962:71–72. See also Baltzell 1987.

33. Domhoff 1974:109.

34. You can have more or less money, and you can have different currencies that have value in different contexts. See Bourdieu 1984.

35. I have used U.S. News and World Report's rankings as a metric.

36. Becker 1988:10.

37. Brooks 2001:11.

38. Duncan et al. 2005; Mazumder 2005.

39. For those who are quantitatively oriented, we can observe that intergenerational elasticity might be as high as 0.62. This indicator looks at the relationship between parents' and children's income as a percentage. So, what percentage of the income difference between families in one generation persists into the next generation? For an intergeneration elasticity of 0.62, a 10 percent difference in parents' income would lead to a 6.2 percent difference in children's incomes. And so the closer the value to zero, the greater a likelihood of a "fair shake"; the closer the value to one, the more one has complete immobility. This level of intergenerational elasticity is reported in Mazumder 2005. Mazumder generates a higher value than many other scholars; he does so by looking at earnings across a ten-year period rather than at a discrete moment. I believe his estimation is quite sound.

40. See Skrentny 2002.

Chapter 2: Finding One's Place

1. Matthew 5:1: "Now when he saw the crowds, he went up on a mountainside and sat down. His disciples came to him, and he began to teach them."

2. In the year of my research, only two students out of five hundred left the school.

3. This American coding of earning one's place through work is similarly observed by Michèle Lamont in her work comparing American and French upper-middle-class workers. She finds that the Americans focus on hard work—in my terms, something the actor does—while the French, by contrast, praise brilliance—in my terms, who the actor is (Lamont 1992).

4. Concord, New Hampshire, is an overwhelmingly white town. Almost all the staff members are white, and so the potential racial dynamics of low-wage, non-white workers serving elites (or future elites) are largely absent.

5. Tocqueville [1831] 2003.

6. For work on symbolic boundaries, see Lamont 1992.

7. For emotion work, see Hochschild 1979. This idea has been expanded into thinking about "emotional labor," in which workers manifest particular emotions as part of their job in order to promote organizational goals. See Rafaeli and Sutton 1987.

8. Aldrich has written thoughtfully on the experience of old wealth in the United States (1988). Our lunch was kindly arranged by Herb Gans after Aldrich had heard about my own project and time at St. Paul's.

9. Online statement about the faculty from the vice rector for faculty.

10. The idea of dispositional "marks" of success comes from Weber 1958. Weber notes the ways in which Calvinists, in responding to the doctrine of predestination, sought to display "marks" of their election.

Chapter 3: The Ease of Privilege

1. Bourdieu 1996:21.

2. Most new students are placed into shared rooms. Some have singles, but in general the benefits of a roommate (someone who knows if you are really struggling and can also be a very quick friend) far outweigh the potential risks (a situation where the roommates hate one another).

3. The application process is very competitive, with around two thousand applicants for about two hundred spaces.

4. The physical differences between students are often dramatic, as many are just entering puberty when they arrive at St. Paul's and many are adults by the time they leave.

5. Mansbridge 2001:1.

6. Massey and Denton 1998.

7. Wilson 1978:1–2, 144.

Chapter 4: Gender and the Performance of Privilege

1. Foucault 1995:26.
2. Bourdieu 2000:141. For Bourdieu's discussions of gender, see Bourdieu 2001.
3. Bourdieu 2001:63.
4. Students have a half day of classes on Saturday.
5. See Buchman and DiPrete 2007; Meadows, Land, and Lamb 2005.
6. This is particularly the case with elite colleges. Though many non-elite colleges now have gender ratios of 60:40 in favor of the more qualified girls, elite schools have continued to accept less qualified boys to maintain an even ratio. I often joke that the biggest affirmative action program in college admissions is for men.
7. We must not be blind to another contradiction: corporeal display and corporeal ease are not equivalent. While ease can be carried through one's life, display is rewarded quite differently as we get older. In short, youth is cherished. Young, healthy bodies make us all happy; some of us may be turned on, some of us may feel nostalgia for our own youth, and some of us may simply appreciate the exuberance of the human body. The aging, sagging body, however, does not thrill us nearly as much. One might ask a question my ethnographic work at a school cannot address: "If corporeal display is important for women, how is this managed later in life, when women with experience are corporeally disadvantaged compared to women with youth?"
8. As C. Wright Mills argued, these different vocabularies marked different interpretive expectations for the act and its consequences: "Men discern situations with particular vocabularies, and it is in terms of some delimited vocabulary that they anticipate consequences of conduct. Stable vocabularies of motives link anticipated consequences and specific actions" (1940:906).
9. Mannheim 1967:249. See also Butler 1990.
10. See Garfinkel 1984.
11. Butler 1990:179.
12. I would like to thank Angela Barian for pointing this out to me.
13. Readers may wonder how common homosexuality is at the school, or perhaps how common sex, drinking, or drugs are. Contrary to the image portrayed of elite kids, drug-fueled orgies and wild parties are rare. They never happen on campus—where the risk of getting caught and punished is high. And upon surveying the students about their health, the school essentially found that its students were like other high school students. They were a little more stressed out, which is not surprising. But their rates of sexual activity, of first sexual contact, and of drinking and drugs were the same as those of students across the nation.

Students usually leave campus to break the rules. If they do so on campus and are caught, colleges may find out about their transgressions, and this could hurt their chances of being accepted. If they do so at home or in a hotel room, colleges are typically never the wiser.

14. Much like Anges in Garfinkel 1984.

Chapter 5: Learning *Beowulf* and *Jaws*

1. See Bryson 1996; Peterson and Kern 1996.

2. L. Levine 1990.

3. See Bryson 1996; Emmison 2003; Gans 1974; Peterson and Kern 1996; and Sintas and Alvarez 2002. This argument assumes that "social stratification and cultural stratification map closely onto each other" (Chan and Goldthorpe 2007:1). As Michael Emmison argues, "the cultural lives of those once deemed to be the 'bearers' of elite or high cultural traditions are increasingly diversified, inclusive or omnivorous" (2003:226).

4. This idea comes from Weber 1958.

5. Plato 1991:518c.

6. Merton argues, "Men respond not only to the objective features of a situation, but also, and at times primarily, to the meaning this situation has for them. And once they have assigned some meaning to the situation, their consequent behavior and some of the consequences of that behavior are determined by the ascribed meaning" (1968:475–76). This idea has antecedents in the "Thomas Theorem." Thomas and Thomas write, "If men define situations as real, they are real in their consequences" (1928:571–72). This idea has been taken up most systematically by those who study deviance, such as Kai Erikson and Howard Becker. Erikson argues, "Deviance is not a property *inherent in* any particular kind of behavior; it is a property *conferred upon* that behavior" (1966:6). Or equivalently, Becker argues that "*social groups create deviance by making the rules whose infraction constitutes deviance.* ... From this point of view deviance is *not* a quality of the act the person commits, but rather a consequence of the application by others of rules and sanctions to an 'offender'" (1963:9). This approach is known to sociologists as "labeling theory," which

> argues that initial acts of delinquency are relatively harmless instances of primary deviance. From the standpoint of the child, such acts are defined as "play" or "mischief"; however, from the standpoint of the larger community, they are viewed as "evil" or as a "law violation." The community's response ... is to label the child as "bad" or "evil." The label, in turn, influences the self-image of the child, who comes to view him or herself as bad or delinquent, which in turn increases the

likelihood of future deviance. ... A hallmark of labeling theory is the proposition that deviant labels are not randomly distributed across the social structure, but are instead more likely to apply to the powerless, the disadvantaged, and the poor. (Matsueda 1992:1588)

However, the positive qualities of being consecrated have been less rigorously applied by sociologists.

7. Durkheim [1912] 1995:243–44.

8. It is not a mistake that the examples provided are all boys. I will address this point in a subsequent section.

9. This is in stark contrast to those at the low end of the stratification system who are often "dressed-down" in school. As Ann Ferguson found in her work on black masculinity and middle school, "I witnessed the discourteous, harassing treatment of pupils by some of the school adults. This verbal disparagement and the heard dressing-down of kids was carried out in the name of school discipline required by certain kinds of children; it was seen as an essential weapon, given the circumstances, in the creation and maintenance of order. It was typically unleashed against children who were black, poor, and already labeled as trouble" (2000:70).

10. See Lareau 2003 for a more thorough accounting of such specialization. Lareau powerfully argues that one of the marks of upper-middle-class parenting (as opposed to working-class parenting) is that parents work to ensure that their children cultivate special skills, talents, or interests.

11. Yet recent books on college admissions processes suggest some of the same collusion and, more important, advantages afforded to elite high school students. See Golden 2006; Stevens 2007; Schmidt 2007; and Soares 2007.

12. Stevens 2007.

13. See Karabel 2006.

14. http://www.sparknotes.com.

15. See Karabel 2006.

16. This should not be read simply as racial insensitivity. When the great British violinist Thomas Bowes came to campus and I was to play for him at a public master class, I hardly practiced. Again, it was a mundane event for me.

17. This was by no means scientific. But given that I asked several students and boys were overwhelmingly named, I do not doubt that the identification of boys with extraordinary talent is mistaken. Girls were more likely to name another girl but were still much more likely to talk about boys (boys were named over 80 percent of the time and 70 percent of the time by girls).

18. Espenshade and Radford (2009) show a significant "Asian penalty" for applicants to elite schools. Put simply, Asian students must be more qualified to enter, as their pool is quite strong, and colleges seek to limit their overall enrollment in college. See chapter 3 of their work.

19. Of course, these points ignore the processes leading to applications. For differences in the rates of application and acceptance, see chapter 3 in Espenshade and Radford 2009.

20. Beisel 1997.

Conclusion

1. Devah Pager's work is a clear indication of this. See Pager 2007; Pager, Western, and Bonikowski 2009. Pager demonstrates the strong negative impacts of having a criminal record on labor market chances (which disproportionately impacts blacks), as well as a persistent bias against blacks in labor market hiring.

2. L. Levine 1990.

3. L. Levine 1990; Beckert 2001.

Methodological and Theoretical Reflections

1. Duneier 2000.

2. Burawoy 1998.

3. Duneier 2000.

4. Wacquant 2004.

5. Harding 1986, 1987.

6. I have developed this idea in concert with Colin Jerolmack. See Jerolmack and Khan 2010.

7. My greatest debts are to Stevens 2007; Gaztambide-Fernandez 2009; Karabel 2006; Cookson and Persell 1985; and Lareau 2003.

WORKS CITED

Aldrich, Nelson. 1988. *Old Money*. New York: Alfred A. Knopf.

Aries, Philippe. 1962. *Centuries of Childhood: A Social History of Family Life*. Trans. Robert Baldick. New York: Vintage.

Baltzell, E. Digby. 1962. *An American Business Aristocracy*. New Haven: Yale University Press.

———. 1987. *The Protestant Establishment: Aristocracy and Caste in America*. New Haven: Yale University Press.

Bamford, T. W. 1967. *Rise of the Public Schools: A Study of Boys' Public Boarding Schools in England and Wales from 1837 to the Present Day*. London: Nelson.

Becker, Gary S. 1988. "Family Economics and Macro Behavior." *American Economic Review* 78(1):1–13.

Becker, Howard S. 1963. *Outsiders*. New York: Free Press.

Beckert, Sven. 2001. *The Monied Metropolis: New York City and the Consolidation of the American Bourgeoisie, 1850–1896*. Cambridge: Cambridge University Press.

Beisel, Nicola. 1997. *Imperiled Innocents: Anthony Comstock and Family Reproduction in Victorian America*. Princeton: Princeton University Press.

Bourdieu, Pierre. 1984. *Distinction: A Social Critique of the Judgment of Taste*. Cambridge, MA: Harvard University Press.

———. 1996. *The State Nobility*. Trans. R. Nice. Stanford: Stanford University Press.

———. 2000. *Pascalian Meditations*. Trans. R. Nice. Stanford: Stanford University Press.

———. 2001. *Masculine Domination*. Trans. R. Nice. Stanford: Stanford University Press.

Bourdieu, Pierre, and Jean-Claude Passeron. 1977. *Reproduction in Education, Society, and Culture*. Thousand Oaks, CA: Sage.

Bowen, William G., and Derek Bok. 2000. *The Shape of the River: Long-Term Consequences of Considering Race in College and University Admissions*. Princeton: Princeton University Press.

Bowen, William G., Martin Kurzweil, and Eugene Tobin. 2005. *Equity and Excellence in American Higher Education*. Charlottesville: University of Virginia Press.

Brandeis, Louis. [1914] 1995. *Other People's Money, and How the Bankers Use It*. New York: St. Martin's Press.

Brim, Orville Gilbert, et al. 1969. *American Beliefs and Attitudes about Intelligence*. New York: Russell Sage Foundation.

Brooks, David. 2001. *Bobos in Paradise: The New Upper Class and How They Got There*. New York: Simon and Schuster.

Bryson, Bethany. 1996. "'Anything But Heavy Metal': Symbolic Exclusion and Musical Dislikes." *American Sociological Review* 61:884–99.

Buchmann, Claudia, and Thomas DiPrete. 2006. "The Growing Female Advantage in College Completion: The Role of Parental Education, Family Structure, and Academic Achievement." *American Sociological Review* 71:515–41.

Buchmann, Claudia, Thomas DiPrete, and Anne McDaniel. 2008. "Gender Inequalities in Education." *Annual Review of Sociology* 34:319–37.

Burawoy, Michael. 1998. "The Extended Case Method." *Sociological Theory* 16(11):4–33.

Butler, Judith. 1990. *Gender Trouble: Feminism and the Subversion of Identity*. Berkeley: University of California Press.

Chan, Tak Wing, and John H. Goldthorpe. 2007. "Social Stratification and Cultural Consumption: Music in England." *European Sociological Review* 23(1):1–19.

Cookson, Peter W. Jr., and Caroline Hodges Persell. 1985. *Preparing for Power: America's Elite Boarding Schools*. New York: Basic Books.

Copley, Terence. 2002. *Black Tom: Arnold of Rugby: The Myth and the Man*. New York: Continuum.

Dale, Stacy Berg, and Alan B. Krueger. 2002. "Estimating the Payoff to Attending a More Selective College." *Quarterly Journal of Economics* 117(4):1491–1527.

Delbanco, Andrew. 2007. "Scandals of Higher Education." *New York Review of Books* 54(5):March 29.

Domhoff, G. William. 1974. *The Bohemian Grove and Other Retreats: A Study of Ruling Class Cohesiveness*. New York: Harper Collins.

Duncan, Greg, Ariel Kalil, Susan Mayer, Robin Tepper, and Monique Payne. 2005. "The Apple Does Not Fall Far from the Tree." Pp. 23–79 in *Unequal Chances: Family Background and Economic Success*, ed. Samuel Bowles, Herbert Gintis, and Melissa Osborne Groves. Princeton: Princeton University Press.

Duneier, Mitchell. 2000. *Sidewalk*. New York: Farrar, Straus, and Giroux.

Durkheim, Emile. [1912] 1995. *Elementary Forms of Religious Life*. Trans. Karen Fields. New York: Free Press.

Emmison, Michael. 2003. "Social Class and Cultural Mobility: Reconfiguring the Cultural Omnivore." *Journal of Sociology* 39:211–30.

Erikson, Kai. 1966. *Wayward Puritans: A Study in the Sociology of Deviance*. New York: Macmillan.

Espenshade, Thomas, and Alexandria Radford. 2009. *No Longer Separate, Not Yet Equal: Race and Class in Elite College Admission and Campus Life*. Princeton: Princeton University Press.

Ferguson, Ann. 2000. *Bad Boys: Public Schools in the Making of Black Masculinity*. Ann Arbor: University of Michigan Press.

Fischer, Karen. 2006. "Elite Colleges Lag in Serving the Needy." *Chronicle of Higher Education,* May 12.

Foucault, Michel. 1995. *Discipline and Punish: The Birth of the Prison*. New York: Vintage.

Friedland, Roger, and Robert Alford. 1991. "Bringing Society Back In." In *The New Institutionalism in Organizational Analysis*, ed. Paul DiMaggio and Walter Powell. Chicago: University of Chicago Press.

Gans, Herbert. 1974. *Popular Culture and High Culture*. New York: Basic Books.

Garfinkel, Harold. 1984. *Studies in Ethnomethodology*. Malden, MA: Polity Press.

Gaztambide-Fernandez, Rubén. 2009. *The Best of the Best: Becoming Elite at an American Boarding School*. Cambridge, MA: Harvard University Press.

Goffman, Erving. 1961. *Asylums: Essays on the Social Situation of Mental Patients and Other Inmates*. New York: Anchor.

Golden, Daniel. 2006. *The Price of Admission: How America's Ruling Class Buys Its Way into Elite Colleges—and Who Gets Left outside the Gates*. New York: Crown Publishers.

Gramsci, Antonio. 1971. *Selections from the Prison Notebooks*. New York: International Publishers.

Harding, Sandra. 1986. *The Science Question in Feminism*. Ithaca: Cornell University Press.

———, ed. 1987. *Feminism and Methodology: Social Science Issues*. Bloomington: Indiana University Press.

Heckscher, August. 1996. *A Brief History of St. Paul's School*. Concord, NH: Trustees of St. Paul's School.

Hobsbawm, Eric. 1989. *The Age of Revolution: 1789–1848*. New York: Vintage.

Hochschild, Arlie Russel. 1979. "Emotion Work, Feeling Rules and Social Structure." *American Journal of Sociology* 85(3):551–75.

Jencks, Christopher. 2002. "Does Inequality Matter?" *Deadalus* 131(1):49–65.

Jerolmack, Colin, and Shamus Khan. 2010. "Culture in Interaction." Unpublished manuscript.

Karabel, Jerome. 2006. *The Chosen: The Hidden History of Admission and Exclusion at Harvard, Yale, and Princeton*. New York: Mariner Books.

Lamont, Michèle. 1992. *Money, Morals, and Manners: The Culture of the French and American Upper-Middle Class*. Chicago: University of Chicago Press.

Lareau, Annette. 2003. *Unequal Childhoods: Class, Race, and Family Life*. Berkeley: University of California Press.

Lemann, Nicholas. 2000. *The Big Test: The Secret History of the American Meritocracy*. New York: Farrar, Straus and Giroux.

Levine, Lawrence. 1990. *Highbrow/Lowbrow: The Emergence of Cultural Hierarchy in America*. Cambridge, MA: Harvard University Press.

Levine, Steven. 1980. "The Rise of American Boarding Schools and the Development of a National Upper Class." *Social Problems* 28:63–94.

Lipset, Seymour Martin. 1996. *American Exceptionalism: A Double-Edged Sword*. New York: W. W. Norton.

Lipset, Seymour Martin, and Gary Wolfe Marks. 2001. *It Didn't Happen Here: Why Socialism Failed in the United States*. New York: W. W. Norton.

Mannheim, Karl. 1967. *Man and Society in an Age of Reconstruction: Studies in Modern Social Structure*. New York: Harcourt Brace.

Mansbridge, Jane, and Aldon Morris. 2001. *Oppositional Consciousness: The Subjective Roots of Social Protest*. Chicago: University of Chicago Press.

Massey, Douglas S., and Nancy A. Denton. 1998. *American Apartheid: Segregation and the Making of the Underclass*. Cambridge, MA: Harvard University Press.

Matsueda, Ross. 1992. "Reflected Appraisals, Parental Labeling, and Delinquency: Specifying a Symbolic Interactionist Theory." *American Journal of Sociology* 97(6):1577–1611.

Mazumder, Bhashkar. 2005. "The Apple Falls Even Closer to the Tree than We Thought." Pp. 80–99 in *Unequal Chances: Family Background and Economic Success*, ed. Samuel Bowles, Herbert Gintis, and Melissa Osborne Groves. Princeton: Princeton University Press.

McLachlan, James. 1970. *American Boarding Schools: A Historical Study*. New York: Scribner.

Meadows, Sarah, Kenneth Land, and Vicki Lamb. 2005. "Assessing Gilligan vs. Sommers: Gender-Specific Trends in Child and Youth Well-Being in the United States, 1985–2001." *Social Indicators Research* 70(1):1–52.

Merton, Robert K. 1968. *Social Theory and Social Structure*. New York: Free Press.

Mills, C. Wright. 1940. "Situated Actions and Vocabularies of Motive." *American Sociological Review* 13:904–9.

———. 1956. *The Power Elite*. New York: Oxford University Press.

Pager, Devah. 2007. *Marked: Race, Crime, and Finding Work in an Era of Mass Incarceration*. Chicago: University of Chicago Press.

Pager, Devah, Bruce Western, and Bart Bonikowski. 2009. "Discrimination in a Low-Wage Labor Market: A Field Experiment." *American Sociological Review* 74:777–99.

Peterson, Richard A., and Roger M. Kern. 1996. "Changing Highbrow Taste: From Snob to Omnivore." *American Sociological Review* 61:900–907.

Piketty, Thomas, and Emmanuel Saez. 2003. "Income Inequality in the United States: 1913–1998." *Quarterly Journal of Economics* 118:1–39.

Plato. 1991. *Republic*. Trans. Alan Bloom. New York: Basic Books.

Putney, Clifford. 2001. *Muscular Christianity: Manhood and Sports in Protestant America, 1880–1920*. Cambridge, MA: Harvard University Press.

Rafaeli, A., and R. I. Sutton. 1987. "Expression of Emotion as Part of the Work Role." *Academy of Management Review* 12:23–37.

Rousseau, Jean-Jacques. [1762] 1979. *Emile, or On Education*. Trans. Allan Bloom. New York: Basic Books.

Sax, Leonard. 2007. *Boys Adrift: The Five Factors Driving the Growing Epidemic of Unmotivated Boys and Underachieving Young Men*. New York: Basic Books.

Schmidt, Peter. 2007. *Color and Money: How Rich White Kids Are Winning the War over College Affirmative Action*. New York: Palgrave Macmillan.

Sen, Amartya. 1999. "Merit and Justice." In *Meritocracy and Economic Inequality*, ed. Ken Arrow, Sam Bowles, and Steven Durlauf. Princeton: Princeton University Press.

Sintas, Jordi Lopez, and Ercilia Garcia Alvarez. 2002. "Omnivores Show up Again: The Segmentation of Cultural Consumers in Spanish Social Space." *European Sociological Review* 18(3):353–68.

Skrentny, John D. 2002. *The Minority Rights Revolution*. Cambridge, MA: Harvard University Press.

Smith, Rogers. 1993. "Beyond Tocqueville, Myrdal, and Hartz." *American Political Science Review* 83(3):549–66.

———. 1997. *Civic Ideals: Conflicting Visions of Citizenship in U.S. History*. New Haven: Yale University Press.

Soares, J. A. 2007. *The Power of Privilege: Yale and America's Elite Colleges*. Stanford: Stanford University Press.

Sombart, Werner. [1906] 1976. *Why Is There No Socialism in the United States?* New York: Sharpe.

Sommers, Christina Hoff. 2000. *The War against Boys: How Misguided Feminism Is Harming Our Young Men*. New York: Simon and Schuster.

Stevens, Mitchell. 2007. *Creating a Class: College Admissions and the Education of Elites*. Cambridge, MA: Harvard University Press.

Thomas, William I., and Dorothy Swaine Thomas. 1928. *The Child in America: Behavior Problems and Programs*. New York: Alfred Knopf.

Tilly, Charles. 1999. *Durable Inequality.* Berkeley: University of California Press.

Tocqueville, Alexis de. [1831] 2003. *Democracy in America.* Trans. Gerald Bevan. New York: Penguin.

Tsay, Angela, Michèle Lamont, Andrew Abbott, and Joshua Guetzkow. 2003. "From Character to Intellect: Changing Conceptions of Merit in the Social Sciences and Humanities, 1951–1971." *Poetics* 31:23–49.

Wacquant, Loïc J. D. 2004. *Body and Soul: Notebooks of an Apprentice Boxer.* Oxford: Oxford University Press.

Weber, Max. 1958. *The Protestant Ethic and the Spirit of Capitalism.* Trans. Talcott Parsons. New York: Scribner.

Wilkinson, Richard, and Kate Pickett. 2009. *The Spirit Level: Why More Equal Societies Almost Always Do Better.* New York: Bloomsbury Press.

Willis, Paul. 1982. *Learning to Labour: How Working Class Kids Get Working Class Jobs.* New York: Columbia University Press.

Wilson, William Julius. 1978. *The Declining Significance of Race: Blacks and Changing American Institutions.* Chicago: University of Chicago Press.

Young, Michael. 1994. *The Rise of the Meritocracy.* New York: Transaction Publishers.

INDEX

PRINCETON STUDIES IN CULTURAL SOCIOLOGY

Paul J. DiMaggio, Michèle Lamont,
Robert J. Wuthnow, and Viviana A. Zelizer, *Series Editors*

*Origins of Democratic Culture: Printing, Petitions, and the Public Sphere
in Early-Modern England* by David Zaret

Bearing Witness: Readers, Writers, and the Novel in Nigeria
by Wendy Griswold

Gifted Tongues: High School Debate and Adolescent Culture
by Gary Alan Fine

Offside: Soccer and American Exceptionalism
by Andrei S. Markovits and Steven L. Hellerman

Reinventing Justice: The American Drug Court Movement
by James L. Nolan, Jr.

*Kingdom of Children: Culture and Controversy in the
Homeschooling Movement* by Mitchell L. Stevens

Blessed Events: Religion and Home Birth in America
by Pamela E. Klassen

Negotiating Identities: States and Immigrants in France and Germany
by Riva Kastoryano, translated by Barbara Harshav

*Contentious Curricula: Afrocentrism and Creationism in
American Public Schools* by Amy J. Binder

Community: Pursuing the Dream, Living the Reality
by Suzanne Keller

*The Minds of Marginalized Black Men: Making Sense of Mobility,
Opportunity, and Future Life Chances* by Alford A. Young, Jr.

*Framing Europe: Attitudes to European Integration in Germany, Spain,
and the United Kingdom* by Juan Dez Medrano

Interaction Ritual Chains by Randall Collins

*Talking Prices: Symbolic Meanings of Prices on the
Market for Contemporary Art* by Olav Velthuis

*Elusive Togetherness: Church Groups Trying to
Bridge America's Divisions* by Paul Lichterman

Religion and Family in a Changing Society by Penny Edgell